The **Jumbo**
Parenting Journal

Developmental Milestones from Birth to 5 Years!

by Becky Daniel

illustrated by Valery Larson

Publishers

Instructional Fair • TS Denison

Grand Rapids, Michigan 49544

Instructional Fair • TS Denison

The Jumbo Parenting Journal was previously published by Instructional Fair • TS Denison under the Celebrate, Play & Share Series of titles: *My Infant, My One-Year-Old, My Two-Year-Old, My Three-Year-Old, My Four-Year-Old, and My Five-Year-Old,* ©1997.

About the Author

Becky Daniel is a parent, teacher, author, and editor—four distinctive yet interrelated professions. After graduating from California University at Long Beach, she taught kindergarten through eighth grade. When she began her family, she left the classroom to care for her first daughter and to pursue a career in writing at home.

Now the mother of three children—Amy, Sarah, and Eric—she edits a magazine and writes educational books from her home in Orcutt, California. Over the past 25 years she has written over 200 educational resource books.

She is also the author of a picture book, *Prince Poloka of Uli Loko,* a Hawaiian story for children, and *I Love You Baby,* a parenting book. In 1989 she was honored to have her biographical sketch and a list of her earlier works featured in Volume 56 of *Something About the Author.*

Credits

Author:	Becky Daniel
Project Director:	Sherrill B. Flora
Illustration Artist:	Valery Larson
Book Cover Design:	Annette Hollister-Papp & Darcy Bell-Myers
Cover Photography:	© Digital Stock

ISBN: 1-56822-963-1
The Jumbo Parenting Journal
Copyright © 2000 by Instructional Fair • TS Denison
A Division of Instructional Fair Group, Inc.
A Tribune Education Company
3195 Wilson Drive NW
Grand Rapids, Michigan 49544

Table of Contents

How to Use This Book

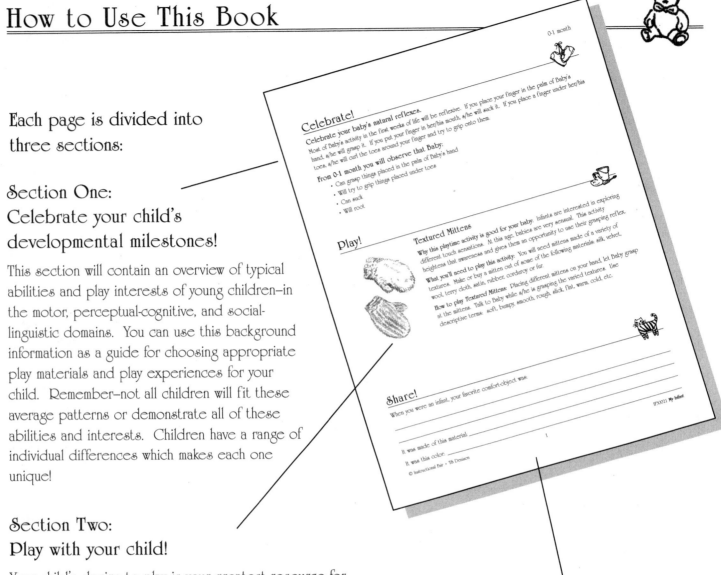

Each page is divided into three sections:

Section One:
Celebrate your child's developmental milestones!

This section will contain an overview of typical abilities and play interests of young children—in the motor, perceptual-cognitive, and social-linguistic domains. You can use this background information as a guide for choosing appropriate play materials and play experiences for your child. Remember—not all children will fit these average patterns or demonstrate all of these abilities and interests. Children have a range of individual differences which makes each one unique!

Section Two:
Play with your child!

Your child's desire to play is your greatest resource for teaching and encouraging cognitive, fine-motor, and gross-motor development. Playing with your child will reveal his or her interests to you, and nourish his or her intelligence and imagination.

Each of the activities or play experiences in this section will in some way relate to and encourage the developmental milestones discussed in Section One of the same page. These activities are quick and easy! Your time is precious now.

Play with your child! These moments of joyful togetherness will support the process of his or her social and language development, creative expression, and information-processing skills.

Section Three:
Share your memories!

This section is a small gift that you can give to yourself. Your child will be grown up so quickly, and memories of his or her early years will fade with time. Take just a moment to record these little milestones. They are precious, and reading them years from now will warm your heart.

So, **celebrate** each day with your child, **play** and be joyful (life is good!), and **share** your memories with the future you!

Celebrate!

Celebrate your baby's natural reflexes.

Most of Baby's activity in the first weeks of life will be reflexive. If you place your finger in the palm of Baby's hand, s/he will grasp it. If you put your finger in her/his mouth, s/he will suck it. If you place a finger under her/his toes, s/he will curl the toes around your finger and try to grip them.

From 0-1 month you will observe that Baby:

- Can grasp things placed in the palm of Baby's hand
- Will try to grip things placed under toes
- Can suck
- Will root

Play!

Textured Mittens

Why this playtime activity is good for your baby: Infants are interested in exploring different touch sensations. At this age, babies are very sensual. This activity heightens that awareness and gives them an opportunity to use their grasping reflex.

What you'll need to play this activity: You will need mittens made of a variety of textures. Buy or make mittens out of some of the following materials: silk, velvet, wool, terry cloth, satin, rubber, corduroy or fur.

How to play *Textured Mittens:* Placing different mittens on your hand, let Baby grasp at the mittens. Talk to Baby while s/he is grasping the varied textures. Use descriptive terms: soft, bumpy, smooth, rough, slick, flat, warm, cold, etc.

Share!

When you were an infant, your favorite comfort-object was:

_____

_____

It was made of this material: _____

It was this color: _____

Celebrate!

Celebrate your baby's developing language/communications skills.

One of the most important developments during Baby's first month will be the appearance of that first smile and giggle. Soon Baby will be smiling spontaneously.

From 0-1 month you will observe Baby:

- Smiling while sleeping
- Smiling when s/he sees familiar faces
- Responding to a smiling face with movement or sounds

Play!

See Baby Smiling

Why this playtime activity is good for your baby: From birth Baby is learning to identify and respond to subtle signals and recognize patterns of responsiveness. S/he is discovering that s/he can affect the world. Reinforcing this message is vital to Baby's developing self-esteem.

What you'll need to play this activity: A hand mirror

How to play *See Baby Smiling*: Hold Baby on her/his back in your lap. Hold a hand mirror 8" to 12" (20 cm to 31 cm) in front of Baby so s/he can focus on the reflection in the mirror. Say, "I see Baby smiling." Remember to wear a big smile for Baby while you are playing this game. When Baby smiles, respond with "I see Baby smiling!" Let Baby gaze into her/his reflection in the mirror as long as Baby is interested.

Variation: Daily, return your baby's smiles with appropriate words of praise, affection and smiles.

Share!

The first time I saw you smile it was like this:

_____

_____

_____

You were this old: _____

Celebrate!

Celebrate your baby's developing gross motor skills.

During the first few weeks Baby's movements will be very jerky. You may notice Baby's chin quivering or hands trembling. By the end of the first month, Baby's nervous system will mature and her/his muscle control will improve. You can help Baby develop gross motor skills by playing exercise games.

From 0-1 month you will observe that Baby:

- Needs help supporting head
- Makes jerky, quivering arm thrusts
- Often keeps hands held in tight fists
- Has strong, exaggerated reflex movements

Play!

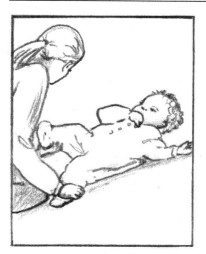

Baby Aerobics

Why this playtime activity is good for your baby: Baby will learn to use her/his muscles only by using them. At first movements will be reflexive and jerky. Helping Baby move body parts—especially arms and legs— in a smooth and particular way will help Baby develop gross motor skills.

What you'll need to play this activity: No special equipment is necessary for playing these two exercise games.

How to play *Baby Aerobics*: Place Baby on a bed or soft surface on her/his back. Begin by "riding a bicycle." Hold Baby's feet with your hands and slowly and gently move the legs in a bicycle-peddling motion while chanting "Ride a bicycle, ride a bicycle." Then exercise by "clapping." Hold Baby's hands in yours. Slowly and gently bring the hands together and say, "Clap your hands." Then open Baby's arms wide and stretch them out to Baby's side. Say, "Open wide." Repeat. Alternate the legs and arms exercises to give equal amounts of exercise to upper and lower body. Play for only a few minutes the first day. Exercises can be extended a bit after Baby is used to them.

Share!

The first time you lifted your head off the bed to look around, it was like this:

_____

Date:_____ You were this old: _____

When you were an infant, one way you exercised by yourself was:

_____

Celebrate!

Celebrate your baby's developing visual skills.

Between birth and three months you will witness Baby's growing interest in the world around her/him by the way s/he focuses and watches things. Baby's vision will go through many changes the first months. Babies are born with peripheral vision (can see to the sides), and gradually they acquire the ability to focus on a single point in front of their visual field. By one month, Baby will be able to focus on things as far away as three feet.

From 0-3 months you will observe that Baby:

- Focuses 8" to 12" (20 cm to 31 cm) away
- Occasionally involuntarily crosses her/his eyes
- Prefers black-and-white or high-contrast patterns
- Prefers the human face to all other patterns

Play!

Hello, I'm Puppet

Why this playtime activity is good for your baby: Stimulation of Baby's visual perception is enhanced with black and white, moving objects. Babies love to follow a puppet's movements and watch a puppet's mouth open and close. This activity is also an excellent language starter for older babies.

What you'll need to play this activity: Make or buy a black and white sock puppet. It is best to use just one puppet with which Baby can become familiar. Use a white sock with black eyes, mouth, and nose, or a black sock with white facial features. The sight of the familiar puppet will help Baby feel secure and increase the fun of this playtime activity.

How to play *Hello, I'm Puppet*: Place Baby on her/his back in your lap where s/he feels secure. Hold the puppet so the puppet's face is about 8" to 15" (20 cm to 38 cm) above Baby's face. Wiggle the puppet to get Baby's attention. Say, "Hello, I'm Puppet." While moving the puppet's mouth, talk for the puppet. Speak in short, simple phrases. Slowly move the puppet's head from side to side. Watch to see if the baby's eyes are following the puppet's movements. If Baby reaches and wants to grasp the puppet, that is okay. Physical contact with the puppet may increase Baby's interest in this play activity.

Share!

When you were an infant and we played with puppets, you responded like this:

_____

_____

_____

Celebrate!

Celebrate your baby's developing fine motor skills.

Immediately after birth Baby will be able to grasp objects, but it will be weeks or even months before Baby can hold onto and manipulate objects placed in her/his grasp and let go at will.

From 0-3 months Baby will develop her/his fine motor skills and abilities to:
- Reach and grasp objects at will
- Hold a rattle and shake it
- Release a grasp at will

Play!

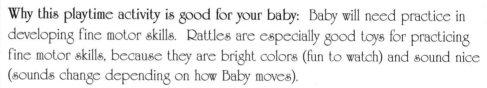

Shake, Rattle, and Roll!

Why this playtime activity is good for your baby: Baby will need practice in developing fine motor skills. Rattles are especially good toys for practicing fine motor skills, because they are bright colors (fun to watch) and sound nice (sounds change depending on how Baby moves).

What you'll need to play this activity: Bright, colorful, see-through rattles are especially nice for this play activity because Baby can see the movement inside the rattle when s/he shakes it.

How to play *Shake, Rattle, and Roll!*: Place Baby in your lap on her/his back. Hold a rattle 8" to 12" (20 cm to 31 cm) above Baby's head and shake (shake it up and down), rattle (move from side to side), or roll (rotate the rattle between your palms by rolling your hands back and forth). Each of these rattle movements will make a different sound. When Baby reaches for the rattle, put it in her/his grasp. As Baby moves the rattle, say "shake, rattle, and roll." If Baby cannot maintain a grasp yet, continue to move the rattle in interesting ways while talking to Baby.

Helpful Hint: Tie a 6" (15 cm)-long ribbon to the handle of a rattle and safety pin the other end of the ribbon to Baby's sleeve. This makes the rattle more accessible for Baby—even if s/he drops it, the rattle is still within reach.

Share!

When you were an infant, the way you played with baby rattles was this:

_____

_____

_____

Celebrate!

Celebrate your baby's developing cognitive skills.

From birth you will notice that Baby has the amazing ability to use a variation in tone and intensity in crying to express different needs. Crying is the only way Baby has to communicate her/his needs to you.

From 0-3 months, crying serves important useful purposes for your baby:

- It is a way to call for help when hungry or uncomfortable.
- It helps Baby shut out sights, sounds, and other sensations that are too intense.
- It helps Baby release tension.

Play!

Ride a Horsey

Why this playtime activity is good for your baby: One of the best ways to soothe a crying baby is to rock her/him back and forth or sway gently from side to side. Slow, calm movement seems to soothe most babies.

What you'll need to play this activity: a rocking chair

How to play Ride a Horsey: Sitting in a rocking chair, place crying baby on her/his back in your lap. As you slowly rock back and forth, recite this rhyme:

> Ride a horsey, ride a horsey,
> Up to town.
> Watch out, Baby, watch out, Baby,
> Don't fall down!

When you reach the last line of the rhyme, spread your legs a bit so Baby moves deeper into your lap. Place Baby securely back in your lap with knees together again and repeat.

Helpful Hint: If this game doesn't quiet Baby, try gently stroking her/his head or patting the back or the chest. Sometimes singing or talking in a quiet voice will calm a crying baby too.

Share!

When you were an infant and you cried, I soothed you by:

_____

_____

Celebrate!

Celebrate your baby's developing language milestones.

By listening to you and others talk, Baby is learning the importance of speech long before s/he understands any specific words. At this age, Baby is already aware of voice tones. Screaming or yelling might make Baby cry. Singing might help relax Baby. Soft, soothing sounds makes babies feel secure.

From 0-3 months you will obverse that Baby:

- Recognizes familiar voices
- Babbles and makes coos, chuckles, and gurgle sounds
- Enjoys hearing animal sounds and environmental sounds

Play!

Old McDonald Had a Farm

Why this playtime activity is good for your baby: Your baby is reassured, comforted, and entertained by the sounds s/he hears. When Baby coos and gurgles back at you, s/he is aware of the smile on your face and is learning that talking is a two-way communication.

What you'll need to play this activity: No special equipment is needed for this game–just a happy singing voice.

How to play *Old MacDonald Had a Farm*: Hold Baby in your lap on her/his back so Baby can see your mouth. Sing this simplified version of the song "Old MacDonald Had a Farm." Sing slowly, and make all of the animal sounds. As your child gets older and you play this game, hesitate before you make the animal sound giving her/him an opportunity to respond with the appropriate sound.

Old MacDonald had a farm, e-i-e-i-o
And on his farm he had a cow, e-i-e-i-o
Moo, moo.
Moo, moo.

Old MacDonald had a farm, e-i-e-i-o
And on his farm he had a cat, e-i-e-i-o.
Meow, meow.
Meow, meow.

Other Animal Sounds to make:
Sheep–baa, baa
Rooster–cock-a-doodle-do
Chick–peep, peep
Dog–bow, wow
Duck–quack, quack
Horse–neigh, neigh
Mouse–squeak, squeak
Crow–caw, caw

Share!

The very first sounds you made were these: _____

_____

You were this old: _____

Celebrate!

Celebrate your baby's developing visual perception.

At one month your baby still can't see very clearly beyond a foot or so. By two months Baby's eyes will be more coordinated and will work together to move and focus at the same time. At three months you will observe your baby following objects with her/his eyes. As Baby's visual focus matures, s/he will continue to gaze in the direction of moving objects that disappear, but s/he will not search for an object hidden from view.

From 1-3 months you will observe that Baby:

• Follows a rattle with her/his eyes for a short distance
• Looks at objects when they are placed in her/his vision

Play!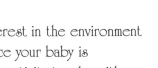

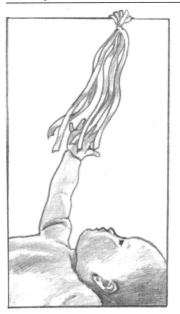

Ribbons in the Breeze

Why this playtime activity is good for your baby: Baby's interest in the environment provides wonderful opportunities for parent/child play. Since your baby is interested in visually following moving objects, this is a great activity to play with your baby. "Ribbons in the Breeze" will promote her/his visual awareness.

What you will need to play this activity: Brightly colored ribbons, needle and thread

How to play *Ribbons in the Breeze*: Cut the ribbons in varying lengths. Sew several together at one end. Hang the ribbons to the right and left, about one foot from your baby's eyes. Watch for the baby to acknowledge that s/he sees the ribbons. Usually there will be an increase in the baby's body movements or language. To make the ribbons flutter, use your hand to move them back and forth or blow on them.

Share!

When you were an infant, the object you most enjoyed watching was: _____

_____

As you grew older, you loved to watch: _____

_____

Celebrate!

Celebrate your baby's discovering the principle of cause and effect.

During the second and third months Baby will enjoy causing things to happen. Baby will become directly aware of the effect of her/his own actions on the physical world. This will hold a special fascination for your baby. Discovering the principle of cause and effect is the beginning of the capacity for Baby to amuse and entertain her/himself.

From 2-3 months you will observe that Baby:

- Is developing visually-directed reaching
- Enjoys creating effects in the environment by her/his own actions
- Will repeat an action over and over to see the effect

Play!

Hear Me Ring

Why this playtime activity is good for your baby: Young infants will use movements of arms and legs to create sounds. Through this experience, the infant will experience cause and effect. For example: If I move my leg, then I hear a pleasant sound.

What you'll need to play this activity: Sew a bell in the middle of each of two 6" (15 cm) pieces of elastic. Attach Velcro™ to the ends of the pieces.

How to play *Hear Me Ring*: Place the elastic bands around one of Baby's ankles and one wrist. Show Baby that when s/he moves one arm there is a sound. Move the other arm and there is not a sound. Repeat with the legs. Although Baby is too young to understand language, always explain to Baby what you are doing. "When you move the leg with the bell you hear a sound. When you move the arm without the bell you do not hear a sound."

Variation: Sew bells to the toes of a pair of Baby's socks. When s/he kicks her/his legs, the bells will ring.

Share!

When you were a baby and I put bells on your wrists and ankles, you reacted like this:

_____

_____

When I put bells on your socks, you reacted like this: _____

_____

Celebrate!

Celebrate your baby's maturing self-awareness.

By the end of the second month Baby will spend most of the day watching and listening to the people around her/him. S/He will begin to show genuine signs of pleasure and friendliness. Baby will feel good when those around smile and talk to her/him.

From 2-4 months you will observe that Baby:

- Enjoys looking at the human face more than anything else–especially Mother's or the main caregiver's
- Will hold a gaze into someone's eyes longer and longer
- Enjoys exploring her/his own body
- Will spend a great deal of time watching own moving hands and fingers
- Enjoys looking at own reflection in mirror

Play!

I See Baby

Why this playtime activity is good for your baby: Crib mirrors and infant wall mirrors encourage self-awareness. Infants as young as two months of age enjoy seeing their own reflections in mirrors.

What you'll need to play this activity: Mirrors are an important piece of equipment in a baby's room. For safety, mirrors for young infants should be unbreakable and have no sharp edges. They should be firmly mounted on the side of a crib or over a changing area at a convenient height for infant viewing. For optimal support in developing self-awareness, mirrors should be large enough for infants to see their faces and their body movements.

How to play *I See Baby*: When you see Baby gazing at her/himself in the mirror, say "I see Baby." Then explain that the image s/he is viewing is her/himself.

Variation: You can also play "I See Baby" by placing Baby in a lying position in your lap and using a hand mirror or holding Baby in front of a mirror.

Share!

The first time you gazed into a mirror at your own reflection, this is how you reacted:

_____

_____

Celebrate!

Celebrate your baby's developing language/communications skills.

The word infancy comes from the Latin, *infantia*, which means an inability to speak. At about two months, you may begin hearing your infant repeat some vowel sounds like *ah* or *ooh*. By four months, Baby will babble routinely with combinations of consonant and vowel sounds like *mama*, *baba*, or *dada*.

From 2-4 months you will observe that Baby:

- Repeats sounds in a rhythmic patterns
- Listens carefully to your voice
- Anticipates your moods by the tone of voice you use
- May say her/his first words

Play!

I See, Do You See?

Why this playtime activity is good for your baby: It is easier to master language when sounds are accompanied by visual clues.

What you'll need to play this activity: Common household objects like a baby bottle, rattle, an apple, etc.

How to play *I See, Do You See?*: As you point to Baby's hand, say "I see your hand." Hold up Baby's hand and ask, "Do you see Baby's hand?" Do the same with other objects such as Baby's foot, an apple, Baby's bottle, Baby's rattle, etc. Introduce one or two new objects each day, and review the others introduced on other days.

Share!

When you were a baby, the first sounds you most liked to make were these:

_____

_____

_____

_____

Celebrate!

Celebrate your baby's developing sensory awareness.

Enjoy playing with your baby through touch! Babies love to be touched and to touch others. Give Baby a back rub; outline her/his legs and arms softly with your fingers; kiss hands and fingers, head and face. Bonding by touching is physically and psychologically healthy for Baby, and it will be so much fun for you!

From 3-6 months you will observe that Baby:

- Enjoys playing with other people and may cry when playing stops
- Uses fingers to explore own face
- Enjoys watching own hands and fingers move
- Will use sense of taste to explore environment
- Will become more communicative and expressive with face and body

Play!

Touch My Nose

Why this playtime activity is good for your baby: Young children need special "one-to-one" time with their caregivers. This activity helps to develop the bond between baby and adult. At this age babies can imitate some movements and expressions, and they recognize some words.

What you'll need to play this activity: No special equipment is needed to play this game.

How to play *Touch My Nose:* Place Baby on her/his back in your lap. Establish eye contact. Say "Touch my nose," and touch your nose. Then say "Touch my ears," and touch your ears. Touch and name several parts of your face. After you have played this game for a while give Baby a chance to touch the appropriate place on your face as you give the commands.

Variation: Play "Touch Baby's Nose." As you name facial features, touch the appropriate place on Baby's face. Eventually Baby will touch the places s/he hears you naming.

Share!

When named, you could touch your nose when you were this old: _____

When named, you could touch your ears when you were this old:_____

When named, you could touch your eyebrows when you were this old:_____

When named, you could touch your chin when you were this old: _____

When named, you could touch your tummy when you were this old:_____

When named, you could touch your feet when you were this old: _____

When named, you could touch your knees when you were this old: _____

When named, you could touch your elbows when you were this old:_____

Celebrate!

Celebrate your baby's developing cognitive skills.

Between three and six months, Baby's memory and attention span will increase. Your baby will understand and use the principle of cause and effect. For example: Baby will learn that when s/he drops her/his bottle, someone gives it back to her/him. When s/he cries, someone picks her/him up. When s/he shakes a rattle, it makes a sound.

From 3-6 months you will notice that Baby is:

- Absorbing information
- Applying knowledge to her/his day-to-day activities
- Accidentally stumbling upon the effect of certain actions

Play!

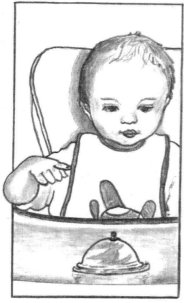

Ring the Bell

Why this playtime activity is good for your baby: Babies enjoy making things happen–discovering cause and effect. When playing this game, Baby will learn that pushing the button on the bell causes it to ring.

What you'll need to play this activity: Desk bell

How to play *Ring the Bell*: This activity works best if you have the baby sitting in a high chair, or supervised in a walker with a tabletop on it. Demonstrate how to ring the bell. See if the baby can do it on her/his own. Stress the word "push" as you are doing this activity. If the baby doesn't understand how to ring the bell, help by taking Baby's hand and pushing the button with one of Baby's fingers. When Baby rings the bell, say "Ring the bell again." Soon Baby will know that pushing the bell is making it ring.

Variation: Use other musical instruments to teach Baby cause and effect. Beat a pot with a spoon, shake a tambourine, ring a bell, and bang sticks together.

Share!

You were very smart when you were a baby. One of the first things you learned to do by yourself was this:

_____

_____

_____

Celebrate!

Celebrate your baby's developing gross motor skills.

During the fourth through the sixth month most babies begin learning how to sit up. Baby will accomplish this challenge in small steps as her/his back and neck muscles gradually strengthen and s/he develops better balance in the trunk, head, and neck.

From 3-6 months you will notice that Baby:

- Can raise legs and arms off the floor while resting on stomach
- Can hold head steady
- Sits up with a little support

Play!

Sitting Up Big!

Why this playtime activity is good for your baby: At this age it is good to help Baby strengthen back and neck muscles and practice balance by sitting up.

What you'll need to play this activity: Soft pillows placed in a baby-sized box, a bean bag chair or anything that is soft like a cushion

How to play *Sitting Up Big*: Place soft pillows or cushions in a box or get out the bean bag chair. Prop the baby securely against the cushions or back of the chair. Both of these ways of supporting Baby are excellent for protecting her/him during the many tumbles that occur while the baby is practicing this new sense of independence and way of looking at the world. By taking soft, formable objects and surrounding the baby, you can create a support where Baby will feel secure and safe. Once the baby has strengthened her/his back muscles and learned to maintain good balance, sitting up without support will be easy. When you sit Baby up say, "Sitting up big!" Tell Baby how proud you are of her/his ability to sit up. In the beginning, don't let Baby sit up too long. It will make her/his muscles tired. Gradually extend the sitting up time each day.

Variation: You can help the baby to practice sitting up in yet another way. Place Baby in a small, round inflatable ring. (These swimming pool rings are available at most discount stores.) This way the baby can feel the light support around her legs while the ring keeps her/him upright.

Share!

You sat up for the very first time with support at the age of: _____

You learned to sit up by yourself at the age of: _____

Celebrate!

Celebrate your baby's visual milestones.

During these early months, Baby's good vision is playing a key role in her/his early motor and cognitive development.

From 3-6 months you will observe that Baby:

- Will have developed full color vision
- Will have maturing distance vision
- Will have the ability to track moving objects for greater lengths of time

Play!

Red, Blue, and Yellow

Why this playtime activity is good for your baby: Baby is beginning to distinguish subtle shades of reds, blues, and yellows. Many babies like increasingly complex patterns and shapes as they get older. Looking at new and unusual pictures will stimulate Baby and provide an opportunity for comparing and contrasting colors, shapes, or sizes.

What you'll need to play this activity: Large pictures from magazines, catalogs, calendars, posters, greeting cards–especially pictures with a lot of primary colors (red, blue, and yellow).

How to play *Red, Blue, and Yellow:* Hold the baby on your lap with her/his back against your chest. Look at the pictures together. Name the objects in the pictures for Baby. Point out the three primary colors. Don't confuse Baby by naming other colors; s/he may not be able to distinguish pastels yet.

Share!

When you were a baby, your favorite color, shapes, and things to look at included:

_____

_____

_____

_____

Celebrate!

Celebrate your baby's developing language/communication skills.

Children learn language in stages. From birth your baby is receiving information about language by hearing people make sounds and watching how they communicate with one another. Baby will listen to the vowels and consonants and will begin to notice the way these combine into syllables, words, and sentences.

By the end of six months, you may notice that Baby:

- Understands the word "no"
- Babbles consonants and vowels
- Will try to imitate sounds s/he hears
- Uses her/his voice to express a wide range of feelings including joy, pain, and anger

Play!

Play Eye Winker

Why this playtime activity is good for your baby: Body parts are some of the first words your baby will learn to recognize, understand, and pronounce.

What you'll need to play this activity: No special equipment is needed to play this game.

How to play *Eye Winker:* As you recite the rhyme, point to the appropriate part of Baby's face. Then say the rhyme and let Baby point to the appropriate parts of her/his face. Gradually speed up the rhyme and see if Baby can follow with her/his finger pointing.

Brow blinker,	(eyebrow)
Eye winker,	(eyes)
Nose dripper,	(nose)
Mouth eater,	(mouth)
Chin chopper,	(chin)
Chin chopper.	(chin)

Share!

You knew the parts of your face when you were this old:_____

Your first word was: _____ Date:_____

Your first phrase was: _____

Date you spoke your first phrase was: _____

Your first sentence was:_____

Date you spoke your first sentence was: _____

Celebrate!

Celebrate your baby's maturing self-awareness.

By three or four months Baby's favorite sound will be her/his own name. S/He will love to hear you saying, calling, and singing it. When you talk to Baby, use her/his name often. Make up little songs and incorporate your baby's name.

From 3-6 months you will observe that Baby:

- Responds to the sound of her/his name
- Recognizes self in mirror
- Enjoys social play
- Likes to listen to rhythmic and rhyming words (nursery rhymes) and songs (simple tunes)

Play!

Pat-a-Cake

Why this playtime activity is good for your baby: Clapping or moving hands and feet in rhythmic ways will help Baby learn coordination. Hearing her/his name in a rhyme will make this playtime even more enjoyable for Baby.

What you'll need to play this activity: No special equipment is needed to play this game.

How to play *Pat-a-Cake*: As you say the rhyme, help Baby clap her/his hands together in time. Make the appropriate hand or arm movements when you say these words: "pat," "prick," "mark it," or "throw it in the oven."

> Pat-a-cake, pat-a-cake, baker's man!
> Make me a cake as fast as you can:
> Pat it, and prick it, and mark it with a (*say the first letter of Baby's name*).
> And throw it in the oven for (*Baby's name*) and me.

Share!

When you were a baby and we played Pat-a-Cake, you reacted like this:

_____

_____

Celebrate!

Celebrate your baby's cognitive development.

By the time Baby is four to six months old, you will probably have a fairly precise daily routine that is comfortable for both of you. A daily routine for eating, napping, bathing, and sleeping provides Baby with needed security. Celebrate your baby's growing sense of security and trust.

From 4-6 months you will observe that Baby:

- Recognizes and trusts familiar people
- May cry if approached by a stranger
- Is sometimes anxious if daily routine is disrupted

Play!

Peekaboo

Why this playtime activity is good for your baby: Babies do not know that things they cannot see still exist. When Mother leaves Baby's sight, s/he doesn't know if Mother will ever return again. The coming and going of family members teaches Baby trust.

What you'll need to play this activity: A transparent cloth like a silk head scarf

How to play Peekaboo: Place Baby in a lying position in your lap. Drape the scarf over Baby's head and ask "Where is Baby?" Lift the scarf and say "Peekaboo!" Then pull off the scarf and say "There s/he is!" Act a little surprised when you see Baby.

Variations: Variations of Peekaboo are almost endless. As your baby gets older, allow her/him to take the lead. Soon Baby will pull off the scarf when asked "Where is Baby?"

Share!

When you and I played Peekaboo, you demonstrated your enjoyment by:

_____

_____

This is how you reacted to strangers: _____

_____

Celebrate!

Celebrate your baby's developing auditory skills.

From four to six months is when participation in your baby's language development is most important. Listening is how Baby will learn speech. Every day s/he records all of the sounds heard. Nursery rhymes, children's songs, and short stories are all especially pleasant for Baby to hear.

From 4-6 months you will observe that Baby:
- Will respond to a sound by imitating it
- Will gaze into your face when you are talking to her/him
- Will turn her/his head in your direction when you enter a room or speak
- Will keep time to music by moving hands or feet

Play!

Nursery Rhyme Games

Why this playtime activity is good for your baby: Nursery rhymes about daily events will help Baby learn common routines like night and day.

What you will need to play nursery rhyme games: Make sure you have a good nursery rhyme book in your home library. A nursery rhyme each night before bed will help Baby relax and look forward to bedtime.

How to play these nursery rhyme games:

In the morning you might welcome Baby awake with this rhyme:

> Come, my dear child,
> Up with the sun,
> Birds are all singing,
> And morning's begun.

At night when it is time to go to bed you might recite this one:

> Go to bed (*Baby's name*),
> Go to bed (*Baby's name*),
> Merry or sober, go to bed (*Baby's name*).

Share!

When you were a baby, your favorite nursery rhyme was this one:

_____

_____

_____

Celebrate!

Celebrate your baby's gross motor movement milestones.

Between four and eight months your baby will develop the muscle control s/he needs to lift her/his head off the floor. S/He will be able to stretch out on her/his tummy and lift both legs and both arms off the floor at once. Most babies learn to roll over in both directions–from stomach to back and from back to stomach–before the eighth-month birthday.

By the end of the eighth month you will observe that Baby:

- Can transfer objects from hand to hand
- Can reach with one hand
- Can support her/his whole weight on legs
- Can roll over both directions at will

Play!

Kick the Balloon

Why this playtime activity is good for your baby: Moving objects often compel a baby to move so that the baby can keep the object going. This activity will promote agility in the baby and is a fun kicking game for Baby to play.

What you'll need to play this activity: A large inflated balloon with a ribbon tied to it

How to play *Kick the Balloon:* Secure the balloon overhead and suspend it from the ceiling about 3" to 5" (76 mm to 127 mm) from Baby's feet. Show Baby how to move her/his legs to make the balloon move. Tell Baby, "Kick the balloon." Give Baby a chance to kick and bat at the balloon all by her/himself.

Variation: You may want to slide Baby down so her/his arms, instead of feet, reach the balloon. Tell Baby "Bat the Balloon."

(Balloon activities should <u>always</u> be supervised by an adult. Never leave a baby alone with a balloon.)

Share!

When you were a baby, your favorite toys included:_____

_____

When you played with balloons, you liked to do this: _____

_____

_____

Celebrate!

Celebrate your baby's language/communications skills.

It is your job to say the names of all the people and objects that Baby comes in contact with each day. Say them and the baby's own name over and over for her/him. Talk to Baby every day with familiar words and sentences. This is one of the most important things you can do for your baby.

From 6-9 months you will observe that Baby:

- Waves bye-bye
- Begins making consonant sounds
- Uses Mama/Dada nonspecifically
- Babbles and coos in "baby talk"
- Recognizes the names of many common objects

Play!

Touch the Apple

Why this activity is good for your baby: At this age, it is important to encourage Baby to listen for all the various sounds s/he can hear during the day. This game will help Baby learn the names of common household objects.

What you'll need to play this activity: Pick three or four common items from the kitchen, including an apple.

How to play *Touch the Apple*: This game is played easily if you sit the baby in a high chair with a tray. Place three or four objects including an apple on the baby's high chair tray. Then say "Touch the apple." Touch the apple so Baby will know what you want her/him to do. If Baby touches the apple say "You touched the apple!" If Baby touches one of the other objects, for example a banana, say "You touched the banana." Touch the apple again. Repeat until Baby can touch the four objects named. If Baby knows the objects, the next day you can choose three new objects plus the apple. If Baby doesn't know the names of the four objects, use the same ones in a game until she/he learns them.

Share!

The first time you waved bye-bye you were this old: _____

When you were six months old, the objects you could touch when they were named included these:

_____

_____

When you were nine months old, the objects you could touch when they were named included these:

_____

Celebrate!

Celebrate your baby's social/emotional developmental milestones.

During this time you may notice that Baby has two different ways of dealing with people. S/He will be outgoing and affectionate with those s/he knows. Unfamiliar faces, on the other hand, may cause Baby anxiety. Remember, it is healthy for Baby to be able to make the distinction between the familiar and the unfamiliar. A strong sense of self will help Baby feel more secure in unfamiliar situations.

From 6-9 months you will observe that Baby:

- Recognizes mother or father as the principal caregiver
- May become shy when in a new place or situation
- May cling to mother and familiar people
- May demonstrate anxiety around strangers

Play!

Show Your Toy

Why this playtime activity is good for your baby: Encouraging Baby to play social games with new people will help her/him become more at ease and familiar with the new faces.

What you will need to play this activity: Whichever toy your baby is holding will be fine.

How to play *Show Your Toy*: When a stranger approaches Baby (and this is an okay person for baby to get to know), tell Baby "Show your toy to (name of person)." That way, Baby will receive a verbal signal from you that being friendly to this person is safe. Presenting a toy instead of her/himself is less threatening to a baby because it puts the focus on the toy instead of self.

Variation: If a toy isn't available, Baby can show her/his shoes, hands, etc.

Share!

When you were a baby, this is how you reacted to strangers: _____

_____

This is how you reacted when left with a babysitter: _____

_____

_____

Celebrate!

Celebrate your baby's developing self-care skills.

During the period between six and nine months, Baby will begin extending arms and legs to help when being dressed and undressed. S/He will have preferences and find ways to let you know what they are. S/He will be able to grasp a toothbrush and brush her/his own teeth.

From 6-9 months old you will observe that Baby:

- Cries when s/he needs help
- Will hold her/his own bottle
- Will begin to feed her/himself
- Will want to hold a cup and drink from it
- Will begin to take off clothing that s/he can remove easily
- Will like to untie own shoes or pull off socks

Play!

Baby's Cup

Why this self-care activity is good for your baby: Learning to hold a cup and drink from it is a difficult task. Practicing holding and pretending to drink from a cup are good exercises to prepare for balancing and sipping from a cup of liquid.

What you'll need to play this activity: It is time for Baby to have her/his own cup. It should be nonbreakable plastic or metal with one or two large handles. It should not be too big. It should be the size that the baby can easily hold in both hands.

How to play *Baby's Cup:* Begin by letting Baby hold the empty cup. Let Baby see you pour a few drops of water in the bottom of the cup. Then show Baby how to tip up the cup and sip the water. Increase the amount of water in the cup until baby becomes better at drinking from it. At first you can hold the cup for her/him, and then both of you can hold it together. Soon Baby will want to hold the cup by her/himself.

Share!

You first learned how to drink from a cup at the age of: _____

When I taught you how to drink from a cup this is what happened: _____

_____

_____

Your first cup looked like this: _____

Celebrate!

Celebrate your baby's developing fine motor skills.

Between six and nine months Baby will begin using the pincher grasp, but s/he won't perfect this fine motor skill until approximately nine months old. Using the thumb and opposing finger, Baby will be able to pick up objects and hold them for extended periods of time.

From 6-9 months you will observe that Baby:

- Likes to bang things together
- Enjoys inserting small things inside larger things
- Will poke, twist, and squeeze soft and pliable toys
- May drop, pour, and throw foods off the high chair tray
- Will like to open/shut, push/pull, and drag objects
- Can pick up very small objects

Play!

Puzzles

Why puzzles are good toys for your baby: Puzzles with two to four pieces with pieces fitting easily into precut outline forms or wooden puzzles with knobs are excellent manipulative toys for babies this age. Puzzles will give Baby an opportunity to practice fine motor skills and eye-hand coordination at the same time.

What you'll need to play this activity: You will need puzzles with two to four pieces or wooden puzzles with knobs. Thick plastic pieces with rounded edges are most useful because they can be put in the mouth and are washable.

How to play with puzzles:

1. Begin by showing Baby the completed puzzle. Take out one piece and then another until the puzzle is completely disassembled. Then put it back together while Baby watches.

2. One of the first ways Baby will learn to play with puzzles is taking them apart. After you put the puzzle together, encourage baby to take it apart.

3. Guide Baby's hand in putting one missing puzzle piece back in the puzzle.

4. Let Baby play with puzzle pieces in free play.

Share!

The first time you played with a puzzle you did this: _____

_____

_____

Celebrate!

Celebrate your baby's exploration play.

During this important developmental stage, Baby will begin looking around at things near and far. S/He will be able to hold onto objects, look at them and use them in an appropriate ways. You will witness Baby learning to hold two toys at once, reaching across her/his body to get the second toy. It is through exploratory play that Baby will learn how things feel and work.

From 6-9 months you will observe that Baby:

- Can sit up for extended periods of time
- Will explore and experiment with toys as tools
- Will discover the size, shape, weight, and feel of things for her/himself

Play!

Baby In a Box

Why this playtime activity is good for your baby: Exploration is one of the best kinds of learning games for Baby.

What you'll need to play this activity: Four large cardboard boxes and a variety of textured objects and toys

How to play *Baby In a Box*: Gather four cardboard boxes large enough for Baby to sit inside. Fill each with a different textured object such as shredded newspaper; several inches of sand; a velvet or silk blanket; cotton balls or any other textured objects that you think will please Baby. Let the baby sit in one of the boxes to play. Talk to Baby about the texture of the objects in the box. After a while, move the baby to a new box with a different texture. Leave the textured boxes available for play. When Baby loses interest in the textured boxes, change the textures inside the boxes.

Share!

When you were a baby, your favorite textures to touch were these: _____

_____

When you were six months old, your favorite comfort-toy was this: _____

_____

You enjoyed playing with: _____

_____

Celebrate!

Celebrate your baby's developing auditory/visual skills.

By six months your baby's vision will be fully developed. Baby will smile at you when you are across the room and spend time studying objects that are several feet away. As Baby's eyesight develops, s/he will seek out more stimulating things to view. Now is the time to nurture Baby's interest in books. Books will provide the visual stimulation that s/he enjoys, while listening to a story will give Baby rich, new vocabulary accompanied by pictures. Weekly trips to the library will provide pleasure and teach Baby the importance of having a variety of books available.

From 6-9 months you will observe that Baby:

- Can sit quietly for a few minutes at a time
- Is interested in large, colorful pictures
- Will like to listen to short stories and books
- Will enjoy different kinds of music

Play!

Lap Reading

Why lap reading is good for your baby: Talking about pictures usually generates more interest than reading stories to babies, but by nine months Baby will enjoy word-for-word reproduction of some rhythmic or rhyming materials, especially nursery rhymes.

What you'll need to play this activity: Books suitable for adults reading aloud to older infants include the cloth, plastic, or cardboard books suitable for babies. Other picture books and nursery rhyme books are suitable, too. The size and construction of books for lap reading need not conform to the standard for books to be handled by infants alone, because the adult holds the book, turns the pages, and can protect the baby and the book from harm.

How to use books with 6-9 month olds: Sit Baby up in your lap, leaning against your chest, so s/he can see the pictures as you hold the book in front of her/him and turn the pages. Begin by discussing the pictures in the book. The amount of lap reading time can be extended as indicated by Baby's interest and ability to sit quietly.

Share!

When you were a baby, your favorite stories/books were these: _____

_____

The first time you went to the library, you: _____

_____

Celebrate!

Celebrate your baby's strengthening gross motor muscles.

When Baby is lying on her/his tummy on a flat surface, you will observe that s/he is always in motion. S/He'll arch her/his neck so s/he can look around. Babies this age aren't content to stay in one position long. S/He will be able to turn over at will and will flip without a moment's notice. All these activities are strengthening muscles for crawling–a skill Baby will probably master between seven and ten months. At eight months Baby will probably be sitting up without support.

From 7-10 months you will observe that Baby:

- Will crawl or creep to reach objects
- Will sometimes do push-ups when placed on tummy
- Will use elbows to hold up the upper body when placed on tummy
- Will roll over from back to stomach or from stomach to back

Play!

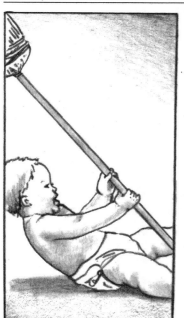

Pull-Up!

Why this playtime activity is good for your baby: Upper body strength is an important key to crawling. You can help Baby get ready to crawl by helping her/him exercise her/his arms and upper body.

What you'll need to play this activity: Broomstick

How to play *Pull-Up!*: Set up a soft environment using pillows or bean bag chairs. Lay the baby on her/his back. Have the baby grab the broomstick. Cover her/his hands with your own, squeezing slightly to show the baby how to hold on. Lift the broomstick slowly, just a couple of inches. As Baby raises up, say "Pull-up!" Hold a few seconds, then lower. Wait and see if Baby will try to lift her/his own body using strong arm muscles. Give the verbal cue each time Baby pulls up her/his body. Repeat several times each day to strengthen Baby's hand, arm, shoulder, and upper back muscles.

Share!

When you were a baby, your favorite way to exercise was this:_____

_____

_____

_____

Celebrate!

Celebrate your baby's developing gross motor skills.

During this developmental stage, you can encourage your baby to crawl. Present her/him with intriguing objects placed just beyond her/his reach. As Baby becomes more agile, make miniature obstacle courses with soft pillows, boxes, and sofa cushions for Baby to maneuver around, between, and over.

From 7-10 months you will observe that Baby:

- Begins to crawl forward on belly
- Will be able to assume the hands-and-knees position
- Will be able to move forward on hands and knees

Play!

Balloon Ball

Why this playtime activity is good for Baby: This game combines curiosity, vision, and crawling action while enhancing Baby's visual awareness.

What you'll need to play this activity: Inflate three or four large, sturdy balloons. Secure the air inside by tying a knot at the neck of each balloon. It is best if the balloons are different primary colors. (Use the heavy, sturdy type of balloon, not the small and flimsy kind.)

How to play *Balloon Ball:* Let the baby explore the balloons with her/his hands. Then toss a balloon, and encourage Baby to crawl after it. If the baby loses track, point to the area where the balloon landed. Repeat with another balloon. (Always supervise this game because an uninflated or broken balloon is dangerous if swallowed. Never leave an infant alone with a balloon.)

Variation: Tie a short length of yarn to a small, inflated balloon, and tie the other end of the yarn around Baby's wrist. Show her/him how to bat the balloon.

Share!

I remember the very first time you crawled. The date was: _____

You were this many months old: _____

This is what happened: _____

_____

_____

Celebrate!

Celebrate your baby's maturing gross motor skills.

In the months before Baby begins walking, s/he will do many different kinds of exercise to make her/his body strong and ready to support and balance the body in an upright position. When placed on her/his stomach, s/he will push up with arms and lock her/his elbows so that her/his arms are straight. This is excellent exercise for back, shoulders, and arms.

From 8-12 months you will observe that Baby:

- Can pull her/himself up to a standing position
- Walks upright holding onto furniture
- Stands momentarily without support

Play!

Walking Through the Maze

Why this playtime exercise is good for your baby: When Baby can stand firmly on her/his feet while holding on, s/he will try walking. If you provide a stand-up maze of things to hold onto while standing, Baby may try to maneuver through the maze in an upright position.

What you will need to play this activity: To make this walking maze, gather a soft sofa, chairs with soft backs, large boxes draped with soft blankets or quilts, soft pillows, etc.

How to play *Walking Through the Maze:* Arrange the furniture in one room so that there is support along the maze. Get on your knees and holding onto the furniture, boxes, and pillows, work your way through the maze. Encourage Baby to "walk" through the maze too. If Baby would rather crawl through the maze for a while, that is okay. Give Baby time to build courage when learning to walk. Leave the maze up for a few days until Baby tires of it.

Share!

The first time you took steps alone it was like this:_____

_____

_____

_____

_____

Celebrate!

Celebrate your baby's cognitive milestones.

At about nine months Baby will be extremely curious about everything. S/He will have a short attention span and will move rapidly from one activity to the next. Two or three minutes is the longest s/he'll spend with a single toy or playing a particular game. By the end of the first year, Baby will probably be able to sit for as long as fifteen minutes.

From 9-12 months you will observe that Baby:

- Will explore toys and use them in appropriate ways (talk on play telephone, comb hair with a brush, etc.)
- Will be able to find partially hidden objects easily
- Will look at an object when it is named
- Will imitate sounds that s/he hears and gestures that s/he sees

Play!

What Happened?

Why this playtime activity is good for your baby: Your baby will learn much from experimenting with objects. If you watch, you will see Baby dropping food off the edge of the high chair to see what happens, pouring milk out of her/his cup to see where it goes, etc. During these important learning days, it is vital that you encourage your baby's experimentation.

What you'll need to play this activity: Large plastic dish pan and toys that float and sink

How to play *What Happened?*: Put several inches of warm water in the dish pan. One at a time place toys that sink and toys that float in the water. Each time ask Baby "What happened?" If the boat floats, you can add, "The boat floats." Your explanations do not have to be long or complicated. Simple terms like *floats*, *splatters*, and *sinks* will do nicely.

Variation: Supervised, let Baby experiment with the toys and water.

Share!

When you were a baby you liked to experiment by:_____

_____

_____

_____

_____

Celebrate!

Celebrate your baby's social and emotional milestones.

By nine months your baby will probably have become quite social. Baby will pick up cues from you about all your different emotional states. If you are happy and smiling, Baby will laugh and babble. If you are depressed or cry, Baby may become sad or anxious. Babies this age are acutely sensitive to their mothers' emotions.

From 9-12 months you will observe that Baby:

- Enjoys social play
- Is interested in viewing self in a mirror
- Responds to other people's expressions of emotion
- Recognizes the faces of family and friends
- May be afraid of strangers

Play!

This is My Happy (Sad, Mad, Sleepy, Hungry, etc.) Face

Why this playtime activity is good for your baby: Early on, it is good for Baby to learn that all feelings are okay. Teaching Baby the words to express feelings will make it easier for her/him to deal with and accept feelings later.

What you'll need to play this activity: A hand mirror

How to play *This is My Happy Face*: Sit Baby in your lap with her/his back leaning against your chest. Hold the mirror in front of Baby so s/he can see your reflection. Make a big happy face in the mirror and say, "This is my happy face!" Make a sad face and say "This is my sad face." Make lots of different faces and give the words for the emotions you are demonstrating. Then hold the mirror so Baby can see her/his face. Look at the faces Baby makes. Tell Baby how beautiful her/his faces are. After you make a particular face, ask Baby if s/he can make that kind of face. "Can you make a happy face? Can you show me your mad face?"

Variation: On a day when Baby is feeling extremely emotional, you might ask, "Are you wearing your sad (sleepy, sick, surprised, mad, worried, anxious) face?" Tell Baby that it is okay to wear that face when s/he is feeling sad (sleepy, sick, mad, etc.).

Share!

When you were a baby you made the cutest faces. One that I especially loved was like this:

_____

_____

Celebrate!

Celebrate your baby's maturing cognitive skills.

During the last quarter of Baby's first year, s/he will become increasingly mobile. Being able to move from place to place will give your baby a new sense of power. While this new independence will be exciting to her/him, it will also put Baby in dangerous situations. You will have to be extra cautious now. Gate rooms where Baby should not go, tops and bottoms of stairways, and doors to outside.

From 9-12 months you will observe that Baby:

- Recognizes her/his own toys
- Likes to move around and feel a sense of freedom and independence
- Can find partially hidden objects
- Will search for a toy removed from sight

Play!

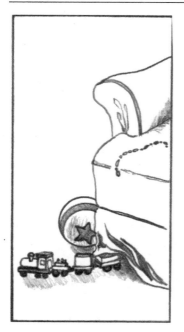

Hide-and-Seek Toys

Why this playtime activity is good for your baby: By this age, Baby recognizes her/his own toys. It will be a surprise to find them hidden around the room. The searching will provide Baby with an opportunity to use visual skills to spot them, gross motor skills to crawl to them, and fine motor skills for picking up and playing with the toys.

What you'll need to play this activity: Brightly colored toys that Baby especially enjoys

How to play *Hide-and-Seek Toys*: Hide toys in low kitchen cupboards where Baby can discover them. Hide toys under sofa cushions, behind furniture, and on low shelves. As Baby moves about exploring the room s/he will find the toys.

Variation: You might want to hide a toy like a doll or stuffed animal (partially exposed with eyes peeking out) behind furniture, under a sofa cushion, etc. Ask "Where is dolly? Do you see Mr. Bear? Can you find the bear?" Help guide Baby's search with verbal clues like: "The bear is over there. You are getting closer. The bear is in a soft place."

Share!

When you were a baby, your favorite toy was this: _____

Your favorite activity was this:_____

You spent most of your time playing this: _____

Celebrate!

Celebrate your baby's developing intellectual skills.

Babies this age usually enjoy playing in the kitchen. They love to rummage through drawers, empty out lower cabinets, and explore broom closets and under sinks. After baby-proofing these areas and making sure they are safe, the kitchen cupboards and cooking utensils will provide a lot of interesting experimentation for your baby. Don't be surprised if suddenly her/his favorite toys are the wooden spoons, egg cartons, and plastic food containers.

From 9-12 months you will observe that Baby:

- Will begin handling things with more awareness
- Will repeat an action if s/he gets people to laugh or respond
- Will enjoy using measuring tools to play in sand, water, or mud
- Will especially enjoy playing with common household objects

Play!

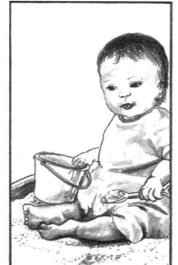

Sandbox

Why this playtime activity is good for your baby: Pouring sand from one container to another is good eye-hand coordination, and babies never tire of pouring, dropping, rolling, and submerging plastic toys in sand and water.

What you will need to play this activity: A large, plastic dish pan with 2" to 4" (51 mm to 102 mm) of sand in the bottom; measuring tools like cups, plastic bowls, and spoons; beach toys like plastic buckets and shovels; and plastic gardening tools like spades and scoops

How to play *Sandbox*: Place Baby in front of the sandbox with toys. Show Baby how to fill a cup with a scoop. Pour sand from cup to bowl, etc. After Baby understands the "Sandbox" game, talk about what s/he is doing. "I see you like to fill the big cup with sand. Can you fill the bucket with sand? Do you see the red cup? Where is the scoop?"

Share!

Your favorite sandbox games were:_____

_____

_____

Your favorite sandbox toys were: _____

_____

Celebrate!

Celebrate your baby's developing gross motor skills.

As soon as your baby has learned to crawl, s/he must begin dealing with obstacles like stairs. Unlike learning to crawl or walk, climbing stairs is something you will have to teach Baby how to do. Climbing stairs is a skill that takes instruction and practice, and if it is attempted without skill or guidance it is dangerous.

From 9-12 months you will observe that Baby:

- Can move arms and legs actively
- Is gradually gaining control of back muscles
- Can sit up without support
- Will move body in rhythmic movements
- Crawls to get from one place to another

Play!

Crawling Up and Down Stairs

Why this playtime activity is good for your baby: If your home has stairs, it is essential that you teach Baby how to safely go up and down the stairs.

What you'll need to play this activity: Let your baby practice crawling up and down steps constructed of heavy-duty foam blocks or sturdy cardboard cartons covered with fabric. You might also use pillows from a sofa placed on the floor in front of the sofa. The sofa then becomes two soft, giant steps.

How to play *Crawling Up and Down Stairs*: Use your hands to assist Baby's crawling up and down the practice stairs you have constructed. Keep the stairs where Baby can practice on them. When Baby has mastered the practice stairs, teach her/him how to go down real stairs crawling backwards. Practice on carpeted steps first.

Share!

The first time you tried to climb down stairs you did this:_____

_____

_____

_____

_____

Celebrate!

Celebrate your baby's developing social/emotional milestones.

Between nine and twelve months babies prefer their mother and/or regular caregivers over all others. You may notice that Baby will extend arms for a hug or to indicate that s/he wants to be picked up and held. These are the developmental months when Baby will begin testing parental responses to her/his actions and behavior. Example: S/He may cry when Mother leaves her/him with a sitter but will stop crying as soon as Mother is out-of-sight.

From 9-12 months you will observe that Baby:

- Demonstrates affection
- Expresses feelings
- Demonstrates preferences such as favorite food, color, toy
- May fear strangers and new places
- May be fearful in new situations

Play!

Peekaboo Umbrella

Why this learning activity is good for your baby: Babies are fascinated by the game of "Peekaboo." Peekaboo is a game which can help Baby to understand the concepts of leaving and returning. When the caregiver is behind the umbrella, she is gone. When the caregiver moves the umbrella away, she has returned.

What you'll need to complete this activity: You will need an umbrella with a smiley face drawn on the top with a magic marker. It is still best to use primary colors when working with Baby, so choose a solid red, blue, or yellow umbrella and use the other two primary colors to draw the face.

How to play Peekaboo Umbrella: Sit the baby in an infant seat. Open the umbrella and show the baby the smiley face you have drawn on it. Spinning the umbrella to get the baby's full attention, play "Peekaboo" with the umbrella. Have fun with this game, and talk a lot about the game with the baby. "Where am I? Can you see me? Can you see me now? Where did I go? Here I am!"

Share!

When you were a baby and I had to leave you with a sitter, you responded in this way:

_____

_____

_____

Celebrate!

Celebrate your baby's developing cognitive skills.

As Baby nears the one-year-old milestone, her/his desire to explore will become insatiable. S/He'll want to touch, taste, and manipulate everything s/he sees–which is, of course, how s/he will learn. But sometimes s/he will get into dangerous situations. You will have to distract Baby often in order to shift her/his focus with minimal resistance.

At 9-12 months you may observe that Baby:

- Will want to touch everything s/he sees
- Will put everything into her/his mouth to see how it tastes
- Will get angry if you take things away from her/him
- Will understand and may say the word "no"

Play!

Roll the Ball!

Why this activity is good for your baby: It is vital for Baby to explore. Babies are naturally curious, and their overall development depends on their experimenting and exploring.

What you'll need to play this activity: A large, soft, colorful ball like a beach ball or a multicolored rubber ball approximately 8" (20 cm) in diameter

How to play *Roll the Ball!*: Sit on the floor and show Baby the ball. Roll the ball a few inches in front of Baby so s/he will crawl to the ball. Tell Baby "Roll the ball." Show Baby how to push the ball along the floor with her/his hand. Repeat rolling the ball and letting Baby go after it.

Variation: Sit Baby up and spread her/his legs apart so the ball can roll between Baby's legs. Sit a few feet in front of Baby and spread your legs in the same way. Roll the ball between Baby's legs. Tell Baby to "Roll the ball back." Lean over and help Baby roll the ball to you. Soon Baby will understand this game and enjoy rolling it to you.

Share!

When you were a baby, your favorite ball game was played like this:

_____

_____

_____

_____

Celebrate!

Celebrate your baby's developing fine motor milestones.

You may remember how Baby used to clumsily grab things with a raking motion. By the end of the first year, s/he'll be able to grasp with the thumb and first or second finger. You may see Baby practicing this movement on small objects like finger food or small bits of dirt, lint, or insects s/he finds on the ground.

At 9-12 months you will observe that Baby:

- Will be able to bang two cubes together
- Will be able to put objects into containers
- Will be able to take objects out of containers
- Will be able to release grasp to let go of objects at will

Play!

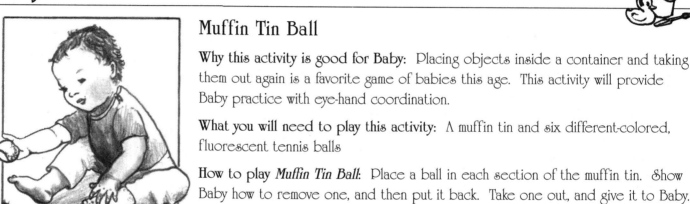

Muffin Tin Ball

Why this activity is good for Baby: Placing objects inside a container and taking them out again is a favorite game of babies this age. This activity will provide Baby practice with eye-hand coordination.

What you will need to play this activity: A muffin tin and six different-colored, fluorescent tennis balls

How to play *Muffin Tin Ball*: Place a ball in each section of the muffin tin. Show Baby how to remove one, and then put it back. Take one out, and give it to Baby. Wait to see if Baby will put the ball back into the empty section in the muffin tin. Let Baby take the balls out and put them back again.

Variation: After Baby understands this game, try putting one ball behind your back to see if Baby realizes that one is missing. Will Baby look for the missing ball? Give Baby the ball and let her/him put it back. Try taking out two balls. Does Baby realize there are two missing balls? Will Baby look for both of the missing balls to put back?

Share!

When you were a baby, you especially enjoyed playing: _____

_____

_____

_____

_____

Celebrate!

Celebrate your baby's emotional milestones.

It is toward the end of the first year when some babies begin to develop fears and phobias. Baby may suddenly become afraid of things that haven't bothered her/him before. Until Baby is older and able to cope with the stress, the best way to subdue these fears is to avoid the situations as much as possible. If Baby is afraid of the dark, put a night-light in her/his bedroom. If Baby doesn't like the sound of the vacuum, do your cleaning when Baby is sleeping. Talking about the fear will sometimes help, too.

From 11-12 months you may observe that Baby:

- Might be afraid of the dark
- Might cry when s/he hears thunder or sees lightning
- Might cry when you turn on loud appliances like vacuum cleaners or garbage disposals
- Might be afraid of the sound of a roaring jet, a backfiring car, or a passing train
- Might become afraid of big dogs or other neighborhood pets

Play!

That's a Scary Sound!

Why this playtime activity is good for your baby: Fears will gradually subside if each time Baby hears or encounters one, you reassure her/him. You will not always be able to avoid Baby hearing certain sounds. A jet flying over your home each afternoon is not something you can avoid. But you can play this game to help distract Baby each time s/he becomes frightened.

What you'll need to play this activity: No special equipment is needed to play this game.

How to play *That's a Scary Sound!*: When you hear a noise that Baby fears, acknowledge it as a scary sound. Say "That is a scary sound!" Then say, "Let's make another scary sound." Give a growl or roar with your voice. Ask Baby to make a "scary sound." Tell Baby that the sound s/he made is a scary sound, too. Tell Baby, "What a scary sound you made!" Make other sounds and call them scary. Whistle, hoot, click your tongue—have fun with this. By playing this game Baby will learn that what s/he hears is just a sound, and sounds are noises that cannot hurt us.

Share!

When you were a baby, you were afraid of these things: _____

_____

You stopped being afraid of these when:_____

_____

Celebrate!

Celebrate your baby's first birthday!

When Baby is one year old, you will want to hold a great celebration. It might be a gathering of two or three family members, or it might include lots of friends and family. But no matter what size the party, be sure to celebrate your baby reaching the first year milestone.

By the end of the first year Baby will have learned to do hundreds of extraordinary things including:

- Crawling fast
- Walking with or without assistance
- Speaking single words and perhaps some phrases
- Eating with fingers and drinking from cup
- Repeating sounds and gestures for attention
- Testing parental responses to positive and negative behavior
- Imitating others
- Using toys and objects in functional ways

Play!

Open Your Presents!

Why this traditional birthday activity is good for your baby: Traditions and rituals are what knit a family together. Birthday cakes and opening presents are traditions that most adults celebrated as children and still celebrate today. Begin a life-long tradition with Baby this year by having a birthday cake (or other traditional birthday food) and presents to open.

What you'll need to play this party activity: A birthday cake with one candle on it and presents wrapped loosely enough that Baby can tear off the paper. Don't tie with ribbons or string that will have to be removed. Bows can be taped on for decorations. Make sure the presents are wrapped so that the task of opening them won't be too frustrating for Baby.

How to play *Open Your Presents!*: Place a birthday present on the floor in front of Baby. Tear away a bit of the wrapping to show Baby how to unwrap it. Tell Baby "Open your presents." There is no hurry, so let Baby open the presents all by her/himself. If Baby wants to take time to play with each present between openings, that is okay. "Open Your Presents" is an activity that can take several minutes or all day!

Share!

Your first birthday party was like this:_____

These are the people who came to your celebration:_____

Your first birthday cake was decorated like this:_____

The gifts you opened at your party included: _____

Celebrate!

Celebrate your toddler's rapidly expanding gross motor skills.

If your baby hasn't started walking at twelve months, s/he will within the next six months. Even if your baby is walking, it will take many more months before s/he can stand up and propel her/himself forward in a smooth fashion. At first, instead of walking, s/he will *toddle*; that is why children this age are called "toddlers."

From 12-18 months you will observe that Toddler:

- Will begin walking
- Will exercise many new physical skills
- Will like to tote, dump, push, pull, pile, knock down, empty, fill

Play!

Follow the Leader

Why this playtime activity is good for your toddler: Toddlers enjoy imitating those they see around them: family, friends, and especially other children. This activity reinforces following direction skills.

What you'll need to play this activity: No special equipment is needed to play this game.

How to play *Follow the Leader*: If your toddler can walk, *Follow the Leader* can be played standing and moving about. If your toddler isn't walking, a crawling or sitting version of the game can be fun, too. Some interesting movements to include in the game: over, under, around, up, down, counting, pointing to body parts, front, and back. Say one- to three-word commands as you are performing a movement you want your toddler to imitate. Example: Say, "round and round" as you spin in a circle or "up and down" as you hop about.

Share!

You took your first steps on this date:_____

You were this many months old: _____

Here is what happened the first time you walked: _____

_____

_____

Celebrate!

Celebrate your toddler's developmental language leaps.

Between twelve and eighteen months your toddler will suddenly seem to understand everything you say. S/He will combine her/his babbling and real words to try to describe what s/he wants or needs you to know. Your toddler will not only recognize the names for things, but s/he will begin to name some familiar objects. At this stage of development it is important not to talk to your toddler in "baby talk." To avoid confusion, use the correct terms for common objects.

From 12-18 months you will observe that Toddler:

- Will understand nearly everything you say
- Will begin to name and point out familiar pictures in books
- Will learn to speak a few words

Play!

Story Time

Why this playtime activity is important for your toddler: You can never start reading too early to children. Research shows that regular reading with expression fifteen minutes a day to toddlers is important to later intellectual development. Young children learn language through repetition, mimicking, and from adult modeling.

What you'll need to play this activity: sturdy, non-toxic, board books. Novelty books such as, textures, scratch and sniff, tab and lift the window, and pop-up books are favorites of toddlers 18 months or older.

How to play *Story Time:* Set aside a time each day–many toddlers prefer a story at bedtime–and make this a part of your daily routine. Hold your toddler in your lap with her/his back against your chest so s/he can see the pictures and watch you turning the pages. Being read to and having opportunities to choose books to look at develops within the young child a love and appreciation for books that will provide a lifetime of reading pleasure.

Share!

When you were a toddler, your very favorite books were these:

_____

_____

_____

_____

Celebrate!

Celebrate your toddler's developing cognitive skills.

At this age you will notice your toddler concentrating very hard on her/his play. Every toy and new game is a learning opportunity. You will see your toddler drawing information learned in previous situations and applying it in new situations.

From 12-18 months you will observe that Toddler:

- Shows interest in causing effects
- Shows curiosity by constantly experimenting with objects
- Shows interest in mechanisms and objects that move or can be moved
- Shows a preference for action toys

Play!

Wind-Up and Go

Why this playtime activity is good for your toddler: At this age your toddler is especially attracted to mechanical devices like wind-up toys, toy boards with buttons and knobs, and things that turn on and off. This activity will provide play with a wind-up toy.

What you'll need to play this activity: a wind-up toy that moves such as a car, truck, or animal

How to play *Wind-Up and Go:* Sit on the floor facing Toddler. Spread your legs and touch toddler's feet with your feet so that your legs make a little fence. Wind up the toy and send it in Toddler's direction. S/He can pick up the toy, turn it around, and send it back to you. Each time the toy runs down, wind it up again. Soon Toddler will be winding it up, too.

Variation: Wind up a toy and send it across the room. Let your toddler crawl or walk to retrieve the toy. Then let Toddler send the toy across the room for you to retrieve.

Share!

When you were a toddler, your favorite wind-up toy was: _____

_____

When you played with this toy, your favorite game was this: _____

_____

_____

_____

Celebrate!

Celebrate your toddler's developing social skills.

Toddlers are at the center of their world. They are only concerned about how things relate to themselves. Toddlers comprehend that other people exist, but the ideas, feelings, and needs of others do not concern children this age. An important part of your toddler's development is to learn self-reliance and how to entertain her/himself.

From 12-18 months you will observe that Toddler:

- Plays in a mostly solitary rather than social way
- Relates to adults better than children
- Shows increasing independence
- Believes that all people think exactly as s/he does

Play!

Busy-Box Toys

Why this playtime activity is good for your toddler: Providing busy-box play will give your toddler an opportunity to be alone and play by her/himself. This kind of toy offers a variety of visual and auditory stimuli to keep her/him amused for extended periods of time.

What you'll need to play this activity: busy-box toys

How to play with busy-box toys: The first step is to show your toddler how the buttons and knobs turn, push, lift, etc. The movement and sounds that the busy-box makes will stimulate your toddler for extended periods of time and help her/him "do" for her/himself.

Variations: As soon as your toddler masters the movements on the busy-box, s/he will quickly tire of it. A variety of toys will be best when teaching Toddler. Present one toy for independent play at a time, and then put it away for a few days. You may find renewed interest when the toy is reintroduced.

Share!

This is what you most often would do when you played alone: _____

_____

_____

_____

Celebrate!

Celebrate your toddler's emotional development.

From twelve to eighteen months you will notice that Toddler will show affectionate responses to you and other familiar people and will start social contacts without your prompting. S/He will increasingly be able to imitate all kinds of actions. Your toddler will be fascinated by your actions and those of other adults s/he sees. Encourage her/him to imitate you. This is the way children learn new skills and build an increased sense of competence.

From 12-18 months you will observe that Toddler:

- Will promptly return a response from you
- Enjoys person-to-person contacts
- Shows preference for certain soft toys and dolls

Play!

Dolly

Why this playtime activity is good for your toddler: Social and fantasy play materials can support the development of simple pretend activities. Playing with dolls is the beginning of make-believe play. Imitation is a big part of a toddler's learning process.

What you'll need to play this activity: doll and accessories such as, baby blanket, doll bed, etc. Some of the soft simple dolls appropriate for infants can also be used for young toddlers. At this developmental stage some children want a more realistic baby doll for their first pretend play. Simply constructed baby dolls should be small enough to hold and made of vinyl or rubber. Hair or moving eyes are not recommended because they are less sturdy, more difficult to clean, and too complex for this age group. (Some young toddlers are even afraid of moving eyes.)

How to play *Dolly*: Show your toddler how to hold Dolly, how to wrap Dolly in a baby blanket, how to rock Dolly in your lap, and how to perform other life-like tasks. Place Dolly in a baby bed, sing to Dolly, etc. After watching you play with the doll, your toddler will be anxious to try some other pretend play.

Special Note: Boys as well as girls should be encouraged to play with dolls.

Share!

Your first doll looked like this: _____

_____

You named your first doll: _____

Celebrate!

Celebrate your toddler's auditory milestones.

From about 15 months toddlers may enjoy true rhythm instruments such as, bells, rattles, and tambourines. Many toddlers this age will sing to themselves and will listen to rhymes and jingles for three to five minutes at a setting.

From 12-18 months you will observe that Toddler:

- Enjoys listening to simple stories read from picture books
- Especially enjoys stories with rhythm, rhyme, and repetition
- Likes to play with simple musical instruments
- Will use household objects like pots and spoons to make sounds

Play!

What's in the Trash Can?

Why this playtime activity is good for your toddler: Toddlers love repetition and enjoy playing games they can join in.

What you'll need to play this activity: a clean, plastic trash can and an assortment of toys or common objects

How to play *What's in the Trash Can?*: Put the toys or common objects in the trash can. One at a time, pull out an object. Ask, "What's in the trash can? Is this a spoon?" Give your toddler time to indicate with nod or head shake or verbally if you have named the object correctly. When the object has been correctly identified, pick out another. You can introduce many new vocabulary words to your toddler this way. When all objects have been removed, name each one as your toddler puts it back into the trash can.

Variation: If you know the song "I Love Trash" and are familiar with the Sesame Street character "Oscar the Grouch," sing the song as items are removed from the trash can.

Share!

When you were a toddler, your favorite song was:_____

When you were a toddler, your favorite objects with which to make sounds were: _____

When we played the What's in the Trash Can? game, you would do this: _____

_____

_____

_____

Celebrate!

Celebrate your toddler's sensory experiences.

During the first half of the second year your toddler will explore with his/her body how small a space her/his body can get in, on top of, beneath, etc.

From 12-18 months you will observe that Toddler:

- Shows off for attention
- Can tear paper and/or magazines
- Enjoys "rough-housing"
- Can discriminate edible materials
- Is aware of body parts and can name some of them

Play!

My Mouth!

Why this playtime activity is good for your toddler: Toddlers discover new things about their bodies when they look in a mirror and examine each part. This activity will teach your toddler things about her/his mouth such as: expressions s/he can make with mouth and face, seeing her/his mouth open and close, seeing and feeling the bumps on the tongue, associating the bumps with taste, and looking at the teeth and gums.

What you'll need to play this activity: unbreakable wall mirror or hand mirror; for variation you will need: napkins; food such as thin slices of carrot, small marshmallows, small crackers, juice or milk, candy, lemon slice

How to play *My Mouth!:* Stand before the large mirror or give your toddler a hand mirror. Allow time for experimenting. Have Toddler point to her/his mouth. Ask if s/he can smile with her/his mouth; laugh with his/her mouth; make his/her mouth open and shut. Open wide and look inside. Have your toddler feel her/his tongue. Tell your child that the little bumps on her/his tongue are the taste buds. "We taste with our mouths and tongues."

Variation: Give your toddler a napkin. Set out the food so s/he will discover opposites like hard and soft (carrot and marshmallow); dry and wet (cracker and juice); sweet and sour (candy and lemon). Talk about the opposite attributes of the food.

Share!

The first time you discovered your mouth and all of the fascinating things it could do, your reactions were:

Celebrate!

Celebrate your toddler's health and well-being.

As Toddler is able to explore with increasing thoroughness, play materials must be safe for her/his use and abuse. Materials must be very sturdy and meet all safety standards for this age group. Carefully maintain toys by examining for breaks, cracks, splinters, etc. Regularly and thoroughly clean all of your toddler's toys.

From 12-18 months you will observe that Toddler:

- Bangs toys together or against the floor and furniture
- Bites, chews, and puts toys in her/his mouth
- Sometimes falls on and trips over toys

Play!

Rub and Scrub

Why this playtime activity is good for your toddler: Children enjoy tactile experiences. Water, soap, bubbles, sponges, and toys provide interesting tactile play. Through water play your toddler will discover concepts such as *float*, *sink*, and *absorb*.

What you'll need to play this activity: plastic wash tub; sponges; mild soap such as baby shampoo; warm water; toys (to be washed)

How to play *Rub and Scrub*: Place the tub of warm water on the floor. You may want to place it on a beach towel to absorb water splashed out of the tub. Begin the game by taking a sponge and washing a toy. Say, "Rub and scrub. Scrub, scrub, scrub the car."

Repeat the rhyme, and invite Toddler to join in as you wash another toy. Next, have your toddler scrub a toy alone. As s/he works, recite the rhyme for her/him. With close supervision, let toddler wash some of her/his toys all by her/himself.

Share!

When you were a toddler, your favorite water game was: _____

_____

When you washed your own toys, this is what happened: _____

_____

_____

Celebrate!

Celebrate your toddler's developing abilities and play interests.

Young toddlers not only are more mobile but also are more likely to notice what other children are playing with and want what they see. The concept of sharing has no meaning to toddlers.

From 12-18 months you will observe that Toddler:

- Is unlikely to relinquish a toy without strong protest
- Does not have the ability to wait
- Cannot use a toy cooperatively
- Cannot take turns

Play!

It Is My Turn

Why this playtime activity is good for your toddler: A toddler's view of the world makes it impossible for her/him to play with other children in a cooperative way. Toddlers can play alongside of others but not interact. Your toddler believes that s/he alone deserves to have everything s/he wants.

What you'll need to play this activity: two similar toys such as dolls, balls, cars, etc.

How to play *It Is My Turn*: Give your toddler one of the toys. You play with the other one for a while. Then say, "It is my turn to have that toy. You can have this one." Trade toys with your toddler. If s/he objects, that is normal and okay. Try playing this game often until your toddler begins to understand the concept of sharing and taking turns.

Special Note: Don't expect this kind of skill to be learned overnight. Your toddler may be two or three years old before grasping this social skill. But sometimes if a difficult concept is introduced early on in a play situation, children embrace the concept more easily.

Share!

The first time I asked you to take turns with a toy, this is what happened:

_____

_____

_____

The one toy you never wanted to share was: _____

Celebrate!

Celebrate your toddler's developing cognitive skills.

Young toddlers like to direct. Your toddler will probably let you know what role you are to play in your games. Sometimes s/he'll bring you a toy so you can help her/him make it work; other times s/he'll take it away from you to try it by her/himself. Watch for cues so you can provide the support and encouragement s/he needs to keep learning.

From 12-18 months you will observe that Toddler:

- Shows interest in ordering and predicting events in his/her environment
- Shows growing interest in repeated routines
- Will use her/his imagination when playing with objects

Play!

Find the Ball

Why this playtime activity is good for your toddler: The feeling of accomplishment is important to your toddler's learning. Providing tasks that s/he can complete successfully will add to her/his positive self-esteem.

What you'll need to play this activity: Picture books with pictures of common objects such as ball, comb, baby, dog, cat, etc.

How to play *Find the Ball*: Hold your toddler in your lap with her/his back against your chest so s/he can see pictures in a book. Open the book and tell your toddler, "Find the ball." If s/he cannot find it, point to the ball so s/he understands how you want her/him to identify an object. Name other objects and point to them. Tell your toddler to find other objects in the picture book. If s/he points to the correct picture, praise her/him, and repeat the name of the object as s/he points. This will make her/him feel good and know that s/he has accomplished something successfully.

Variation: You can point out, too, the names of objects with which s/he may not be familiar, so that s/he can also learn about them. You may want to mark pages in some way so that you can find things that you know the baby can recognize. It's important that you are sure that your toddler can point out things with which s/he is already familiar before you move on to new and unfamiliar ones.

Share!

When you were a toddler and we looked at pictures in books, your favorite objects to find were:

Celebrate!

Celebrate your toddler's developing gross motor skills.

In the first half of the second year, toddlers begin to use furniture. They can climb into adult furniture, and they enjoy using child-sized furniture. They can rock in rocking chairs and ride rocking toys.

From 12-18 months you will observe that Toddler:

- Likes to climb and can manage small indoor stairs
- Enjoys pushing or pulling toys while walking
- Stoops to pick up objects
- Likes to crawl into large boxes or under furniture to play

Play!

Tunnel

Why this playtime activity is good for your toddler: Your toddler will enjoy crawling through a box tunnel. As your toddler explores and investigates an interesting collection of boxes, s/he will become aware of color, shape, size, texture, top, bottom, lid, and the inside and outside in relation to a box. In the eyes of a toddler, a box can become a barn, airport, or garage. It may suddenly be inverted to become a tea party table or worktable.

What you'll need to play this activity: several large boxes or a tall appliance box with both ends removed from the boxes; duct tape; paint and brushes or wide-tip felt markers

How to play *Tunnel:* Using duct tape, secure the boxes together to create a long tunnel. Paint or use markers to decorate the outside of the boxes. (You may want to have Toddler help you decorate the outside of the boxes.) Show your toddler how to climb through the tunnel. If the tunnel is too small for you to crawl through, put your toddler at one end and look at her/him from the other end as you call and coax her/him to come to you.

Variation: A sturdy cardboard box can form the basis of many appropriate activities for Toddler. Through imaginative play, a box can become a car, airplane, train, house, or dog house where one can climb in and out, or play the role of the driver or occupant. Or it can be a quiet, private place to sit and rest.

Share!

When you were a toddler, your favorite game to play with cardboard boxes was:

_____

_____

_____

Celebrate!

Celebrate your toddler's developing language skills.

By one and a half years, most toddlers use language in play and in expressing wishes to others. At this age a toddler's desire to communicate verbally is increased greatly. Keep in mind that boys generally develop language skills more slowly than girls. Your toddler's first few words will include the names of family, favorite toys, and parts of her/his body.

From 12-18 months you will observe that Toddler:

- Can follow simple commands
- Uses words and gestures to get what s/he wants
- Will add consonants (t, d, n, w, and f) to vocabulary
- Demonstrates an interest in music and rhythm

Play!

"The Wheels on the Bus"

Why this playtime activity is good for your toddler: Children this age need many finger plays and songs to learn how to coordinate their body actions and voices. This is important in language learning. Finger play activities also help toddlers learn the names of everyday actions. There are many good songs and finger plays that you can use, or make up your own. Begin with "The Wheels on the Bus."

Verse 1: The wheels on the bus go round and round.
Round and round. Round and round.
The wheels on the bus go round and round, all through the town.

Verse 2: The kids on the bus go up and down.
Up and down. Up and down.
The kids on the bus go up and down, all through the town.

What you'll need to play this activity: No special equipment is needed to play this game.

How to play "The Wheels on the Bus": Sing the song and make the movement of the wheels going round and round with hands and arms. When you sing the second verse, make the movement of bouncing up and down.

Variation: Make up other verses for the song. For example:

- The hands on the bus go clap and clap.
- The feet on the bus go stomp and stomp.
- The eyes on the bus go blink and blink.

- The driver on the bus goes shhh and shhh.
- The horn on the bus goes honk and honk.

Share!

When you were a toddler, your favorite finger play game was:

Celebrate!

Celebrate your toddler's increased interest in active exploration.

During this important developmental stage, your toddler will begin to master objects and the objects' capacities. S/He will watch you to discover how you use tools and imitate these motions. When you notice your child is watching you do something, verbalize what you are doing and why.

From 12-18 months you will observe that Toddler:

- Will use a brush to brush hair
- Will hold a telephone receiver to ear and talk into the mouthpiece
- Begins to sort by shapes and colors

Play!

How Do We Use It?

Why this playtime activity is good for your toddler: At this age instead of simply holding objects, your toddler will actually try to use objects in the appropriate ways. You can help your child learn the function of things by playing this game.

What you'll need to play this activity: book (to read), hairbrush (to brush hair), cup (to sip from), play telephone (to listen and talk), flower (to sniff), and hat (to wear)

How to play *How Do We Use It?*: Sit Toddler on the floor. Place the objects on the floor in front of her/him. Pick up one object, and use it in an appropriate way. For example: brush your hair with the hairbrush. Then hand that object to Toddler and ask "How do we use it?" Let Toddler make the motion. Then place the object back on the floor. Pick up the hat, and place it on your head. Then give the hat to Toddler, and repeat the procedure. Pretend to drink from the cup before handing it to Toddler. Then ask "How do we use it?" Play the game with your toddler for awhile, and then let her/him use the objects to play alone.

Share!

When you were a toddler, the first objects that I noticed you used in a functional way were:

_____

_____

This is how you used each one: _____

_____

Celebrate!

Celebrate your toddler's developing social/linguistic skills.

It is important during this developmental stage that you provide many opportunities to use new words and to relate them to her/his actions. Encourage your toddler to name things. Play games that require your toddler to listen and then respond by following directions.

From 12-18 months you will observe that Toddler:

- Will begin to point to and name her/his body parts
- Begin to understand when you ask her/him to do something
- Begin to understand ownership (Daddy's car, Mother's computer, my bottle)

Play!

Inventions

Why this playtime activity is good for your toddler: Now is the time to provide your toddler with lots of boxes; old pots and pans; and old clothes such as hats, shoes, scarves, neckties, and other accessories. S/He needs all of these things and many more to provide props for pretending and imagining. Making objects that represent other things—but are not exactly duplicates—will force Toddler to use her/his imagination.

What you'll need to play this activity: recycled goods such as boxes, grocery bags, strings, plastic containers with lids

How to play *Inventions*: Let your toddler help you invent toys. Show her/him how to make a homemade stethoscope out of an old film canister and a piece of string. Attach the string to the canister with tape, and let your toddler "listen" to your heart. Make a telephone from two pieces of wood and attach a piece of hose. The toddler can "talk" to you or to others through the hose. Use lunch-sized bags to make hand puppets or large grocery bags to make costumes for play. Use your imagination plus recycled objects to make toys and costumes for imaginative play. Allow plenty of time for your Toddler to play with each invention.

Share!

When you were a toddler, one of your favorite homemade toys was: _____

_____

It looked like this: _____

_____

_____

Celebrate!

Celebrate your toddler's discovery/exploration experiences.

At this age toddlers are interested in looking for hidden objects. It is during this developmental state that toddlers begin to comprehend the fact that things exist even when out-of-sight.

From 12-18 months you will observe that Toddler:

- Can find an object by looking in the right place when hidden in different places
- Can find a hidden object even if it is covered completely
- Will remember where certain things are kept and return to them day after day

Play!

Cigar Box Hide-and-Seek

Why this playtime activity is good for your toddler: This game provides good eye-hand coordination practice.

What you'll need to play this activity: a cigar box or box with a lid that opens and closes; a small doll that will fit inside the box

How to play *Cigar Box Hide-and-Seek*: Put the doll inside the cigar box. Show your toddler how to open the lid. Both show and tell Toddler how to do this. When s/he can do it, ask her/him to hide the doll in the box for you to find. When s/he sees how the whole thing works, let her/him play with the box and doll alone. S/He'll enjoy putting it in and taking it out over and over again. S/He will discover, in yet another way, that something doesn't disappear forever just because s/he can't see it.

Variation: Hide a cotton ball inside a match box, and play hide and seek again. Teach your toddler how to push the little drawer out of the box to see the cotton ball.

Share!

When you were a toddler, your favorite Hide-and-Seek game was played like this:

_____

_____

_____

_____

_____

Celebrate!

Celebrate your toddler's auditory/gross motor milestones.

Toddlers this age enjoy looking at books and magazines with pictures of people–especially babies–and animals. When you look at animal picture books, name the animals and make the sounds the animals make. See if your toddler can make the animal sounds, too.

From 15-18 months you will observe that Toddler:

- Likes listening to stories and nursery rhymes
- Moves to music (bounces)
- Bounces when s/he hears music
- "Dances" to music by bouncing, running, turning in circles, and bounding about

Play!

Move Like an Elephant

Why this playtime activity is good for your toddler: Coordinating listening and keeping a beat is good auditory/gross motor practice for toddlers.

What you'll need to play this activity: marching music

How to play *Move Like an Elephant*: Play the marching music. Bend over at the lower back and swing one arm (as a trunk) in front of your face. Move ponderously to the music like a heavy elephant. Encourage Toddler to move like an elephant, too.

Variations: On different occasions, try moving to music like other animals.

- Move like a bunny (little hops around the room).
- Move like a snake (wriggle on the floor).
- Move like a bird (quickly flap arms like wings while running around the room).
- Move like a penguin (take tiny steps with heels almost together and toes pointed out).
- Move like a snail (scoot along the floor).
- Move like a kangaroo (big leaps around the room).
- Move like a squirrel (move fast on all fours across the floor).
- Move like a duck-billed platypus (move slowly on all fours across the floor).
- Move like a butterfly (slowly flap arms like wings while gliding around the room).
- Move like an iguana (move on all fours, right limbs and then left limbs).
- Move like a bear (walk on all fours then on two, all fours and then on two, etc.).

Note: This is a good time to get out picture books of animals and look at the illustrations. Guess how other animals might move and move those ways, too.

Share!

When you were a toddler, one of your favorite dance movements was:

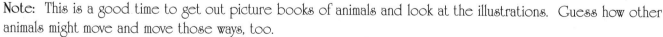

The animal you most liked to imitate was: _____

Celebrate!

Celebrate your toddler's health and safety.

At fifteen months toddlers should receive vaccinations for measles, mumps, rubella (MMR), and Haemophilus influenza bacteria. At eighteen or nineteen months toddlers need the fourth dose of the DTP vaccine and the third dose of oral polio vaccine.

From 15-18 months you will observe that Toddler:

- Can climb out of bed
- Will move furniture to make steps for climbing up high
- Has no fear of jumping from high places
- May not like to be restrained in a car seat

Play!

I Love You; I'll Keep You Safe

Why this safety activity is good for your toddler: Now that your toddler is mobile there are many safety rules s/he will have to learn. When you are teaching your toddler a safety rule, if you preface it with "I Love You; I'll Keep You Safe," your child will see that you are doing this out of love and will more likely be cooperative.

What you'll need to play this activity: patience

How to play *I Love You; I'll Keep You Safe*: Strap your toddler in a seat belt and say, "I love you; I'll keep you safe." When you hold your toddler's hand crossing a street, say, "I love you; I'll keep you safe." When you gate a child out of a room where s/he wants to go, say, "I love you; I'll keep you safe." Although this may make your toddler angry sometimes, it will at the same time give her/him a sense of security.

Variation: Sometimes when your toddler wants to do something that is not safe, you will have to object. For example, if s/he wants to get out of the car seat while the car is moving. Tell her/him "No" and then add, "I love you; I'll keep you safe."

Share!

When you were a toddler, the safety rule you disliked the most was:

_____

_____

Celebrate!

Celebrate your toddler's developing eye-hand coordination.

From 16-18 months you will observe that Toddler:

- Enjoys scribbling with crayons
- Can hold a crayon with a pincher grip
- May scribble in imitation
- Will scribble spontaneously
- May display a hand preference

Play!

Let's Scribble

Why this playtime activity is good for your toddler: Scribbling is good eye-hand coordination practice, and scribbling spontaneously will give your toddler an opportunity to be creative with designs and colors.

What you'll need to play this activity: large sheet of drawing paper taped to work surface; large, preschool crayons; classical music

How to play Let's Scribble: Play the music for Toddler. In time to the music, use the crayon to scribble on a sheet of paper. Make large circles and lines. Move to the music with your upper body as well as hands and arm. Give your toddler one crayon and encourage her/him to scribble to the music. (If given a choice of crayons s/he may test out colors instead of creating scribbles to the music.) Allow sufficient time for Toddler to "work." After a few minutes you may want to give your toddler a second color of crayon.

Variation #1: Save some of your toddler's scribbling so someday you can share it with her/him.

Variation #2: Frame one of her/his first works and hang it in a prominent place in your home.

Variation #3: Have your toddler scribble in the space at the bottom of this page.

Share!

Here is how your first scribbling looked:

Celebrate!

Celebrate your toddler's developing abilities and play interests.

Toddlers are very curious and constantly experimenting with objects. They can operate more complex mechanisms than infants and want more challenge and variety in their play materials.

From 16-20 months you will observe that Toddler:

- Is interested in operating mechanisms
- Is interested in fitting things into other things
- Can sort shapes (round and square)

Play!

Boxes Inside Boxes

Why this playtime activity is good for your toddler: As your toddler explores boxes s/he will discover differences in size, color, and texture. Through play s/he will learn that some boxes fit inside others and others do not. Other learning opportunities in playing this game include: sorting, stacking, opening and closing, filling and emptying.

What you'll need to play this activity: You will need an assortment of small boxes such as those that contained toothpaste or shaving cream, kitchen flavoring and spices; a large shoe box. Optional: round boxes in assorted sizes and colors such as a five-gallon, round ice cream carton, an oatmeal box (cut to fit inside the ice cream carton), and assorted tissue paper rings of various sizes.

How to play *Boxes Inside Boxes*: Fill the large shoe box with small boxes with lids. Replace the lid on the shoe box and set out for your toddler to investigate.

Variation: Fill a five-gallon, round ice cream box with round boxes in different sizes and colors with lids. Replace the lid on the ice cream box and set out for your toddler to investigate.

Share!

When you were a toddler, your favorite way to play with boxes was:

_____

_____

_____

_____

_____

Celebrate!

Celebrate your toddler's gross motor skills.

During the first half of the second year some children are beginning to be able to play simple ball games: either grasping and letting go of a ball, or to-and-from activities. By around 18 months some children can hurl a ball. Young toddlers enjoy the same kinds of soft, small lightweight balls that are appropriate for infants. In addition, toddlers like large, lightweight balls such as beach balls. Children this age are motivated by moving objects.

From 16-20 months you will observe that Toddler:

- Is interested in the movement of varying types and sizes of balls
- Is fascinated by balls that roll in unpredictable ways such as a football
- Will begin learning how to kick and throw a ball at a target

Play!

Beach Ball Roll

Why this playtime activity is good for your toddler: Playing with a beach ball gives a toddler opportunities to run, walk, kick, and move in a variety of ways. Watching the ball move in different directions and at different speeds will help increase your toddler's agility.

What you'll need to play this activity: beach ball

How to play *Beach Ball Roll*: Roll, throw, and kick the beach ball to Toddler. S/He can bring the ball back to you or try to return it using the same method you used to get it to her/him.

Variation: Roll balls down ramps such as a slide at a park. Have your toddler stand at the end of the slide and try to catch the beach ball as it rolls down the ramp.

Share!

When you were 18 months old, your favorite game to play with a ball was:

_____

_____

_____

_____

Celebrate!

Celebrate your toddler's natural creativity.

Scribbling is extremely enjoyable for toddlers this age. Scribbling will support developing representational abilities. Your toddler will feel great pride in her/his work and enjoy seeing it displayed in the home.

By the end of 20 months you will observe that Toddler:

- Likes using large, nontoxic preschool crayons
- May still need paper taped to work surface
- Will hold up work for you to admire
- Enjoys sensory experiences like finger painting

Play!

Finger Painting Place Mats

Why this playtime activity is good for your toddler: By this age toddlers feel a sense of belonging to the family and like to feel as though they are contributing to the family.

What you'll need to play this activity: finger paints in primary colors; paper place mats; plastic wrap

How to play *Finger Painting Place Mats*: For easy clean up, cover the high chair tray with plastic wrap. Dip a paper place mat in water and place it on the top of the tray. Place a large tablespoon of thick, red finger paint on the center of the paper. Invite Toddler to use her/his hands and fingers to move the paint around. For added sensory awareness, add flavoring extracts or spices to the finger paint. Allow time for Toddler to make a place mat for one member of the family. Talk about whose place mat Toddler is making. Place the painting where it will dry. Dip another place mat in water and place it on the tray. This time place a large tablespoon of thick, blue finger paint on the center of the paper. Repeat with yellow. Encourage Toddler to make a place mat for each member of the family. When the paint is dry, use the place mats. Praise the art work while the family uses the place mats.

Variation: Mix primary colors to make secondary colors. Place ½ tablespoon (8 ml) of red and ½ tablespoon (8 ml) of blue finger paint in the center of a wet paper. Encourage Toddler to mix the colors to discover that red and blue make purple. Talk to Toddler as s/he is mixing colors to make pictures. "What color does red and blue make?" Experiment with other combinations. "What color does yellow and blue make?"

Share!

When you were 18 months old, your favorite color was: _____

The first time you finger painted your reactions were: _____

Celebrate!

Celebrate your toddler's growing self-awareness.

During this important developmental stage, it is important to provide an appropriate range of materials to support and nurture your toddler's play. It is during these months that you will notice s/he is beginning to engage in pretend and role-play activities.

From 18-24 months you will observe that Toddler:

- Shows growing awareness of others
- Shows interest in imitation of others
- Demonstrates responsiveness to others

Play!

Look At Me!

Why this playtime activity is good for your toddler: Full-length (unbreakable and securely mounted) mirrors are suitable for your toddler because s/he can stand and move about and is increasingly aware of her/himself. Very sturdy hand-held mirrors with no sharp edges or parts (like mirrors that are appropriate for older infants) are also appropriate for this age range.

By approximately 20 months, toddlers begin to enjoy dressing up and seeing themselves in various costumes.

What you'll need to play this activity: mirror; dress-up clothes such as hats, caps, capes, scarves, button-up-the-front shirts, large boots, wigs, gloves, etc.

How to play *Look at Me!*: Show your toddler how to put the scarves around her/his head, cape around the shoulders, cap on her/his head, etc. Demonstrate how to wear the various costumes. Show your child how to pull on the gloves and boots. Play with the dress-up clothes and Toddler for awhile. Then let your child play with the dress-up clothes alone.

Share!

When you were a toddler, your favorite dress-up costume was:

_____

_____

_____

Celebrate!

Celebrate your toddler's developing fine motor skills.

From 18-24 months you will observe that Toddler:

- Enjoys rolling, pounding, and squeezing clay
- Can string beads together
- Can turn single pages of books

Play!

Roll-A-Dough, Pat-A-Dough

Why this playtime activity is good for your toddler: While working with play clay, your toddler will observe how the rolling pin flattens the dough and makes it smooth and how the cookie cutter leaves its identical imprint as it is pressed into the dough. This activity also gives your toddler an opportunity to experience the concepts *rolling* and *patting.*

What you'll need to play this activity: Play clay; rolling pin; large, simple cookie cutters; plastic place mat

How to play *Roll-A-Dough, Pat-A-Dough*: Find a work surface that is comfortable for your toddler. Cover the worktable with a plastic place mat. Give your toddler a round handful of dough. Show her/him how to roll out the dough with the rolling pin. Use a cookie cutter to cut out a shape. Then pick up the play clay and roll it into a round ball again. Help Toddler learn how to use the rolling pin and cookie cutters. Allow time for your toddler to play with the dough and tools.

Variation: Instead of using play clay, you can make peanut butter dough. Mix one part peanut butter and one part honey with two parts powdered milk. Form into balls. If the dough is too sticky, add more powdered milk.

Share!

When you were a toddler and you played with modeling materials, you liked to do this:

_____

_____

_____

_____

Celebrate!

Celebrate your toddler's sensory/gross motor experiences.

Toddlers have a natural desire to move and explore. At this developmental stage it is important that you provide lots of opportunities that will encourage gross motor development, promote body awareness, and stimulate creativity through movement.

From 18-24 months you will observe that Toddler:

- Enjoys moving freely
- Enjoys moving to music
- Can keep time to many kinds of music

Play!

I Can Move

Why this playtime activity is good for your toddler: With minimal directions your toddler will learn to move freely. With practice your toddler will become very creative in her/his movements. Both movement and dance are natural expressions of the young child.

What you'll need to play this activity: music

How to play *I Can Move:* Play music and encourage Toddler to move about to the music. Suggest big steps, little steps; moving slowly, moving quickly. Introduce movement concepts such as tip-toeing, jumping, spinning, and twirling.

Variation: Make movements and let Toddler imitate your movements. Then encourage your child to be the leader and show you a movement to imitate. This game should use simple, slow moves to quiet, soft music.

Share!

As a toddler, you liked to move to this kind of music: _____

_____

As a toddler, this is how you would move to the music: _____

_____

_____

Celebrate!

Celebrate your toddler's newly developing cognitive skills.

As your toddler carries out various explorations, s/he is increasing her/his understanding of the space around her/him and the objects within that space. S/He is learning how to get from one room to another and how to hunt for somebody or something. It is up to you to give your toddler every opportunity to engage in this learning process of exploration and discovery.

From 18-24 months you will observe that Toddler:

- Can point to objects that match or are almost like a familiar sample
- Likes to build towers and buildings with blocks
- Understands the meaning of the word "another"

Play!

Matching Animal Crackers

Why this playtime activity is good for your toddler: Young children learn to recognize and identify the shapes of things more quickly when they are working with edible objects.

What you'll need to play this activity: a box of animal crackers

How to play *Matching Animal Crackers*: Place three different shapes of animal crackers on the table in front of your toddler. From the box of crackers, pick out one of the three shapes that are on the table and show it to your toddler. Say, "Which one of those is the same as this?" Or, "Which one of the crackers on the table is an elephant-shape like this one?" Help your toddler learn to match the shapes of animal crackers.

Variation #1: Place several crackers in a pile and say, "Crackers." Put one by itself and say, "One cracker." You can teach the concept of *many* and *few* or *one* and *three* in this way.

Variation #2: If animal crackers are too much alike for your toddler to sort by shape, try using pretzel sticks, square crackers, round crackers, and fish-shaped crackers to sort.

Share!

When you were this age, you could sort animal crackers: _____

Your favorite snack was: _____

_____

Celebrate!

Celebrate your toddler's newly acquired social skills.

The best way you can help your toddler learn how to make choices is to offer her/him many opportunities to try both sides of various actions and activities so s/he can learn about the results of her/his choices.

From 18-24 months you will observe that Toddler:

- Has contrary impulses
- Is often not able to make choices
- Changes her/his mind and moods quickly

Play!

Pick One

Why this daily activity is good for your toddler: This informal game is to be played during the day. Whenever possible, give your toddler a choice between two things. The only way one can learn to make choices is to have opportunities to choose.

What you'll need to execute this activity: two choices of foods such as different kinds of dry cereal, fresh fruit, crackers, kinds of cheese, etc.

How to play *Pick One*: When you are preparing a meal or snack for your toddler, show her/him two choices. Explain the difference. Then say, "Pick one." Let toddler have the one s/he chooses.

Variation #1: When dressing your toddler let her/him choose between two different shirts, dresses, colors of socks, etc. Don't give choices between more than two or three things because making a decision between too many things is extremely frustrating for most toddlers. Always let toddler wear the thing s/he chooses.

Variation #2: If your toddler doesn't want to do something, for example, take a bath, give her/him a choice. "Would you like to take your bath now or take your bath after you have some juice?" Giving your toddler a choice will sometimes get her/him to do something she/he would choose not to do at all.

Share!

When you were a toddler and you were given a choice of colors to wear, you would usually choose:

_____

_____

When you were given a choice about what to eat, you would usually choose:

_____

Celebrate!

Celebrate your toddler's social/emotional development.

Toddlers need opportunities to be alone–to play by her/himself, but with you nearby so s/he knows where you are. It is also important at this stage of development to give your toddler opportunities to try to imitate actions that s/he sees going on around her/him. When you and your toddler are playing together with toys, gradually stop playing and just sit and watch. Soon you should be able to get up and do something else in the room while s/he plays contentedly on her/his own. The next step is to leave the room, but be close enough to hear her/him calling to you. Check in every few minutes. Providing toys that you know s/he especially enjoys will extend the time playing alone.

From 18-24 months you will observe that Toddler:

- Will be able to play alone for short periods of time
- Will feel insecure if you are not in close proximity
- Will imitate the actions and activities that you and others perform

Play!

Bake a Cake

Why this playtime activity is good for your toddler: It provides the opportunity for your toddler to entertain her/himself using kitchen measuring tools and sand.

What you'll need to play this activity: tub of sand; measuring tools such as a plastic cup, plastic jar, plastic bowls, large spoons, scoops; large cookie cutters; small bucket of water

How to play *Bake a Cake*: Show your toddler how to mix sand and water in a bowl. Stir it with a spoon. Pour the mixture into a mold like a cup or small bowl, then tip it over and turn it out. To make a cookie, press a cutter into wet sand. Push away all of the sand around the cutter. Lift the cutter from the sand. As soon as your toddler understands the game, let her/him play with the sand, water, and tools anyway s/he chooses.

Share!

One of your favorite things to do when you played in sand was:

_____

_____

_____

_____

Celebrate!

Celebrate your toddler's auditory/gross motor experiences.

During the second year toddlers show an increasingly active interest in and response to simple music and movement activities.

From 18-24 months you will observe that Toddler:

- Can jump and stand on tiptoes
- Can stand on either foot and balance
- Can walk between parallel lines approximately 8" (20 cm) apart
- Is very active and cannot sit still very long

Play!

Scarves In the Wind

Why this playtime activity is good for your toddler: This activity gives your toddler the opportunity to practice her/his skill of balance. It will also help her/him release energy in a creative and pleasurable fashion.

What you'll need to play this activity: music; sheer, colorful scarves

How to play Scarves In the Wind: Play the music. Show your toddler how to wave scarves (one in each hand) through the air while moving to the music.

Variation #1: Make streamers by stapling one end of several 36" (91 cm)-long strips of crepe paper streamer inside a folded 3" by 5" (76 mm by 127 mm) index card. Cover the staples with tape. Use the streamers to move to music.

Variation #2: Make ribbon streamers by taping three or four strips of ribbon to one end of a drinking straw. Wave the ribbon streamers to music.

Share!

When you were a toddler one of your favorite things to do to music was:

_____

_____

_____

_____

Celebrate!

Celebrate your toddler's visual learning experiences.

Toddlers need much practice with paper and crayons. They should have a supply of old magazines that can be easily torn plus form boards with circles and squares in the primary colors. Provide as many manipulative experiences as you can for your toddler.

From 18-24 months you will observe that Toddler:

- Will be able to imitate a vertical stroke on paper
- Will enjoy looking at magazines and tearing out pictures
- Will correctly place circles and squares in a form board

Play!

Tear, Poke, and Punch

Why this playtime activity is good for your toddler: Tearing and poking or punching holes in paper is extremely fun for toddlers. These three activities give toddlers exercise for small hand muscles and are good ways to get rid of aggressive feelings and extra energy.

What you'll need to play this activity: old magazines with colorful pictures; newspapers; wooden spoon (with a handle for poking holes in paper); a hole punch

How to play *Tear, Poke, and Punch*: Show Toddler how to tear pictures from the magazines. Demonstrate how to poke holes in the newspaper with the handle of a wooden spoon. Then show her/him how the hole puncher works, and let her/him punch holes in newspaper. S/He'll have a wonderful time and make a paper snowstorm all around.

Share!

When you were a toddler, your favorite thing to do with old magazines and newspapers was:

_____

_____

_____

_____

Celebrate!

Celebrate your toddler's abilities and play interests.

During the second year most toddlers learn to walk and climb with increasing proficiency. In the second half of this period toddlers become very interested in exploring and expressing their capacities for gross motor movement. They are especially interested in exploring positions in space and particularly like the experience of being up high. Some toddlers can also descend a small, low slide. Low toddler stairs with handrails and low slides with side rails may be appropriate after 18 months but always needs close supervision.

From 18-24 months you will observe that Toddler:
- May be able to climb a three-step ladder or go up a few stairs
- Will have difficulty coming down stairs
- Enjoys the sensation of swinging
- Will have poor judgment about the consequences of actions and may easily hurt her/himself

Play!

Jump Up!

Why this playtime activity is good for your toddler: Mini-trampolines provide a safe environment for practicing her/his newly developed jumping skills.

What you'll need to play this activity: exercise mini-tramp

How to play *Jump Up!:* Place the mini-tramp in the middle of the room away from all obstacles. To begin this activity, the toddler should hold onto both of your hands and jump. The next step is to have the toddler jump holding only one of your hands. The final, big step is to let your toddler try to jump by her/himself. Balance in children this age is often unpredictable, so for the sake of safety, the use of a mini-tramp should always be closely supervised.

Note: There are mini-tramps available through some toy stores and school supply stores that are designed especially for the very young child. These tramps come with a handlebar so the baby or young child is always able to hold on and steady her/his balance.

Share!

When you played on a mini-tramp, this is what happened:

_____

_____

Celebrate!

Celebrate your toddler's exploration and creativity.

At this age you will need to demonstrate how to do things for your toddler. Although they seem very simple to you, everything is still a mystery to your child. Some days s/he may enjoy watching your lesson, but on other days s/he may not seem to pay attention at all and will insist on doing things "all by myself."

From 18-24 months you will observe that Toddler:

- Will enjoy playing with sand/water toys
- Will enjoy playing with 20-40 piece block sets
- Especially enjoys art projects that are tactile

Play!

Make A Collage

Why this playtime activity is good for your toddler: Making collages gives toddlers an opportunity to discover the principle of adhesion (different kinds of material will make paper stick to paper).

What you'll need to play this activity: one kind of adhesion (glue stick, squeeze bottle of white glue, or liquid starch); large sheet of heavy paper or light cardboard; construction paper or tissue paper cut in large geometric shapes (circles, squares, triangles); wet paper towels for clean up

How to make a collage: To make a glue stick and paper collage, set out the glue stick and paper pieces which are cut into geometric shapes. Place the large sheet of heavy paper or light cardboard in front of the toddler. Demonstrate for Toddler how to use the glue stick to put glue on the shape pieces, turn them over, and place them on the large sheet of paper. Overlap several shapes in a pleasing fashion.

Variation #1: To make a liquid glue and paper collage, show Toddler how to squeeze a small amount of glue on a paper cut-out, turn it over, and place it on the large sheet of paper. Repeat with other shapes.

Variation #2: To make a liquid starch and tissue paper collage, give your toddler a large sheet of paper. Pour a circle of starch in the center of the paper. Show your toddler how to "finger paint" the paper with the starch. Wash and dry Toddler's hands. Then drop tissue paper cut-outs into the wet starch. Press to smooth the tissue paper on the starch. Let dry.

Share!

The first time you made a collage this is what happened:

_____

_____

Celebrate!

Celebrate your toddler's advancing gross motor skills.

During the second half of the second year play games that require your toddler to move in many different ways. Let her/him invent games. If s/he wants you to, join in the games your toddler invents. Demonstrate how to kick and throw balls. Schedule times for her/him to walk upstairs but don't take her/his hand unless s/he seems insecure or frightened. You will be able to do much to promote your toddler's gross motor skills.

From 18-24 months you will observe that Toddler:

- Walks with more direction to her/his movements
- Goes to places knowingly and with remembrance
- Can kick a ball forward without losing balance
- Can throw a small ball forward

Play!

Stepping Stones

Why this playtime activity is good for your toddler: Your toddler can learn much from a stepping stones game. S/He will experience the concepts: in, on, around, and over; learn to follow directions; learn to listen for music as a signal; and receive practice in gross motor and eye-foot coordination.

What you'll need to play this activity: large sheets of colored construction paper in primary and secondary colors; tape; marching music

How to play _Stepping Stones:_ Lay out sheets of colored construction paper on the floor to create stepping stones. Tape them in place if necessary. Explain that the object of the game is to step on each paper as s/he walks the path from end to end. Explain that s/he is to walk or move when s/he hears the music and stop when the music stops. Begin the music for a few seconds, and then stop the music. Repeat. Older children may be able to tell you the color of the paper where they stop, but toddlers need only enjoy the colorful stepping stones.

Share!

When you were a toddler, you liked to play musical games. This is how we played one musical game together:

_____

_____

Celebrate!

Celebrate your toddler's cognitive skills.

It is important to use picture books with toddlers because the pictures give them a chance to relate what they see to themselves. If your toddler sees a picture of a foot, let her/him feel her/his own foot or your foot. When looking at books, be sure to point out familiar objects and name them. Strengthen this experience for her/him by showing real objects that are the same as the ones s/he sees in a book.

From 18-24 months you will observe that Toddler:

- Will be able to follow three simple directions
- Will use a stick to reach a toy out of her/his reach
- Will be able to understand longer and harder sentences
- Will be more and more interested in books

Play!

Parade of Animals

Why this playtime activity is good for your toddler: Listening to simple directions, interpreting the directions, and then following the directions will help your toddler learn sequencing and how to work from left to right.

What you'll need to play this activity: cardboard covered with felt or flannel, pictures of animals cut from old storybooks (backed with strips of flannel so they will stick to the flannel board)

How to play *Parade of Animals*: Begin by giving only one simple direction. For example: "Put the frog on the board." After you think your toddler knows the names of all of the animal pictures you have prepared, use multiple directions. For example: "Place the frog and the kitten on the board." Later name three objects to be put on the board in a particular order. For example: "Put the dinosaur on the board. Then put the horse next to the dinosaur. Put the frog after the dinosaur." Teach your toddler to place the pictures from left to right. (Always work from left to right as though reading a book.)

Share!

When you were a toddler and we played with a flannel board, your favorite pictures were:

_____

_____

_____

Celebrate!

Celebrate your toddler's social/emotional milestones.

Don't be surprised if it seems your toddler's emotions change from one moment to the next. S/He may turn her/his back on you and walk away and then the next minute turn around and come running back for reassurance. At this age a toddler has mixed feelings about growing up and leaving Mother. Brief separations from Mother may help the toddler become more independent.

From 18-24 months you will observe that Toddler:

- Demonstrates increasing independence
- Begins to show defiant behavior
- Has episodes of separation anxiety that increase toward midyear
- Episodes of separation anxiety will begin to fade when Toddler is about 24 months

Play!

Hide-and-Seek

Why this playtime activity is good for your toddler: Playing Hide-and-Seek will help your toddler understand that you may be there even though s/he cannot see you and that people come and go.

What you'll need to play this activity: No special equipment is needed to play this game.

How to play *Hide-and-Seek:* Hide in a room of your house, and tell your toddler "Come and find me." If s/he is having trouble finding you, give verbal signals so s/he can locate you. "Here I am; can you find me?"

Variation: Tell your toddler to go and hide. Close your eyes and count to five slowly. When you reach the number five announce "Here I come, ready or not." Take turns hiding.

Share!

When you were a toddler and we played Hide-and-Seek, your favorite place to hide was:

_____

_____

_____

_____

Celebrate!

Celebrate your toddler's self-care skills.

At one year your baby was probably feeding her/himself with a spoon and her/his fingers. By eighteen months s/he could get food into her/his mouth consistently. By 18-20 months your toddler could probably use a spoon, fork, and unbreakable glass or cup when s/he wanted to. By her/his second birthday your toddler will still be a messy eater but may not like it if s/he accidentally spills something.

From 18-24 months you will observe that Toddler:

- Will learn to use a spoon and fork to feed her/himself
- Will learn to drink from a cup or glass without spilling

Play!

Make Peanut Butter and Jelly Sandwiches

Why this playtime activity is good for your toddler: Toddlers are usually very motivated by food. Letting your toddler make her/his own peanut butter and jelly sandwich is fun and will give the toddler an opportunity to do something for her/himself.

What you'll need to play this activity: bread (frozen, if bread would easily tear apart); plastic serrated knife and plastic spoon; peanut butter and jelly

How to play *Make Peanut Butter and Jelly Sandwiches*: Help your toddler wash her/his hands. Always begin all food projects by washing hands; this is an important health habit to teach your child. On a bread board, place the bread, peanut butter, jelly, and tools. Make a sandwich while your toddler watches. Explain what you are doing. Then give your child two slices of bread and let her/him make a sandwich. Cut the sandwiches in half. Put half of each sandwich on a plate. Serve with milk. Talk about how delicious the sandwich is that your toddler made.

Share!

The first time you made a peanut butter and jelly sandwich, this is what happened:

_____

_____

_____

_____

Celebrate!

Celebrate your toddler's abilities and play interests.

By fostering the natural creative desires within your toddler, you are helping your child grow up to be a happier, more creative individual.

From 18-24 months you will observe that Toddler:

- Enjoys a variety of art mediums
- Is free and creative when using art materials
- Doesn't have the need to produce a project that can be saved
- Derives great pleasure from the "doing" of an art project

Play!

Sidewalk Chalk Drawing

Why this playtime activity is good for your toddler: Chalk on the concrete will provide a new surface for experimenting with color and design and will allow for huge drawings without the limitations experienced when chalking on a piece of paper.

What you'll need to play this activity: big square chunks of chalk (for easy grasping); sidewalk

How to play *Sidewalk Chalk Drawing*: Let your toddler have several hard chunks of chalk. Use the sidewalk, patio, or other concrete surface for drawing. Chalk will eventually wear off the concrete or it can be hosed off with water.

Variation: Use white chalk to draw on black paper.

Share!

When you were a toddler and you drew pictures on the sidewalk with chalk, you played about this long:

_____

Your chalk picture was:_____

_____

Celebrate!

Celebrate your toddler's social/emotional development.

At the end of the first year your toddler may have began to tell you "no." By the end of the second year her/his protests may have escalated to screaming fits or full-blown tantrums.

Between 18-24 months you will observe that Toddler:

- When defiant, may throw her/himself onto her/his back on the floor and kick and scream
- When defiant, may even hold her/his breath to get what s/he wants
- Believes the world revolves around her/him

Play!

I'm Leaving Now. I'll Be Back When You Stop!

Why this activity is important for your toddler's emotional development: When toddlers throw tantrums they want two things: your attention and to get what they want. Look at the tantrum as a performance.

What you need to do this activity: patience

How to play *I'm Leaving Now. I'll Be Back When You Stop!*: When your child begins to throw a tantrum, after making sure s/he is in a safe place, tell her/him "I'm leaving now. I'll be back when you stop!" Then immediately leave the room and occupy yourself in another area of the house. Don't go back into the room with your toddler until s/he stops crying. Never give in and give your toddler what s/he was having a tantrum to get. If you give in, your toddler will learn very quickly that throwing a tantrum is how to get what s/he wants. If throwing a tantrum doesn't work, s/he will soon stop having them.

Share!

When you were a toddler, here are some of the ways you showed defiance:

_____

_____

The first time you threw a temper tantrum it was: _____

_____

Celebrate!

Celebrate your toddler's self-care skills.

During the second half of the second year, your toddler will begin to do many things for her/himself. Because her/his language skills are developing your toddler will be able to tell you when s/he is hungry, is tired, and needs the toilet.

By the end of 24 months you will observe that Toddler:

- Will help when you wash her/his hands
- Will be able to dress her/himself in simple garments
- Will begin to help you pick up toys

Play!

Picking Up the Toys

Why this playtime activity is good for your toddler: At this age it is important to children to please you. Toddlers want to do what you, a grown-up, can do. S/He'll soon learn that doing things for you brings her/him rewards in the form of pats, hugs, and finally, inward satisfaction because s/he has pleased you.

What you'll need to play this activity: toy containers such as large colorful laundry baskets, large cardboard boxes covered with colorful adhesive paper, or a toy box

How to play *Picking Up the Toys*: You can make the chore of picking up toys into a game that your toddler will enjoy playing. At first you will need to pick up the toys and put them away while your toddler watches. The next step will be to help your toddler pick up the toys. After playing the game at this level, gradually begin watching as your toddler picks up the toys alone.

Variation: Sort toys by different attributes such as colors, big/little, round/square, light/heavy, soft/hard, wheels/no wheels.

Share!

When you were a toddler and it was time to pick up your toys, you would do this:

_____

_____

_____

_____

Celebrate!

Celebrate your toddler's language development.

When addressing your toddler, always use her/his own name. When you talk to her/him, name objects and toys that you and s/he use together during the day. As long as s/he understand you, keep increasing the length of your sentences and conversations with your child. Remember, you are your child's main language model.

By the end of 24 months you will observe that Toddler:

- Will have mastered at least fifty spoken words
- Will speak in sentences of three to four words
- May communicate in a way that no one but you can understand

Play!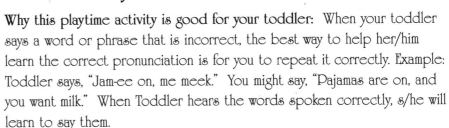

"Pajamas are on, and you want milk."

"Jam-ee on, me meek."

Echo Correctly

Why this playtime activity is good for your toddler: When your toddler says a word or phrase that is incorrect, the best way to help her/him learn the correct pronunciation is for you to repeat it correctly. Example: Toddler says, "Jam-ee on, me meek." You might say, "Pajamas are on, and you want milk." When Toddler hears the words spoken correctly, s/he will learn to say them.

What you'll need to play this activity: No special equipment is needed for this game.

How to play *Echo Correctly*: Listen carefully to what your toddler is saying to you. Then repeat her/his sentence enunciating every word correctly. You are your child's main language model. The more words s/he hears spoken correctly, the easier it will be for her/him to learn language.

Share!

Something you said when you were a toddler that no one but me understood was:

_____

_____

_____

Celebrate!

Celebrate your toddler's second birthday.

It is extraordinary how much your child has learned in one short year! Celebrate how hard your child has worked to learn all of the new things s/he has mastered. Have a birthday gathering and show photographs of how much your toddler has grown in twelve short months.

By the end of 24 months you will observe that Toddler:

- Has learned to walk with confidence, run, jump, and hop
- Has learned to talk in short sentences
- Has learned many self-care skills such as dressing, eating, brushing teeth
- Has become aware of her/himself as separate from others
- Has developed imagination and can play in a creative way

Play!

Blow Out Your Candles!

Why this birthday tradition is good for your toddler: Family rituals and holiday traditions are the threads that weave childhood memories into a beautiful fabric that will wrap your child in warmth all through her/his adult life.

What you'll need to play this activity: birthday cake with two candles

How to play *Blow Out Your Candles!*: At the birthday party, light the candles on your toddler's cake. Put the cake in front of the birthday child. If s/he doesn't know how to blow out candles, show her/him. Then relight them, and let your toddler blow out the candles.

Share!

Here is what happened when it was time to blow out your birthday candles:

_____

These are the people who came to celebrate at your second birthday party:

_____

Here is what happened at your second birthday party:

_____

_____

Celebrate!

Celebrate your two-year-old's gross motor development.

In the year ahead your toddler's gross motor skills will become smoother and more coordinated. S/He'll learn to kick and direct the motion of a ball, walk up and down steps, walk backward and turn corners, and do multiple things like using hands, talking, and looking around at the same time. Every day you will see she/he is becoming more and more adept at maneuvering her/his body.

From 24-30 months you will observe that your toddler:

- Will demonstrate skill in most simple, large muscle activities
- Will engage in lots of physical testing
- Will enjoy jumping from heights, climbing, hanging by the arms
- Will especially enjoy rough-and-tumble play

Play!

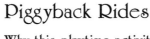

Piggyback Rides

Why this playtime activity is good for your two-year-old: Close physical contact with parents is good for children this age. Rough-housing gives toddlers the opportunity to release extra energy and aggression in a socially acceptable way.

What you'll need to play this activity: No special equipment is needed for this activity.

How to play Piggyback Rides: Get on the floor on all fours. Have your two-year-old climb up on your back and wrap her/his arms around your neck. Carefully move around the room on your hands and knees. Ask your two-year-old if you should go faster. Teach her/him to guide you with verbal commands such as "Go," "Slow," "Stop," and "Faster!" If your toddler isn't verbalizing yet, watch for signals like the squeezing of your neck which may indicate that s/he thinks you are moving too fast or joyful sounds that tell you s/he is having fun and can handle more of this kind of play.

Variation: You can give "horsey rides" while sitting. Sit in a chair and cross your legs. Have your youngster sit on the ankle of the leg that is dangling. Hold your toddler's hands and move her/him up and down by lifting your leg up and down.

Share!

When you were a child and we played Piggyback Rides, your favorite way to play was:

_____

_____

Celebrate!

Celebrate your two-year-old's developing fine motor skills.

Finger plays are a fun and entertaining way to help your toddler learn fine motor and sometimes gross motor skills. Through repetition offered in finger plays, youngsters quickly learn the rhymes and the movements that correspond to the action words. When using rhymes and finger plays do not try to "teach" them, but rather present the rhyme with actions and invite your youngster to join in at the level of participation that is appropriate for her/him.

From 24-30 months you will observe that your toddler:

- Will learn to draw vertical and horizontal lines with a crayon
- Will begin to try curved motions when drawing and coloring
- Will be able to turn book pages one at a time

Play!

Open and Shut/Handy Hands

Why this playtime activity is good for your two-year-old: When doing these finger plays, your toddler will practice controlling the movement of small muscles in her/his hands and fingers and will physically experience opposites such as *open, shut, come, go, stop.*

What you'll need to play this activity: rhymes

How to play *Open and Shut/Handy Hands*: Recite the rhymes while performing the appropriate hand movements.

Open and Shut
Open, shut them, open, shut them.
   (With palms facing up, open, and shut hands.)
Put them on your head.
   (Place hands on head.)
Open, shut them, open, shut them.
   (With palms facing up, open and shut hands.)
Put your hands to bed.
   (With palms together, place back of hands to one cheek and tilt head.)

Handy Hands
Come, come, come.   *(With palms up, pull fingers toward you as if beckoning.)*
Go, go, go.   *(With hands in front of you, push hands away.)*
Stop, stop, stop.   *(Hold open hands up and in front of you.)*
Clap, clap, clap.   *(Clap hands three times.)*
Bye, bye, bye.   *(Wave good-bye with both hands.)*

Share!

When you were two, your favorite finger play was:

_____

Celebrate!

Celebrate your two-year-old's abilities and play interests.

During this developmental stage your toddler should have available a wide variety of small motor tools. Use a plastic dishpan to keep play things such as: colored plastic, snap clothespins; kitchen basters and large medicine droppers; plastic measuring cups such as 1 cup, ½ cup, ¼ cup (240 ml, 120 ml, 60 ml); Styrofoam egg cartons with lids removed; kitchen tongs (both metal and wooden); small rubber balls; large cotton balls; plastic objects; plastic containers will lids containing sea shells and smooth stones (not small enough to swallow).

From 24-30 months you will observe that Toddler:

- Will have fine motor skills required to open clip clothespins
- Will be able to squeeze water from basters and medicine droppers
- Will enjoy hiding and finding small objects in water or sand

Play!

Experimentation

Why this playtime activity is good for your toddler: Using small motor tools is good exercise for the small muscles of the hands and fingers. Your toddler will be fascinated with the principle of suction. S/He will enjoy learning about objects that *sink* and *float* and physically experiencing these opposite concepts.

What you'll need to play this activity: tub of water; basters and medicine droppers; objects that float and sink; empty containers; egg cartons

How to play *Experimentation*: Set out the tub of water, basters, medicine droppers, measuring cups, empty containers, and egg cartons. Demonstrate how the basters and droppers work. Experiment to see which objects float and which ones sink. Then let your toddler experiment with all of the water tools alone.

Share!

When you were two years old, one of your favorite ways to experiment was:

_____

_____

_____

_____

Celebrate!

Celebrate your two-year-old's language development.

As your toddler's language skills develop s/he will ask hundreds of questions every day. Be patient with these questions. Try to answer each one. Remember, one of the most important ways your toddler can learn about things is to ask questions.

From 24-30 months you will observe that your toddler:

- Will begin telling you in sentences about her/his needs
- Will begin to use courtesy in speech such as "please" and "thank you"
- Will continue asking many questions such as "What?" "Where?" and "Why?"

Play!

Feely Box

Why this playtime activity is good for your toddler: At first, your toddler will enjoy pulling all the material from the kit and then returning it. Later, s/he will be able to identify the items and to describe the textures. Your toddler will experience a variety of textures and "feel" how they are different. Later, s/he will be able to select textured items to be placed inside the kit.

What you'll need to play this activity: large shoe box, with a hole big enough for a small hand cut in the lid; three or four textured, household objects to be placed in the box such as plastic pot scrubber, pieces of velvet and silk cloth, hair brush, piece of sandpaper, sponge, apple, cotton balls, sawdust, fake fur, feather

How to play *Feely Box*: Place three to five of the textured items you have collected in the feely box. Place the lid on top. Have your toddler put her/his hand inside the box. Allow time for her/him to feel the objects. Have her/him choose one item and hold it. See if she/he can name it. Pull it from the box. Name the object for your toddler. Put it back into the box. Repeat with other objects. Allow time for your toddler to play with the box alone.

Variation: Put new objects in the box each day. Encourage your toddler to select things to put in the box. Put your hand inside and try to guess what is in the box.

Share!

When you were a toddler, you enjoyed playing with things that had these textures:

When I let you choose things to put inside the "feely box," these are the objects you choose:

Celebrate!

Celebrate your two-year-old's developing social skills.

Children this age enjoy being with other children, but they may not be able to do so without getting into trouble. While playing with other small children, your two-year-old will need constant supervision. It is normal that children this age have difficulty controlling their aggressive impulses so s/he'll need to have you help her/him learn how to do that.

From 24-30 months you will observe that your toddler:

- May offer materials to others, but is usually protective of materials in own possession
- May "hoard" toys
- Is at the "snatch and grab" stage
- Will sometimes be shy and other times aggressive

Play!

Play Group

Why this playtime activity is good for your two-year-old: This activity will give your toddler an opportunity to practice playing with other children. If the play group meets at your home, have plenty of equipment and supplies for all to use. If three children are playing together, there should be three of each kind of toy. For example, if the children are playing in a sandbox, provide three buckets, three plastic shovels, etc.

What you'll need to play this activity: one or two playmates for your toddler; identical toys

How to conduct a play group: Invite a child or two to play with your two-year-old. In the beginning, the play group should meet for a short period of time– not more than 20 or 30 minutes. Close supervision is required to keep everyone safe.

Variation: If a play group is not possible for your youngster, playing at a park or nearby playground will give your toddler the opportunity to see other children at play. However, added caution is needed when your toddler is playing with strangers.

Share!

Your first peer playmate was: _____

Your favorite things to do together were: _____

_____

_____

Celebrate!

Celebrate your two-year-old's emotional development.

It is during this developmental stage when your toddler will discover that society has rules, and s/he is expected to observe them. This fact will present an emotional challenge for both you and your youngster. While many consider these years the "terrible twos," if you can think of them as the "terrific twos," it will be an easier time for both you and your toddler.

From 24-30 months you will observe that your toddler:

- Likes to tell you "No!"
- Doesn't like to be told "No!"
- Will flip-flop between the extremes of clinging and running in the opposite direction

Play!

Yes!

Why this playtime activity is good for your two-year-old: The word your toddler says and hears the most each day is most likely "No." Hearing the word "Yes" teaches your child that there is a choice besides the negative one.

What you'll need to play this activity: No special equipment is needed to do this activity.

How to play *Yes!*: When you need to tell your youngster "No," try this game. Rephrase your commands so that you can tell your toddler something positive instead of something negative. For example, if you do not want your toddler to touch a photograph, instead of saying "No!," point to a magazine near the photograph and say, "Yes, you may touch the magazine. The photograph is not a toy, but the magazine is something for you to hold and see." Or if your toddler wants to go outside, but it is time for a nap, instead of saying "No," say, "Yes, you can go outside as soon as you take your nap." Try to phrase as many of your statements in a positive way as possible.

Variation: Give your two-year-old many opportunities each day to tell you "Yes." Ask questions that s/he will be able to answer with a positive. For example, "Are you a big girl/boy?" or "Do you like coloring with these crayons?"

Share!

You were this old, when you began telling me "No!" _____

When you were two and I told you "No," you usually responded: _____

_____

_____

Celebrate!

Celebrate your two-year-old's communication skills.

It is during this developmental stage that your toddler will begin to understand two-part sentences and be able to perform two-part directions. Remember, children talk more frequently if they have something to talk about. Be sure to give your toddler plenty of interesting activities in which s/he can take part. Sand and water play, finger painting, outdoor play, walking, and visiting nearby places of interest will give your youngster many exciting things to talk about and will speed her/his language development.

From 24-30 months you will observe that your toddler:

- Will frequently ask for the names of various objects and activities
- Understands longer sentences such as, "After you have a nap, you can go outside."
- Will talk more and more–speech is coming in a rush
- Sings or says nursery rhymes, songs, and finger plays

Play!

Let's Go On an Outing!

Why this playtime activity is good for your two-year-old: Your toddler's language development is directly affected by the amount of interesting things s/he has to talk about. A weekly trip to a park, library, mall, zoo, farm, aquarium, circus, bakery, supermarket, vegetable stand, flower shop, pet shop, music store, puppet show, etc., will greatly stimulate your toddler's language development.

What you'll need to play this activity: transportation and imagination

How to play *Let's Go On an Outing!*: Announce the outing destination the day or evening before the outing. To prepare, look in picture books and magazines for pictures of things you might see on the outing. For example, if you are visiting a farm, look at books of farm animals. When you get to your destination, point out for your toddler the things that you discussed beforehand. For example, "Look, Eric, there is a cow. Remember what sound a cow makes? Listen and we might hear the cow make the 'moo' sound."

Variations: If possible, take photographs while you on the outing. When you get the photographs back, look at them with your youngster. Talk about the photographs and the outing again.

Share!

When you were two and we went on outings, your favorite places to go were:

_____

_____

Celebrate!

Celebrate your two-year-old's fantasy play.

Two-year-old children are developing a self-identity and an awareness of themselves as separate from others, but they are still very egocentric. They are beginning to play with other children but need adult help and supervision during these interactions. Some children this age begin working through problems during fantasy play. For example, a toddler will take on the role of a grown-up and act out the things that person does to her/him that are pleasing or upsetting to the child. If you watch your toddler playing with a baby doll, you may see that s/he is imitating gestures and speaking words that you speak to her/him.

From 24-30 months you will observe that your toddler:

- Uses more imagination–toys and dolls may represent other things
- Enjoys playing with dolls and puppets that portray familiar persons or characters

Play!

Puppet Storytelling

Why this playtime activity is good for your two-year-old: Using puppets to tell stories will help extend your toddler's attention span. Additional learning takes place if you use the puppets with concept books for counting, identifying colors, or reciting nursery rhymes. Watch, and you will see that your toddler will talk to and quickly become absorbed in the puppet character as though it is alive. For some children this age, puppets are less threatening than adults, and they will speak frankly to a puppet. Puppets help toddlers gain confidence, foster self-esteem, and aid in developing language skills.

What you'll need to play this activity: puppet, story or concept books

How to play *Puppet Storytelling:* Instead of just telling or reading a story, let a favorite puppet tell your child a story. Sit your toddler in a chair or on the floor in front of you. Hold the book in one hand so your child can see the pictures. Place the puppet near the book as if it is reading the book. Tell or read the story. When your child has a question, let her/him communicate with the puppet.

Variation: Make paper bag puppets for your child's pretend play. Use felt markers to trace the heads of animals or people from coloring books and attach them to paper bags. Decorate them to represent the characters needed for a particular story.

Share!

When you were a two-year-old, your favorite fairy tale was:

Celebrate!

Celebrate your two-year-old's high level of energy.

It is important each day during this developmental stage to provide your toddler with an opportunity for outside play. Outside play allows your youngster plenty of room to move around and celebrate her/his high level of energy.

From 24-30 months you will observe that your toddler:

- Enjoys crawling through tunnels
- Enjoys rolling on mats
- Enjoys going down small slides
- Likes to climb on low structures (with your help)
- Enjoys any game that involves running and climbing

Play!

Outdoor Gym Equipment Exercise

Why this playtime activity is good for your two-year-old: At this stage of development your child especially enjoys swinging, climbing, sliding, and tunneling. Exercising on outdoor gym equipment will give your child and opportunity to use a level of energy not possible indoors.

What you'll need to play this activity: tunnels; swings with seats curved or body shaped and made of energy-absorbing materials; low climbing structures; small slides (All outdoor play equipment needs to have soft material such as sawdust or sand underneath it.)

How to exercise with outdoor gym equipment: In the beginning, stand very close to your toddler as s/he explores outdoor gym equipment. Stay close enough to catch your youngster if s/he decides to try to jump from a high place or cannot get down after climbing to the top of a structure. Use the equipment with your child so s/he can learn how to use it properly. For example, the first time swinging, hold your child in your lap, and swing with her/him until your toddler is used to the sensation. Praise your child for using equipment in safe ways.

Caution: Children this age are likely to get themselves to the top of a climbing structure without being able to get down, so they need constant and careful adult supervision when using outdoor and gym equipment.

Share!

When you were two and we went to the park, your favorite outdoor gym equipment was:

_____

This is how you played on the gym equipment: _____

_____

Celebrate!

Celebrate your two-year-old's self-care abilities.

Now that your child has had her/his second birthday, s/he'll show real progress meeting basic needs such as dressing, eating, and taking care of toys. If you provide what your toddler needs, s/he will most likely be happy to try to get dressed, eat, and put away toys. S/He will still have to have assistance finishing up when dressing with things such as tying shoes, snapping snaps, buttoning buttons, and zipping zippers. When eating s/he will still need help with things such as cutting up meat and pouring milk.

From 24-30 months you will observe that your toddler:

- Will be able to remove much of her/his clothing without assistance
- Will be able to eat and drink quite well, with hardly any spills

Play!

Put Your Little Sock

Why this playtime activity is good for your two-year-old: Talking and doing at the same reinforces what a toddler needs to learn about dressing her/himself.

What you'll need to play this activity: rhyme, appropriate clothing

How to play *Put Your Little Sock*: Talk to your toddler as s/he is being undressed or dressed. Tell her/him about what you and s/he are doing together. Say, "Now, Amy, we'll pull up these socks; you help me," or "Push your foot into your pant's leg, Amy; make your foot come out the other end." Sing the rhyme to the tune of "Put your Little Foot Right Out." You can sing this song if you are putting your child's clothes on, if you are helping her/him put on clothes, or if you are watching her/him dress on her/his own.

Put Your Little Sock
Put your little sock,
Put your little sock,
Put your little sock right on.
Put your little shoe,
Put your little shoe,
Put your little shoe right on.

Share!

When you were this old, with assistance, you could undress yourself. _____

When you were this old, with assistance, you could dress yourself. _____

When you were this old, without assistance, you could undress yourself. _____

When you were this old, without assistance, you could dress yourself. _____

Celebrate!

Celebrate your two-year-old's learning about safety.

Although children this age have greatly increased gross and fine motor skills and are interested in and capable of a wider range of activities, they still have little understanding of what might be dangerous. They may be able to entertain themselves for short periods of time, but because they can get into trouble so quickly, they still must be closely monitored.

From 24-30 months you will observe that your toddler:

- Will have trouble sitting still for extended periods
- May resist restraints such as car seat belts
- Will not understand the danger of playing in the driveway or near the street

Play!

I Spy

Why this playtime activity is good for your two-year-old: Playing "I Spy" while traveling along in a car will keep your toddler entertained so s/he won't mind sitting in restraints for extended periods of time. It will also give her/him practice matching words and objects.

What you'll need to play this activity: No special equipment is needed to play this car game.

How to play I Spy: As you are driving along tell your toddler, "I Spy (name something you see)." Your child looks for the object named, and when s/he sees it s/he points to it. Soon instead of pointing, your toddler will be saying "I Spy."

Examples: I spy a tree; I spy a school bus; I spy a tall building; I spy a red car; I spy our house; I spy snow; I spy a cow.

Variation #1: If you are driving, you may want to have another passenger (such as older sibling) play this game with your child.

Variation #2: When your child is capable, s/he can tell you what s/he spies, and you can look for it.

Note: Any games you play with your child while s/he is riding in the car will make sitting still and being restrained easier for her/him to bear.

Share!

When you were two and we played "I Spy," you liked to: _____

_____

_____

Celebrate!

Celebrate your two-year-old's health and well-being.

Beginning at twenty-four months, your toddler should see a pediatrician and dentist for routine exams once a year. By age two your youngster should have received the HBCV vaccine series against Haemophilus Influenzae B. In addition to the screening tests performed during your toddlers earlier examinations, s/he'll undergo the following laboratory tests: a blood test to check for anemia, urinalysis to check for infection and kidney and metabolic diseases, and a skin test for TB.

From 24-30 months it may be of concern if you observe that your toddler:

- Falls frequently
- Is unable to build a tower of more than four blocks or has difficulty manipulating objects
- Fails to understand simple instructions
- Has little interest in others or is unable to communicate in short phrases

Play!

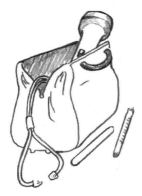

Doctor/Dentist

Why these playtime activities are good for your two-year-old: To reduce anxiety of visits to the doctor and dentist, pretend play about office visits.

What you'll need to play this activity: stethoscope, tongue depressor, small mouth mirror, flashlight

How to play *Doctor*: When playing Doctor, have your child remove her/his shirt and shoes. Sit her/him up on a table. Use the stethoscope (or facsimile) to listen to your youngster's heart. Use the tongue depressor and flashlight to look inside her/his mouth.

How to play *Dentist*: When playing dentist, have your toddler sit in a chair. Use the mouth mirror and flashlight and have the child "open wide." The more conversations you have about visits to dental offices, the more comfortable your toddler will feel in the real situation.

Share!

When you were two and went to the doctor's office, your reactions were: _____

_____

When you were two and went to the dentist's office, your reactions were:_____

_____

When you went for your very first haircut, your reactions were: _____

_____

Celebrate!

Celebrate your two-year-old's abilities and play interests.

Two-year-olds love active, physical play and will have significantly more advanced gross motor skills than they did last year. Your toddler's fine motor skills have also improved, and s/he can now manipulate and explore objects with more deliberate experimentation and demonstrates purposeful efforts at mastery.

From 24-30 months you will observe that your toddler:

- Likes games using her/his whole body
- Plays games to practice balance
- Prefers action toys such as cars, push/pull toys, tricycles, wagons, swings, rocking-horses, and boats
- Enjoys climbing apparatus

Play!

Obstacle Trail

Why this playtime activity is good for your two-year-old: Children this age need gross motor games of high energy. This activity will give your toddler practice walking forward and backward, balancing on one foot, walking tiptoe, turning around, and jumping over or from a low platform. All of these activities are good for your toddler to practice her/his balancing skills.

What you'll need to play this activity: Create an obstacle course by taping lines about 18" (46 cm) apart on the floor, patio, or in the garage. Include boxes to climb through, objects to climb over, and low platforms to climb on and jump from. You may want your child to help you build the obstacle course. Let her/him choose some things to put on the course.

How to play *Obstacle Trail*: Have your toddler stand at the start of the obstacle course. Explain that you will be giving verbal instructions for moving through the obstacle course. For example: "Tiptoe to the box." (Wait until your toddler gets to the box.) "Crawl through the box." (Wait.) "Hop to the platform." (Wait.) "Step up onto the platform, and then jump off." (Wait.) "Walk backwards to the cushions." Etc.

Share!

When you were two and we made an obstacle course, you liked to:_____

_____

Celebrate!

Celebrate your two-year-old's natural artistic abilities.

Children show their first really creative drawings and constructions between the ages of two and three, but at this age it is the process of creating rather than the end product that is important to children. During this important developmental stage, you will notice that your toddler will begin thinking and planning instead of simply acting on objects.

From 24-30 months you will observe that your toddler:

- Will begin making color distinctions
- Will like to paint with brushes and finger paint
- Will probably enjoy using felt-tip markers (nontoxic, washable, and with a large point)
- May make "V" and "H" strokes on paper

Play!

Sponge Mural

Why this playtime activity is good for your two-year-old: Using a sponge as a painting tool will provide your toddler with a tactile experience as well as introduce her/him to the dabbing and smearing movements used in the process. With practice your youngster will discover how s/he can make separate or overlapping prints plus prints in different colors, shapes, and sizes.

What you'll need to play this activity: large sheets of paper such as shelf liner or butcher paper taped to the wall; newspapers, spread on the floor in front of mural; sponges cut into different sizes and geometric shapes; flat pan; paper towels; liquid tempera paint

How to play *Sponge Mural:* Tape large sheets of paper to a wall. Put newspaper down on the floor in front of the mural. Pour about three large spoonfuls of tempera paint into the flat pan. Wet the sponges and place them in the pan. Show your child how to press a sponge in the paint and then press it against the paper on the wall. Try different colors and shapes. The mural can be an ongoing project to be worked with different colors, a few minutes each day.

Share!

When you were two and we painted with sponges on a mural, it looked:

_____

_____

Celebrate!

Celebrate your two-year-old's musical talents.

Music is an important part of your toddler's world. It is one of the first sounds (lullabies) a child hears. Music is soothing and comforting to the young child. It helps her/him relax and go to sleep. Through music a child learns about rhythm, harmony, tone, rhyme, and pitch; and through repetition s/he learns the words and tunes of new songs. Repetition impresses young minds and helps toddlers develop language skills.

From 24-30 months you will observe that your toddler:

- Will join in the singing of nursery rhymes and songs
- Will enjoy finger plays and singing the words
- Will use her/his mouth and voice to make music

Play!

Singing Time

Why this playtime activity is good for your two-year-old: While singing songs your toddler will learn about rhythm, harmony, tone, rhyme, and pitch. While expressing the action parts in the finger plays, s/he will learn to listen and follow directions (given in the song) and to be creative in dramatizing the song.

What you'll need to play this activity: repertoire of ten to twelve simple songs, including songs that contain parts that can be dramatized

How to conduct *Singing Time*: Make singing time a part of your daily routine. This daily activity can take as little as five minutes or last as long as twenty to thirty minutes depending on your toddler's level of interest. Following are some ways to conduct singing activities:

Sing a Song–Your toddler will soon pick up on the rhythm and words to simple songs like "The Farmer In the Dell" and "Old MacDonald Had a Farm."

Action Songs–Dramatize songs such as, "Row, Row, Row Your Boat," and "The Mulberry Bush." Use exaggerated body movements for verbs.

Create a Song–Use a familiar tune such as "Twinkle, Twinkle Little Star," or "Mary Had a Little Lamb" and sing original verses about your toddler. Include your child's name in the made-up songs.

Share!

When you were two, your favorite musical game was: _____

When you were two, your favorite song was: _____

Here is how we played your favorite musical game. _____

Celebrate!

Celebrate your two-year-old's interest in books.

Older toddlers enjoy simple stories read from picture books. They attend to short stories with repetition and/or rhymes and familiar subjects. They especially enjoy stories about what they do themselves.

From 24-30 months you will observe that your toddler:

- Enjoys books with pictures hidden behind movable windows or doors
- Enjoys simple pop-up books and is beginning to like "dress-me" books
- Enjoys looking at books individually as well as having stories read to her/him

Play!

Storytelling with Props

Why this playtime activity is good for your two-year-old: Visual aids used with oral storytelling help youngsters focus on the story and puppets stimulate the listener's imagination.

What you'll need to play this activity: simple, short stories such as fairy tales and fables; props, including any items or objects that relate to the story

Some suggested stories and props are:

The Gingerbread Boy–Use a large decorated cardboard gingerbread cut-out. After telling the story, snack on small gingerbread cookies or bake gingerbread.

The Three Little Pigs–Three plastic pigs in different colors. After telling the story, eat bowls of bean soup.

The Three Bears–Three stuffed bears in different sizes. After telling the story, have oatmeal or porridge.

The Little Red Hen–Plastic animals for each character (hen, goose, cat, pig). After telling the story, enjoy slices of wheat bread with butter.

How to tell stories with props: Place the props in a paper bag or large shoe box. As you read or tell the story, pull out the appropriate prop and show it to your toddler.

Share!

When you were two years old, your favorite fairy tale was: _____

_____

When we had storytime, you especially enjoyed: _____

_____

Celebrate!

Celebrate your two-year-old's sensory experiences.

Materials that can be used for fantasy play in sand or water are appropriate for children this age. Natural materials such as stones, sea shells, sand, water, etc. are wonderful for teaching children many skills. Household materials (funnels, unbreakable measuring cups and spoons, sturdy mixing spoons, basters, strainers, etc.) can be used for sand and water or dramatic play.

From 24-30 months you will observe that playing with natural materials:

- Will have positive effects for your toddler beyond reducing costs
- Will increase your toddler's attention to the natural world
- Will increase your toddler's respect and care for playthings

Play!

Sandbox

Why this playtime activity is good for your two-year-old: As your toddler experiments with sand tools, s/he will learn how each tool works. S/He will discover the change in appearance and texture of sand when water is added–wet sand can be molded, and that when molded, sand will have the same shape as the molding container.

What you'll need to play this activity: sandbox (can be a plastic dish tub); measuring tools such as cups and spoons; beach toys such as buckets and shovels; molding tools such as bowls and boxes; natural objects such as seashells and smooth stones

How to play Sandbox: There are many games to be played in a sandbox. Here are a few appropriate games for your two-year-old:

Sand Play–To a pan of sand, add small, plastic cars, animals, and people. Allow for free play and exploring.

Sand Tools–To a pan of sand, add assorted sizes of plastic measuring spoons and cups, mixing spoons, slotted spoons, strainers, and funnels. Show your child how to use the different tools to sift, measure, and move sand.

Sand Molds–To a pan of sand, add enough water to the sand so that when molded it will hold its shape. Add small containers in different sizes and shapes to be used as sand molds. Demonstrate how to pack the sand into the container, how to invert, and how to remove the mold from the wet sand.

Share!

When you were two playing in a sandbox, your favorite game was: _____

_____

Celebrate!

Celebrate your two-year-old's high level of energy.

Most of your toddler's activities now will be walking, running, climbing, carrying, etc. This is a very active developmental stage, and your child is now capable of thinking of and carrying out a wide variety of activities. Be sure each day s/he spends time both indoors and (weather permitting) outside in self-planned play.

From 24-30 months you will observe that your toddler:

- Enjoys mobile toys like tricycles and wagons (small)
- Loves to run, climb, jump, and hop
- Enjoys toys on which s/he can sit and push her/himself

Play!

Tag

Why this playtime activity is good for your two-year-old: Playing tag allows your child to exert a high level of energy and enjoy her/his favorite pastime–running.

What you'll need to play this activity: No special equipment is needed for this game.

How to play *Tag*: There are many ways to play tag with a two-year-old. Here are several appropriate tag games:

Racing–Running to a destination (side by side) and tagging something and then turning to run back to the starting point is a good tag game. It will motivate your toddler to maintain a fast pace with you. Don't let her/him win every race, but don't let her/him be discouraged by never winning a race with you.

You're It!–Traditional tag where a runner chases someone until s/he tags him/her is a good game for youngsters. When tagged, reverse the roles and chase your toddler. Although you may be able to outrun your toddler, s/he will probably be able to run for longer amounts of time without tiring.

Statue Tag–This game is played like stoop tag except instead of stooping to be safe, one must stop and stand perfectly still like a statue. A person standing still cannot be tagged; only a person in motion can be tagged by the runner.

Share!

When you were two and we played tag, your favorite tag game was: _____

_____

Celebrate!

Celebrate your two-year-old's exploration and play experiences.

Between two and three years of age most children begin to make constructions. Wooden unit blocks (often called kindergarten blocks) are appropriate for this age group. The basic unit is the block measuring $1\frac{3}{8}$" x $2\frac{3}{4}$" x $5\frac{1}{2}$" (35 mm x 70 mm x 140 mm). The blocks may be hard or soft wood. Hardwood blocks are heavier and more durable, but more expensive. Children of this age tend not to use the specialized forms, such as triangles and arches. Recognition of size, shape, and color concepts are reinforced through block play.

From 24-30 months you will observe that your toddler:

- Enjoys interlocking blocks or bricks
- Enjoys interlocking logs

Play!

Block Building

Why this playtime activity is good for your two-year-old: Building with blocks will give your toddler practice in large and fine muscle development; encourage building towers and other structures; and will stimulate creative play. As s/he erects fences, houses, and other buildings, your child will be gaining valuable concentration skills and learning patience when balancing blocks.

What you'll need to play this activity: Set of 50 to 60 blocks; cardboard squares, rectangles and ovals for roofs, patios, lawns, pools, floors, ramps, bridges, and roads.

How to play *Block Building*: Demonstrate for your toddler how to stack, line up in different ways, and stand blocks end to end. Use the blocks in a variety of ways as you play with your toddler. Talk to your toddler about the colors and shapes of the blocks. Count the blocks as you stack them.

Variation: You can use milk cartons to create giant blocks. Begin by opening the milk cartons and washing them with warm, soapy water. Rinse in lemon water and let dry. Stuff the cartons full of newspapers. Fold the top flat and tape in place. Cover the milk cartons with white adhesive-backed paper. Draw or cut from construction paper or colored adhesive-backed paper geometric shapes, numerals, or letters of the alphabet. Using only once concept for each carton, attach the same cut-out to all four sides of the carton.

Share!

When you were a two-year-old and we played with blocks, your favorite game was:

Celebrate!

Celebrate your two-year-old's extended memory span.

By two years of age a child's memory span has improved so that s/he can remember things from a previous day. Older toddlers learn to concentrate and begin to remember three-part directions.

From 24-30 months you will observe that your toddler:

- Grasps simple cause-and-effect relationships
- Is eager to learn new skills
- Will ask many questions

Play!

Make a Pair

Why this playtime activity is good for your two-year-old: Matching is good eye-hand coordination. Working with shoes will give you the opportunity to discuss the owner of each pair of shoes and reinforce concepts such as large, small, soft, hard, new, and old.

What you'll need to play this activity: Gather a bag of about a dozen pairs of shoes. Include: men's work shoes, athletic shoes, ballet slippers, high heels, baby shoes, house slippers, rubber rain boots, cowboy boots—the more varied the shoes the better!

How to play *Make a Pair:* Begin by removing four shoes from the bag (two should match and two should not match) and placing them randomly on the floor. Show your toddler the matching pair of shoes. Then mix up the four shoes and see if s/he can make a pair again. Gradually remove other shoes from the bag and make pairs. Line up the pairs. Talk about which shoes are the biggest, smallest, softest, hardest, newest, and oldest. Play a game of "Whose Shoes are These?" One at a time, show the shoes to your toddler and ask, "Whose shoes are these?" If s/he cannot reply verbally, ask questions that can be answered with a nod or shake of the head. For example, "Are these my shoes? Are these your shoes? Are these Daddy's shoes?"

Share!

You were this old when you wore your first pair of shoes._____

When you were two years old, your favorite pair of shoes was: _____

Celebrate!

Celebrate your two-year-old's developing audio/visual skills.

Older toddlers may learn to sing phrases of songs, often on pitch. They may try to sing along with recorded or "live" nursery rhymes and songs and love to "dance" or perform other actions to music. Movement to music may include running, galloping, swinging, swaying heads, and tapping feet.

From 24-30 months you will observe that your toddler:

- Will listen to simple recorded stories
- Will sit and watch a video segment of ten minutes or even longer
- Will get up and dance or sing along during a video when s/he hears familiar songs

Play!

You're the Star!

Why this playtime activity is good for your two-year-old: Older toddlers are very interested in viewing themselves on video. Watching themselves help children develop positive self-esteems.

What you'll need to play this activity: camcorder, music, costumes

How to play You're the Star!: Let your toddler choose an attractive costume such as a hat, cape, or wig. Play the music and have your toddler move to the music. Practice the "dance" s/he will do on video. Then videotape your toddler. Play the video for your toddler to watch. If s/he wants to do another show, play the music again and repeat the process.

Variation: Have a "You're the Star!" party to share the video with friends and family. Compliment your child in the presence of others.

Share!

The first time I video recorded you, this is what you did: _____

_____

_____

The first time you saw yourself on video, this is how you reacted: _____

_____

_____

Celebrate!

Celebrate your two-year-old's emotional development.

Young children this age are selfish and self-centered. A two-year-old will often employ temper tantrums, pushing, shoving, crying, screaming, or quarreling to get her/his way. During the "terrific twos" your toddler will test not only her/his limits but yours as well. Remember, reasoning with a two-year-old is difficult if not impossible.

From 24-30 months you will observe that your toddler:

- Expresses a wide range of emotions
- May object to major changes in daily routine
- Still confuses fantasy with reality
- Views everything in extremely simple terms
- Will act out to get attention or her/his own way

Play!

Fabric Fun

Why this playtime activity is good for your two-year-old: Tactile games ground children. This activity will bring your toddler to the here-and-now. Playing this game will also teach your toddler in a physical way about differences and similarities. As you play this activity you can explain that each person is also unique and has her/his own special "feel."

What you'll need to play this activity: lightweight poster board cut in 4" (10 cm) squares; scissors; glue; six to eight different pieces of fabric such as fur, terry cloth, velvet, corduroy, denim, burlap, satin, or angora (Instead of making fabric squares, if available, a variety of carpet squares can be used to play this activity.)

How to play *Fabric Fun:* Cut two matching 4" (10 cm) square pieces of fabric from each kind of material. Glue the fabric to the poster board squares. Give your child one set of fabric cards to examine and feel. Talk about how each card feels. Use words such as "fuzzy," "rough," "smooth," and "soft." Discuss the colors of each square. After letting your child play with the fabric cards, give her/him one and see if s/he can find the matching square from the second set of squares.

Share!

There are many things that make you unique and different from all other children. Here are just a few:

_____

_____

_____

Celebrate!

Celebrate your two-year-old's gross motor development.

Toddlers this age can push themselves on wheeled objects like tricycles and wagons with good steering. Older toddlers engage in lots of active play and enjoy moving in a variety of ways such as rolling, galloping, somersaulting, spinning or running in circles, and marching to music.

From 30-36 months you will observe that your toddler:

- Runs easily and climbs well
- Walks up and down stairs, alternating feet
- Can kick balls
- Pedals a tricycle
- Can bend over easily without falling

Play!

Roadway

Why this playtime activity is good for your two-year-old: Using toys like tricycles to practice gross motor skills is fun and easy. Challenge your toddler's play on her/his tricycle by making a "roadway."

What you'll need to play this activity: Use chalk to draw road dividers on a patio, porch, or other safe place. Use a large utility box to build a parking structure. (Cut out two adjacent sides so your child can her/his drive tricycle into the box.) Use your imagination to create a real driving situation like stop signs, etc. Post a speed limit.

How to play Roadway: Talk to your toddler about the roadway. Talk about the road signs and speed limit. Show her/him how to pull in and back out of the "garage." Talk about steering the tricycle so it stays on the right side of the divider. Let your child play with the tricycle obstacle course.

Variation #1: While driving in the car talk about the simple road signs such as "stop," "curve," "slow," and "speed limits."

Variation #2: Show your toddler the hand signals for turning and stopping.

Share!

When you were two and you rode your tricycle, your favorite games were:

_____

_____

_____

Celebrate!

Celebrate your two-year-old's maturing social skills.

Children this age who have older siblings often will begin to show signs of hero worship. Two-year-olds see an older sibling as a strong and independent person who still plays like a kid. Your child may want to tag along with older children, but this is only appropriate once in awhile.

From 30-36 months you will observe that your toddler:

- Displays pride in accomplishments
- Shows a strong desire for independence
- Will mimic actions of older children–especially siblings

Play!

Tent Building Buddies

Why this playtime activity is good for your two-year-old: If your toddler has an older brother or sister, once in awhile, involve them in a game together. If your toddler doesn't have an older sibling, a young babysitter or neighbor may like to play this game with your toddler. Tent building is a game that amuses children of all ages. As your toddler experiments with the covering materials, s/he will discover that if the children want to hide, large covers are needed for large pieces of furniture. Children find satisfaction in making a place where they think they cannot be seen and in playing hiding games. Crawling inside a tent is an experience that may help some children overcome fear of the dark. Many toddlers spend more time making and remaking the tent than they do playing inside the tent. Each time your toddler makes a tent, s/he will be using great imagination and gross motor skills.

What you'll need to play this activity: tent coverings such as blankets, colored bed sheets, sheer curtains, pieces of net fabric or other lightweight fabric; kitchen chairs or card tables; an older sibling, another child who is older, or a babysitter

How to play *Tent Building Buddies*: Give the building materials to your toddler and the older child. Let them be creative in the way they drape tables, sofas, etc., to create a tent.

Share!

The first time you built a tent, here is what happened: _____

_____

The first time you built a tent, the person who helped you was: _____

_____

Celebrate!

Celebrate your two-year-old's developing intellectual maturity.

Toddlers enjoy simple learning games that require one skill such as matching colors or shapes. Some simple learning games will hold their short attention spans and are fun, but most games require interaction with an adult. However, once introduced to the game, children will continue using it and be capable of adding their own creative rules. Young children enjoy playing the role of "teacher" and should be given opportunities to have a turn at doing so.

From 30-36 months you will observe that your toddler:

- Will begin counting to two, and be aware of how many makes two
- May be able to repeat two numbers in order
- Is interested in numbers and amounts of things

Play!

Thumbkin

Why this playtime activity is good for your two-year-old: This finger play will help your toddler learn to count her/his five fingers.

What you'll need to play this activity: rhyme

How to play _Thumbkin_: Recite the rhyme and use the appropriate movements.

Dance, Thumbkin

Dance, Thumbkin, dance,	(Wiggle thumb.)
Dance, ye merrymen, everyone;	(Wiggle all fingers.)
For Thumbkin, he can dance alone;	(Wiggle thumb.)
Thumbkin, he can dance alone.	(Wiggle thumb.)
Dance, Foreman, dance,	(Wiggle first finger.)
Dance, ye merrymen, everyone;	(Wiggle all fingers.)
But Foreman he can dance alone;	(Wiggle first finger.)
Foreman, he can dance alone.	(Wiggle first finger.)
Dance, Longman, dance,	(Wiggle second finger.)
Dance, ye merrymen, everyone;	(Wiggle all fingers.)
For Longman he can dance alone;	(Wiggle second finger.)
Longman, he can dance alone.	(Wiggle second finger.)
Dance, Ringman, dance,	(Try to wiggle third finger without others.)
Dance, ye merrymen, dance;	(Wiggle all fingers.)
But Ringman cannot dance alone;	(Try to wiggle ring finger without others.)
Ringman, he cannot dance alone.	(Try to wiggle ring finger without others.)
Dance Littleman, dance,	(Wiggle little finger.)
Dance, ye merrymen, dance;	(Wiggle all fingers.)
But Littleman, he can dance alone;	(Wiggle little finger.)
Littleman, he can dance alone.	(Wiggle little finger.)

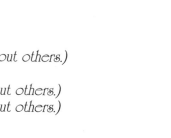

Share!

When you were two and we played Thumbkin, you would: _____

Celebrate!

Celebrate your two-year-old's rapidly developing language skills.

Try not to measure your toddler's verbal abilities against those of other children her/his age. There is more variation at this time in language development than in any other area. Some two-year-olds develop language skills at a steady rate. Others master words in an uneven fashion. It is very important to remember that more verbal children are not necessarily smarter or more advanced than the quieter ones.

From 30-36 months you will observe that your toddler:

- Will begin to name colors (primary, secondary), sizes (big, little), shapes (circle, square, triangle)
- Can match verbs with actions, nouns with objects
- Comprehends the difference between one, few, and many
- Will begin to use plurals and proper tenses in speech

Play!

This Is the Way We Wash Our Clothes

Why this playtime activity is good for your two-year-old: One important way you can help your child learn vocabulary is to match words with the objects. When you are putting on your toddler's sock, say, "Sock." While peeling an apple say, "Apple."

What you'll need to play this activity: rhyme

This Is the Way We Wash Our Clothes
This is the way we wash our clothes, wash our clothes, wash our clothes,
This is the way we wash our clothes, early in the morning.

New Version:
This is the way we dress the baby, dress the baby, dress the baby,
This is the way we dress the baby, early in the morning.

Other verses might include:
This is the way we wash the dishes, . . .
This is the way we tie our shoe, . . .
This is the way we drink our milk, . . .
This is the way we paint a picture, . . .
This is the way we read a book, . . .

How to play *This Is the Way We Wash Our Clothes*: This game is to be sung to the tune: "Here We Go 'Round the Mulberry Bush." Use your imagination to make up additional verses about the things you and your child do every day. Sing the verses when you are performing household tasks.

Share!

When you were two and helped me with household chores, your favorite jobs were:

_____

Celebrate!

Celebrate your two-year-old's self-care abilities.

During the second half of the third year, toddlers become more and more independent. Dressing themselves is a good way for youngsters this age to express independence. Children this age can undress more quickly than dress. Let your toddler undress and dress her/himself as much as possible. This is a good time to formally begin teaching your child the difficult dressing skills such as tying, buttoning, zipping, and snapping.

From 30-36 months you will observe that your toddler:

- Can dress and undress her/himself
- Still has difficulty tying, buttoning, zipping, and snapping
- Understands how to use potty chair

Play!

Button, Zip, and Snap

Why this playtime activity is good for your two-year-old: Begin with unbuttoning, unzipping, untying, etc., before the opposite is taught, because it is easier to take off clothes than to put them on. Tying shoes is a skill often mastered at age five or six, so don't frustrate your child with trying to tie shoes yet.

What you'll need to play this activity: a doll with clothes that button, zip, and snap.

How to play *Button, Zip, and Snap*: Begin by demonstrating how to unbutton the buttons, unzip the zipper, and unsnap the snaps. Don't expect your child to learn these difficult skills overnight. After s/he has played with the doll and can unbutton, unzip, and unsnap, begin showing her/him how to button, zip, and snap. It will take many months or years for little fingers to learn these fine motor skills. Be patient, and praise every effort your child makes to button, zip, and snap her/his own clothes.

Share!

When you were this old, you could unbutton: _____

When you were this old, you could unzip: _____

When you were this old, you could unsnap:_____

When you were this old, you could button: _____

When you were this old, you could zip:_____

When you were this old, you could snap: _____

Celebrate!

Celebrate your two-year-old's learning about safety.

Because your child can now run, jump, and ride a tricycle, her/his natural curiosity will drive her/him to explore many new things, including some dangerous places. Unfortunately, your child's self-control and ability to rescue her/himself are not yet fully developed, so s/he still needs careful supervision. Your toddler's preference for independence may also lead her/him to try to do things alone that s/he is not yet ready to do. Although your toddler wants more independence, s/he will need extra supervision during this developmental stage.

From 30-36 months you will observe that your toddler:

- Is curious and will explore dangerous places
- Is brave and will climb to great heights and not be able to get down
- Is adventurous and will jump into bodies of water like pools and lakes without knowing how to swim
- Will taste medicines or poisonous materials if they are within her/his reach

Play!

Mr. Yuck

Why this playtime activity is good for your two-year-old: Visual signals of danger will help your toddler stay away from dangerous substances.

What you'll need to play this activity: adhesive labels; marking pen; or Mr. Yuck stickers

How to play *Mr. Yuck*: Of course the best way to avoid having your toddler ingest poisonous substances is to lock them away on a high shelf in a cabinet in the garage or a storage shed. Explain to your child that certain things are poisons and will make her/him very sick or even cause death. Draw some Mr. Yuck faces on the labels with markers or use Mr. Yuck stickers. Go around the house with your child and put stickers on the medicine chest, on all household cleaners, and on substances that your child is not to taste. You can put Mr. Yuck stickers on vinegar and other foods that would cause your child harm. Put Mr. Yuck stickers on the stove knobs, iron, and ironing board. Mark electrical outlets with Mr. Yuck stickers. Talk about the fact that Mr. Yuck is there to remind your toddler of great danger.

Share!

Here are the ways I made our home a safe place for you to play:_____

_____

_____

Celebrate!

Celebrate your two-year-old's health and well-being.

By age two and a half your child should have all of her/his primary teeth. The second molars usually erupt between twenty and thirty months. Since the number-one dental problem among preschoolers is tooth decay, you will need to teach your child good dental hygiene.

From 30-36 months your toddler:

- Will need her/his teeth brushed at least once a day
- Will need a soft, multi-tufted nylon-bristle brush
- Will especially enjoy candy and sweets
- Will need her/his first visit to the dentist

Play!

This Is the Way We Brush Our Teeth

Why this playtime activity is good for your two-year-old: With proper coaching your toddler will quickly adopt good oral hygiene as part of a daily routine. However, at this age s/he won't have the concentration or control to brush teeth all by her/himself. Making tooth brushing a game will turn the chore into something fun and entertaining.

What you'll need to play this activity: toothpaste, toothbrush

How to play *This Is the Way We Brush Our Teeth*: Sing the song to the tune of "Here We Go 'Round the Mulberry Bush."

> **This Is the Way We Brush Our Teeth**
> This is the way we brush our teeth, brush our teeth, brush our teeth,
> This is the way we brush our teeth, early in the morning (in the
> afternoon/late in the evening)

Sing the verse while performing each of these steps: Brush the outside of the upper front teeth. Brush the inside of the upper front teeth. Brush the outside of the upper back teeth on the right side. Brush the inside of the upper back teeth on the right side. Brush the outside of the upper back teeth on the left side. Brush the inside of the upper back teeth on the left side. Brush the outside of the lower front teeth. Brush the inside of the lower front teeth. Brush the outside of the lower back teeth on the right side. Brush the inside of the lower back teeth on the right side. Brush the outside of the lower back teeth on the left side. Brush the inside of the lower back teeth on the left side.

Stop between each verse and show your toddler where to move her/his toothbrush by holding your own brush in that spot in your mouth.

Share!

When you were two and a half, this is how you brushed your teeth: _____

Celebrate!

Celebrate your two-year-old's abilities and play interests.

During the second half of the third year, children have better developed representational skills. They can use one object to represent another: a block can be a car and a stick can be a broom. Children this age begin to exhibit more complex repertoire of pretend activities, including sequenced episodes such as "feeding" a doll and then putting it to bed.

From 30-36 months you will observe that your toddler:

- Can match and sort objects into simple functional and perceptual categories
- Can put together materials in more complex and ordered configurations, creating simple patterns and constructions with blocks or other materials
- Can imitate and elaborate on simple patterns observed in social and physical environments.

Play!

Tisket-A-Tasket, Which Basket?

Why this playtime activity is good for your toddler: Sorting provides experiences in recognizing attributes such as colors, sizes, textures, and shapes.

What you'll need to play this activity: baskets in assorted sizes, shapes, colors, and textures; box of assorted objects to place in the baskets such as small dolls, blocks, small boxes, large round beads, small trucks, plastic animals, etc.

How to play *Tisket-A-Tasket, Which Basket?*: Set out the baskets for Toddler to explore. Add the box containing the collection of small items. Place one thing from each group in a basket. For example, one basket is for beads, one is for blocks, and one is for little cars. Then hand Toddler an object and ask "Which basket?" Let your toddler sort the toys into the baskets. At first sorting will probably be random. Later s/he may sort all of the cars into one basket, the animals in another, the blocks in yet another.

Variation: Be creative and sort by color or by size instead of function. Talk about how the toys are sorted. "Let's put all the red toys in this basket." Or "Let's put all the big objects in this basket." Always praise all efforts your toddler makes to sort.

Share!

When you were this old, you could sort by color (primary colors):_____

When you were this old, you could sort by shape (round/square):_____

When you were this old, you could sort by size (big/little): _____

When you were this old, you could sort by function: _____

When we played sorting games you liked: _____

Celebrate!

Celebrate your two-year-old's creative and artistic abilities.

During the two and a half to three year period, children develop good hand and finger coordination and may move fingers independently. Appropriate art supplies for children this age include large crayons and felt-tip pens with large tips; paper for drawing; finger paints and paper; an adjustable easel, with tempera paints, large paper, and brushes; easy-to-use blunt-ended scissors; an unbreakable chalkboard, with large chalk and an eraser; and modeling clay or dough.

From 30-36 months you will observe that your toddler:

- May copy circles and crosses
- Will begin drawing stick people with heads, arms, and legs
- Will begin to be able to use child-safety scissors
- Enjoys working with clay and molding materials

Play!

Creating Ornaments

Why this playtime activity is good for your two-year-old: While making and working with play dough your toddler will learn terms such as "small," "large," "sticky," "smooth," and "roll". S/He'll practice fine motor skills and feel a sense of accomplishment for creating the play dough and then an ornament to be hung on a Christmas tree.

What you'll need to play this activity: play dough ingredients (flour, salt, water); tools such as a rolling pin and cookie cutter; waxed paper

How to create sun-dry dough: Begin by having your youngster help you make the play dough. Mix 2 cups (474 ml) flour and 1 cup (237 ml) salt together in a bowl. Your child can stir these ingredients together. Slowly add 1 cup (240 ml) of water until it becomes a soft workable dough. Food coloring can be added to the water or powdered tempera paint mixed with the dry ingredients.

How to create ornaments: Give your child a ball of dough. After your child has had an opportunity to explore and manipulate the dough, give her/him a rolling pin and a cookie cutter. Working on wax paper, roll the dough flat with the rolling pin. (The dough should be approximately ½" [13 mm] thick.) Show your child how to use the cookie cutter to make a final cut-out. Use a pencil to punch a hole in the top of the figure. Scratch your child's name and the date on the back of the ornament. Place on a rack in the hot sun to dry. When the dough is dry, give your child a choice of yarn or ribbons to insert through the hole.

Share!

When you were two and worked with play dough, you especially enjoyed: _____

Celebrate!

Celebrate your two-year-old's musical talents.

As your toddler becomes more adept, you can introduce her/him to playing musical instruments such as drums, sticks, triangles, etc. in time to music. This takes a lot of concentration, and it will probably be a long while before s/he can do this. Play music frequently during the day, sing and encourage your child to sing with you. Be sure that you also provide some special quiet times during the day.

From 30-36 months you will observe that your toddler:

- Will try to sing as you are singing (pitch your own voice higher than normal)
- Comprehends the difference in sounds such as loud, soft, harsh, soothing, high, low, fast, slow, etc.

Play!

Marching Band

Why this playtime activity is good for your two-year-old: Simple body movements such as stamping the feet, marching, jumping, or swaying are good for children to learn rhythm. This activity will allow your two-year-old the opportunity of experiencing different sounds and movements.

What you'll need to play this activity: marching music; sticks

How to play *Marching Band*: Play marching music. Give two sticks to your toddler and show her/him how to hit them together in time to the music. Use your own pair of sticks to accent the beat of the music. March around while playing the sticks. It will take a great deal of practice before your child will be able to keep time with hands and feet at the same time. Repeat this marching band game often until your child can coordinate her/his hands with her/his feet to the beat of a march.

Variation: Give your toddler the opportunity to march and play other instruments, too. Instead of beating sticks, try ringing bells, shaking a tambourine, clicking spoons together, or blowing a whistle.

Share!

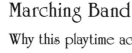

When you were two and we marched around to music, you liked to: _____

_____

When you were two and we marched around to music, your favorite musical instrument to play was:

_____

Celebrate!

Celebrate your two-year-old's role playing and fantasy play.

Most child development experts designate this period as the beginning of true doll play. As the child begins to assign more important meaning and characteristics to the doll, it takes on more complex roles in pretend play. As a result, more representational dolls (that look more like babies or whatever they are intended to be) with more accessories and props become appropriate (particularly as children near three years of age).

From 30-36 months you will observe that your toddler:

- Will enjoy playing with dolls that have removable clothes with easy-to-fasten closings
- Will enjoy simple feeding and care accessories for supporting doll play
- Will enjoy playing with a doll that can be washed, has rooted hair, and movable eyes
- Cannot yet manipulate articulated limbs

Play!

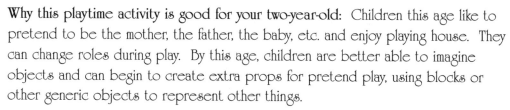

Playhouse

Why this playtime activity is good for your two-year-old: Children this age like to pretend to be the mother, the father, the baby, etc. and enjoy playing house. They can change roles during play. By this age, children are better able to imagine objects and can begin to create extra props for pretend play, using blocks or other generic objects to represent other things.

What you'll need to play this activity: appliance box with a door and windows cut out to represent a house; poster paint and brushes; smaller boxes to represent tables, beds, furniture; doll; snack

How to play *Playhouse*: You may want your toddler to watch you cut the "door" and "windows" in the box. Let your youngster help you decorate the outside of the box with poster paints or markers. Place boxes inside for table, doll bed, etc. Get inside the "house" with your child. Have a snack of crackers and milk. Play with the doll. Then let your child play in the "house" alone.

Variation: If you do not have an appliance box to build a play house, hang blankets over the edges of a picnic or card table, and use that enclosure for a playhouse.

Share!

When you were two and you played in your playhouse, you liked: _____

_____

_____

Celebrate!

Celebrate your two-year-old's physical growth and nutritional needs.

At age two, children of the same age begin to vary a lot in size and weight. Do not compare your toddler's measurements with those of her/his playmates. As long as s/he is maintaining her/his own individual rate of growth, there in no reason to be concerned. Daily provide a variety of healthful foods from which your child may choose.

From 30-36 months you will observe that your toddler:

- May eat less than you think s/he should
- Needs fewer calories at this time because s/he is growing more slowly

Play!

This Is a Healthful Choice

Why this playtime activity is good for your two-year-old: It is never too early to begin teaching your toddler to make healthful food choices. This activity will help your child appreciate good, nutritious foods.

What you'll need to play this activity: No special equipment is needed to play this activity.

How to play *This Is a Healthful Choice*: This activity should be played in a supermarket while your child is riding in the cart and you are doing your regular shopping. As you look at foods, when you put something especially good for you into your cart say, "This is a healthful choice." For example, when buying whole-wheat bread, you might explain to your toddler that brown bread is a better choice than white bread. When choosing fresh vegetables and fruits, let your toddler point to the ones s/he would like to try. When you put her/his selections into the cart say, "That was a healthful choice, Max." Praise your toddler for asking for and eating healthful foods.

Variation: Cut out pictures of healthful foods from magazines or grocery store newspaper ads. Paste them on sheets of construction paper. Put the pages together like a book and staple along the left-hand edge. Look at the "Healthful Choice" book together.

Share!

When you were two and a half and we went grocery shopping, your healthful choices included:

_____

_____

Celebrate!

Celebrate your two-year-old's perceptual-cognitive milestones.

As toddlers get closer to age three, they are interested in attributes of objects such as textures, shapes, sizes, and colors. Children this age often begin working out solutions to problems mentally rather than by using a trial-and-error method.

From 30-36 months you will observe that your toddler:

- Will learn to match a group of similar objects
- Will enjoy playing with patterns, and sequencing
- May demonstrate first counting skills
- Uses objects to carry out actions on other objects

Play!

Attribute Logic Blocks

Why this playtime activity is good for your two-year-old: At around 2½ years, children begin to play with patterns, sequences, and order. Playing with paper attribute logic blocks will give your toddler an opportunity to work with the attributes–size, color, and shapes.

What you'll need to play this activity: two construction paper cut-outs of each of the following:

Big red circle, blue circle, yellow circle   Little red circle, blue circle, yellow circle

Big red square, blue square, yellow square   Little red square, blue square, yellow square

Big red triangle, blue triangle, yellow triangle   Little red triangle, blue triangle, yellow triangle

How to play *Attribute Logic Blocks:* Begin by using just some of the paper cutouts; sorting through all 36 would be frustrating for a two-year-old. There are numerous ways to use these paper cutouts to teach your child. Here are a few ways that are appropriate for two-year-olds:

Exactly the Same–Show your child an attribute logic block. Ask her/him to find the one exactly like it. (Give her/him three or four from which to choose.)

The Same Color–Place one of each color in front of your child. Show her/him an attribute block and say, "Which one is the same color?" Repeat with other colors.

The Same Shape–Place one of each shape in front of your child. Show her/him an attribute block and say, "Which one is the same shape?" Repeat with other shapes.

The Same Size–Place four attribute blocks (two big and two little) in front of your child. Show her/him a large attribute block and say, "This is a big shape, which ones are big, too?" Repeat with a small shape.

Share!

When you were two, your favorite attribute block was this color: _____

When you were two, your favorite attribute block was this size: _____

When you were two, your favorite attribute block was this shape: _____

Celebrate!

Celebrate your two-year-old's bedtime rituals.

Children this age usually hate to go to bed. They are afraid they will miss some fun that the family is having without them. Most toddlers will do anything they can think of to put off going to bed.

From 30-36 months you will observe that when it is bedtime your toddler:

- Might ask for drinks and use other tricks to stay up
- Might climb out of her/his bed or crib to get you
- Might cry when it is time to go to bed

Play!

Bedtime Story Time

Why this playtime activity is good for your two-year-old: Soothing your toddler with a bedtime ritual will help her/him fall asleep more quickly. A bedtime story is especially good to include during the bedtime ritual because hearing a story told in a low, monotone voice can help relax your child.

What you'll need to play this activity: books

How to play *Bedtime Story Time*: When you read a story to your toddler as part of a bedtime ritual, first have your child climb in bed. Pull up the covers, and have her/him stretch out and begin relaxing. This way when the story is over there won't be a lot of commotion and moving about which might wake her/him. Sit in a chair by the crib or on the edge of the bed and show the pictures as your read the story. Stories with repetition are especially good at bedtime since the rhythm tends to be soothing. (Avoid scary stories at bedtime.)

Variation: A bedtime song and/or prayer may become part of your bedtime ritual. The important thing is to keep the ritual rigid. Bedtime should be a certain time, and the elements of the ritual should be something on which your toddler can always depend.

Share!

When you were two and a half, your bedtime ritual was:_____

_____

_____

_____

Celebrate!

Celebrate your two-year-old's sensory experiences.

Older toddlers are interested in all sensory activities and can learn to discriminate between various stimuli. They are fascinated by different smells, tastes, and textures, and enjoy trying to guess what they are smelling, touching, or tasting.

From 30-36 months you will observe that your toddler:

- Will bring food to her/his nose and sniff it
- Will ask about new aromas she/he experiences
- Will sometimes rub the satin trim of a blanket or other pleasing texture while falling asleep
- When hearing a new sound will ask about it

Play!

Guess That Aroma/Flavor/Sound

Why this playtime activity is good for your two-year-old: Identifying an aroma, flavor, or sound is a good way to reinforce sensory awareness. These three activities will give your toddler an opportunity to use sensory clues rather than visual clues to identify familiar foods or objects.

What you'll need to play this activity: a bag with a sniff hole or feeling hole cut in the side; aromatic foods, textured toys, and musical instruments

How to play *Guess That Aroma*: Put a familiar aromatic food in a bag. Cut a sniff hole (about halfway up the side of a lunch-sized bag) just big enough to stick a nose through. Close the top of the bag. Let your toddler put her/his nose in the sniff hole and smell the food. Then show her/him three foods, and ask which one of the foods is inside the bag.

How to play *Guess That Flavor*: Cut tiny pieces of food that your child especially enjoys. (Don't trick her/him by putting something in her/his mouth that s/he doesn't enjoy eating.) Have your toddler close her/his eyes. Place the food on her/his tongue. Then show her/him three foods and have her/him point to the food s/he thinks she is tasting.

How to play *Guess That Sound*: Put three or four musical instruments on the floor in front of your toddler. Ask her/him to close her/his eyes tightly. Play one of the instruments, and then place it back down on the floor. When your child opens her/his eyes, ask her/him to point to the instrument s/he heard.

Share!

When you and I played guessing games about aromas, flavors, and sounds, your favorite game was:

_____

This is how we played the game: _____

_____

Celebrate!

Celebrate your two-year-old's fine motor skills.

Older toddlers can put together simple wood and plastic fit-in puzzles, in which one piece fits in each space. Puzzles with four or five pieces are suitable for children younger than 30 months. As children approach age three, puzzles with six to ten or more pieces may be used. Puzzles with knobs are easier, but the knobs should be firmly attached. Most three-year-olds will be able to distinguish between basic shapes (circle, square, triangle), colors (blue, yellow, green, orange, purple), and size (big, little).

From 30-36 months you will observe that your toddler:

- Can match an object in her/his hand or in the room to a picture in a book
- Completes puzzles with six to twelve pieces
- Can sort by shape, size, or color

Play!

Copy Cat

Why this playtime activity is good for your two-year-old: This activity will teach your youngster about duplicating the shape, size, and color of paper patterns.

What you'll need to play this activity: two sets of construction paper shapes of circles, squares, and triangles in primary and secondary colors. One set is to be cut about 5" (127 mm) in diameter (big) and the other one is to be cut about 3" (76 mm) in diameter (little); drawing paper; pencil; red, blue, yellow, orange, green, and purple crayons

How to play *Copy Cat*: Show your toddler the pattern of the big, red circle. Trace around the shape on a sheet of drawing paper. Have your toddler color the shape the same color as the pattern. As your child is coloring the shape, talk about its color, shape, and size. Repeat with other patterns. Use the patterns for several weeks until your toddler is familiar with all of them.

Variation: If this task is too difficult for your toddler, trace a shape and color it. Then have your toddler find the matching pattern from three or four choices. As your child becomes more proficient at matching colors, shapes, and sizes, increase the number of patterns from which s/he is to choose.

Share!

When you were two years old and we played with colored shapes, you especially enjoyed:

_____

_____

Celebrate!

Celebrate your child's third birthday.

Invite friends and family to celebrate the hard work your toddler has put into her/his growth and development this year. Make the party festive and focus on your child's wide range of impressive accomplishments.

During your child's third year you will observe that s/he has learned many extraordinary things:

- Has learned to draw and hold pencil and crayons with pincher grip
- Has learned to dress and undress her/himself
- Can feed her/himself
- Has learned to play with focus for extended periods of time
- Has become potty trained
- Has learned to talk in four, five, or six word sentences

Play!

Sing Happy Birthday!

Why this birthday party activity is good for your three-year-old: Taking time to pause and celebrate yearly growth, development, and learning is important for your child's positive self-esteem. Birthdays are a perfect time to pause and take stock of your child's growth and development. When everyone stops and sings a song while your toddler stands in the spotlight, s/he will learn how special s/he is to you and others.

What you'll need to play this activity: birthday cake with three candles

How to play *Sing Happy Birthday!*: At the birthday party, have everyone sing "Happy Birthday" three times, one for each year. Let your toddler blow out her/his own candles on the cake and open her/his own presents. Take lots of photographs and look at the photographs taken at her/his last two birthdays and the day Baby was born. Display pictures of your toddler for all of the party guests to view. An appropriate present for a three-year-old includes a big scrapbook that you can put art projects in during the next year.

Share!

Your third birthday party was: _____

The people who shared the day with you were: _____

_____

What you had to say about your party was: _____

_____

Celebrate!

Celebrate your three-year-old's gross motor development.

Three-year-olds are still in the process of developing good gross motor coordination. Children this age seem to be in constant motion. To a great extent, the continuous movement is because children use their bodies to convey thoughts and emotions that they cannot yet convey with language.

From 36-42 months you will observe that your child:

- Likes to test her/his own physical strength
- Enjoys acrobatics
- Enjoys outdoor equipment

Play!

Up! Down! All Around

Why this playtime activity is good for your child: Three-year-olds need a great deal of physical exercise. On the days when the weather prohibits outdoor play, this playtime activity will give your child some good exercise and also challenge her/his gross motor and following directions skills.

What you'll need to play this activity: two chairs facing each other

How to play *Up! Down! All Around*: Have your child sit in one of the chairs while you sit in the other one. Slowly give directions. In the beginning perform the exercise with your child. Then after your child gets good at following directions, sit and only give verbal commands.

Example of Exercises:

Stand up; stretch arms up; reach for the sky; stand on tip-toes; reach up, up, up; hold it there.

Bend down; touch your knees; touch your toes, stretch down, down, down; hold it there.

Turn round and round; march around the chair; march around the room; around, around, around; stop and hold it there.

Share!

When you were three years old, one of your favorite ways to exercise indoors was:

_____

_____

Celebrate!

Celebrate your three-year-old's fine motor skills.

Three-year-olds have more control and can better direct movements. Self-care skills like dressing, eating, and toilet training are developing and will insure that your child can take proper care of her/his own body for the rest of her/his life. The best way you can help build your three-year-old's positive self-image and guide her/his self discipline, is to let your child practice these new self-care skills so s/he feels confident and capable. Praise all your child's efforts to get dressed, feed her/himself, and meet her/his own needs.

From 36-42 months you will observe that your child:

- Is developing increased finger control
- Can pick up small objects using the pincher grip
- Can hold a pencil using adult grasp
- Is building a self-image (positive or negative)

Play!

Treasure Hunting with Fingers and Toes

Why this playtime activity is good for your child: While exploring different kinds of materials with hands and feet, your child will discover creative ways to work with the materials and thus become more aware of textures in her/his everyday world. Plus your youngster will discover that textures do not "feel" the same when experienced with her/his feet and toes as they do with the hands and fingers.

What you'll need to play this activity: large, plastic dish pan; something to bury treasure under such as cornmeal, sand, sawdust, foam packing pieces, or shredded newspapers; treasures such as seashells, gemstones, coins, coin-shaped chocolates wrapped in foil, or small plastic prizes.

How to play *Treasure Hunting with Fingers and Toes:* Fill the tub with cornmeal, sand, or whatever textured material you choose to use. Hide one treasure (seashell, stone, coin, chocolate, etc.) under the material. Have your child close her/his eyes and use fingers to feel for the prize. The next time you hide a prize, have your child use her/his toes instead of fingers, to search for the treasure. Alternate fingers and toes during additional searches.

Share!

When you were three years old and we played treasure hunt, your favorite textured material was:

_____

Your favorite treasure to find was: _____

Celebrate!

Celebrate your three-year-old's abilities and play interests.

Children this age like climbing structures that have secret places for imaginative, role-playing activities. For instance, climbing structures with walled enclosures are wonderful props for fantasy play.

From 36-42 months you will observe that your child:

- Loves to build with small construction materials
- Is vigorously active with units and large construction materials
- Likes to play in an enclosed structure

Play!

Build a Fort

Why this playtime activity is good for your child: Children this age have a high level of interest in building their own play places. They enjoy hiding in small places when engaging in imaginative, role-playing activities.

What you'll need to play this activity: construction materials such as a large appliance box, card table draped with blankets, small pup tent, or picnic table covered with cloths

How to play *Build a Fort*: Provide construction materials, and help your child create a small, enclosed "fort" for play. Your child will have as much fun creating the structure as actually playing inside of it. Be imaginative, and let your child direct the building of the "fort." Give her/him a choice in the materials to use; let her/him decide where the structure will be built; as much as possible, let your child do the construction work.

Variations #1: Blankets hung from the edge of a top bunk bed make a good enclosure, and the bottom bunk provides a soft place to play.

Variation #2: Natural "forts" like those found under grape arbors, behind big bushes, and in between low branches of small trees all make excellent "forts." If your child enjoys building a play place, help her/him build many different ones. Each "fort" can be a secret hiding place.

Share!

When you were three years old, you liked to build "forts." One particular fort you built was:

_____

_____

Celebrate!

Celebrate your three-year-old's language development.

By three, most children have mastered basic rules of language and have an impressive vocabulary that increases daily as the children experiment with words. Instead of crying, throwing tantrums, and grabbing what they want, children this age will often express their needs and feelings verbally.

From 36-42 months you will observe that your child:

- Will offer sympathetic words if someone who is close to her/him gets emotional
- Will try to bargain to get what s/he wants
- Will begin demonstrating a strong sense of justice

Play!

Pick It, Name It, Keep It!

Why this playtime activity is good for your child: This game will help hold your child's attention for a time and will serve as a distraction for her/him when s/he is throwing a tantrum or being highly emotional. This activity is a good, one-to-one game that teaches basic vocabulary.

What you'll need to play this activity: a small object that will fit into your fist (preferably an object which you would like to teach your child to name)

Examples: jelly bean (or other colorful candy); crayon; or a natural object such as a seashell, smooth stone, or gemstone

How to play *Pick It, Name It, Keep It!*: Show your child the object to be used in the game. Let her/him hold and feel it. Ask for the object back. Place your hands behind your back, and hide the object in one fist. Bring both closed hands in front of you and say, "Pick it." When your child picks a hand, open it. If the hand is empty, put your hands behind your back and replay this step of the game. When your child chooses the hand with the object, say, "Name it." If your child can name the object, say, "Keep it." S/He gets to keep the prize. If s/he cannot name the object, name the object for her/him, and begin the game again.

Share!

When you were three years old and we played "Pick It, Name It, Keep It!" your favorite prize was:

_____

Your favorite way to play the game was:_____

Celebrate!

Celebrate your three-year-old's developing social skills.

During this developmental stage you may notice that your child is much less selfish than s/he was at age two. At age three your child will begin playing with other children–interacting rather than playing simultaneously. One of the most difficult and less obvious skills your child will need to acquire in this stage of development is learning how to handle anger and aggression. Learning this difficult social skill can only happen in a peer setting.

From 36-42 months you will observe that your child:

- Will begin making her/his own friends
- Will discover the special things about her/himself that makes her/him desirable as a playmate
- Will begin choosing her/his own playmates
- Will test both parents to the point of a reaction

Play!

Cracker Snack

Why this playtime activity is good for your child: While playing with peers your child will learn important skills like sharing, taking turns, cooperation, etc. Having the opportunity to serve others will help your youngster learn manners and important social skills.

What you'll need to play this activity: two of your child's peers (could be siblings or adult family members if peers are not available for play); crackers of various shapes such as fish-shaped crackers, squares, rounds, pretzel sticks, etc.; small plates; napkins

How to play *Cracker Snack*: Place the different kinds of crackers on separate plates. For example, put round Ritz™ crackers on one plate. Place the square soda crackers on another plate. Have the children take turns passing out one of each cracker to each child including her/himself. Since the crackers are different shapes, it will be easy to see who didn't get one of each cracker. When everyone has a sample of each kind of cracker, the children may enjoy their cracker snack.

Variation: Play this game with slices of different kinds of fruit. Each child has a plate of fruit and serves each peer and then her/himself one slice.

Share!

When you were three years old and you had the opportunity to serve some other children crackers, this is what happened:

_____

_____

Celebrate!

Celebrate your three-year-old's developing communication skills.

At this age your child will spend most of the time asking questions. S/He will want to know "Why?" "How?" "When?" "What?" and "Who?" When you tell your child what to do, s/he will expect an explanation, "Why?" Take the time to give your child a simple, clear answer. If it is bedtime and your child asks, "Why do I have to go to bed?" a simple, "Because it is bedtime," is explanation enough. If your child asks a question that you cannot answer, for example, "Why is the sky blue?," answer that you do not know. Then make this a challenge to find out the answer. That way you are teaching your child two important things: Not knowing all of the answers is okay. There are sources for finding answers to all questions.

From 36-42 months you will observe that your child:

- Will speak in sentences of four or six words
- Will imitate adult speech patterns
- Will understand nearly every word s/he hears
- Will use correct grammar

Play!

Do You Remember?

Why this playtime activity is good for your child: When hearing a story, children this age enjoy recalling the details. Talking about the facts given in the story reinforces sequencing with terms such as "before," "after," and "at the beginning/end" of the story.

What you'll need to play this activity: fairy tales with predictable, sequenced events such as "Little Red Hen," "Three Little Pigs," "The Three Bears," "Three Billy Goats Gruff," and "The Gingerbread Man."

How to play *Do Your Remember?*: While reading a familiar fairy tale, stop often to ask simple recall questions:

"Do you remember what the first pig used to build his house?"

"Do you remember the first thing the Gingerbread Man ran past?"

"Which Billy Goat Gruff crossed the bridge first?"

"Whose bed did Goldilocks crawl into last?"

When your child cannot recall answers, look in the book and find the answers. Talk about the characters and the events in the stories you read.

Share!

When you were three years old, your favorite fairy tale was: _____

Celebrate!

Celebrate your three-year-old's developing gender identification.

While role-playing during make-believe games, your youngster will begin to identify with her/his own sex. Boys this age often choose to play the "father," while girls will prefer to play the "mother." Young children need to identify with one sex so they can grow to identify with each parent. For example, "I am a girl; I will grow up to be a woman. I am not a boy; I will not grow up to be a man." It is extraordinary to see how a little boy absorbs his father's behavior or how a little girl will imitate her mother. This strong identification speaks highly of the power of imitation and early awareness of a child's own sexuality.

From 36-42 months you may observe that:

- The average preschool boy is more aggressive than the same-age girl
- Girls are often more verbal and cooperative than boys the same age
- Your child will find conventional male or female role models in family, friends, neighbors, television, magazines, books, etc.

Play!

House

Why this playtime activity is good for your child: While playing "House" and using dolls, your child will demonstrate her/his ability to use symbolic play. Children use dolls to imitate the people in her/his life. Symbolic play brings out imitation. In her/his use of sexual differences and the doll's "behavior," your child will demonstrate her/his fantasies regarding each family member. Playing "House" will give your child an opportunity to learn how to handle strong feelings in a safer and more mature way than s/he could a year ago.

What you'll need to play this activity: playhouse setting including: scaled-down furniture or representations; dolls

How to play *House*: Ask your child what role s/he will play. Ask her/him what role s/he wants you to play. Use the dolls to represent the children in the family. Pay close attention to how s/he role-plays the mother and father. How are the "children" treated? How do the "children" feel about family happenings? Ask your child, "How does Dolly feel about taking a nap?" Verbally give your child options from which to choose. "Does Dolly feel angry that she has to take a nap? Does Dolly feel happy that she is being held and rocked by the mother?" Encourage your child to play "House" alone and with peers.

Share!

When you were three years old and you played house, you would:_____

_____

_____

_____

Celebrate!

Celebrate your three-year-old's cognitive milestones.

During this developmental stage children need an increasing variety of natural materials such as rocks, shells, leaves, seeds, pressed flowers, and sterilized bones (saved from meals or found in natural settings) for play. Many parents are anxious to teach three-year-olds to recognize and write numerals and the letters of the alphabet. Don't attempt this kind of teaching unless the desire to learn is coming from your child. Instead, during this developmental year, continue working with attribute blocks, puzzles, building blocks, and measuring sand and water games.

From 36-42 months you will observe that your child:

- Will show an increasing interest in simple number and quantity activities
- May count to three or more
- Will enjoy measuring activities
- Will play in order to learn

Play!

Sand Tracing

Why this playtime activity is good for your child: Drawing in a tray of sand will offer a new experience as your child discovers s/he can use fingers to make marks and designs, and that the imprints can be erased easily by shaking the tray of sand. Your youngster will physically experience drawing basic shapes such as circles, squares, and triangles.

What you'll need to play this activity: a flat pan with sides (pizza pan); aluminum foil; sand or cornmeal; large, cardboard geometrical shapes (circle, square, triangle)

How to play *Sand Tracing:* Place a sheet of aluminum foil in the bottom of a flat pan. Cover this with a thin layer of sand or cornmeal. Show your child how to use one finger to draw lines and reveal the aluminum foil at the bottom of the pan. Suggest that your child use her/his "pointer finger" for drawing. Then show your child a basic cardboard shape. Lay the pattern on the sand, and trace around it with your finger. Remove the pattern, and look at the outline left in the tray. Show your child how to erase the lines by shaking the tray of sand. Then let your child experiment with outlining the cardboard patterns in the sand.

Share!

When you were three years old and you traced shapes in the sand, you liked:

_____

_____

Celebrate!

Celebrate your three-year-old's fantasy play.

In this age range, costumes for creative and cooperative dramatic play (as well as for other forms of cooperative social interaction) will allow a variety of uses. Dress-up clothes should evolve as your child's interests and abilities mature. A box of dress-up clothes and a full-length, unbreakable mirror mounted on wall or in a sturdy stand will contribute in a very positive way to your three-year-old's fantasy play.

From 36-42 months you will observe that your child:
- Will recognize the uniforms of a variety of professions
- Will enjoy dressing up and playing in front of a mirror

Play!

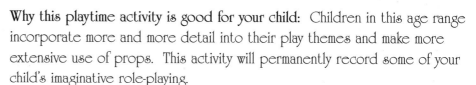

Portfolio of Fun

Why this playtime activity is good for your child: Children in this age range incorporate more and more detail into their play themes and make more extensive use of props. This activity will permanently record some of your child's imaginative role-playing.

What you'll need to play this activity: camera; dress-up clothes

How to play *Portfolio of Fun*: Encourage your child to use dress-up clothes to "become" a particular character. Encourage your child to dress by her/himself. Then take a photograph of your child. Talk about the costume and "who" the child is role-playing. Take notes. Then have your child dress up in yet another costume of her/his choice. Again take a photograph, and talk about the clothing. Take notes on this second costume too. Ask questions to stimulate your child's creativity. For example, "When you wear this hat do you feel like dancing? Does this dress make you feel fancy? When you wear the fireman's hat, do you feel especially brave?" Each time your child gets dressed-up take a photograph. If your child is bored, this game can be played over an extended period of several days. When you have used your roll of film and taken notes on each of your child's costumes, have the film developed. Then mount each photograph and your child's thoughts about the costume on a page of construction paper or on separate pages of a scrapbook. Show your child the photographs and read the "stories." This portfolio of fun will become a treasured book for your three-year-old to "read" and "reread."

Share!

When you were three years old and we made a portfolio of you in dress-up costumes, your favorite seemed to be:

Celebrate!

Celebrate your three-year-old's high level of energy.

Early in this age range most children learn to pedal, which opens the door for all sorts of three- to four-wheeled pedal vehicles. Children this age like realistic ride-ons (car, trucks, horses, etc.); however, these toys are not always practical. Sturdy, realistic ride-ons typically are very expensive and a real-looking truck cannot, for example, be used to play car or fire engine. So generic ride-on toys will be more flexible and practical in your child's fantasy play. Exercising on pedal toys will give your child an opportunity to exert a high level of energy while practicing steering and balancing.

From 36-42 months you will observe that your child:

- Will enjoy using vehicles to get from place to place
- Will enjoy using vehicles (wagons) to move things from place to place

Play!

Tricycle, Mother, May I?

Why this playtime activity is good for your child: During this important stage of learning your youngster will develop a longer attention span and learn to follow a simple plan of action. "Tricycle, Mother, May I?" will teach your child to remember to ask permission and give her/him the opportunity to follow simple directions while riding on her/his tricycle.

What you'll need to play this activity: tricycle

How to play *Tricycle, Mother, May I?*: This game is played exactly like "Mother, May I?" except instead of advancing on foot, the player moves forward on her/his tricycle. Have your child sit on the tricycle. Give a command. If s/he remembers to ask permission, ("Mother, May I?") you give the go-ahead. ("Yes, you may.") Then s/he proceeds to follow the instructions. If s/he forgets to ask permission, you remind her/him to go back to the starting point. ("You forgot to ask, 'Mother, May I?' so go back to the start.")

Examples of directions:

Pedal to me slowly.

Pedal to me as fast as you can.

Pedal three times.

Pedal to the end of the porch.

Pedal down the driveway to the sidewalk.

Pedal to me using only one foot (or one hand to steer).

Share!

When you were three years old and played on your tricycle, you enjoyed:

_____

_____

Celebrate!

Celebrate your three-year-old's positive attitude.

At this age many children's negativism and adversity practically disappears. Three-year-olds seem to be more tranquil and cooperative in ways they could not be when they were two-year-olds. In many instances, this year of development will be an easier, calmer parenting period for you and a more peaceful stage for your child.

From 36-42 months you will observe that your child:

- Is involved in rapid learning
- May begin to demonstrate a positive, strong self-image
- Is easier to handle than s/he was last year

Play!

Rainbow Race

Why this playtime activity is good for your child: At age three, some simple board games become appropriate. Because your child has a longer attention span, is learning to take turns, and can follow a simple plan of action, board games may become great learning tools.

What you'll need to play this activity: colored dice (made by placing a different color of paper on each of the six sides of a cube); a game board (with a trail of the six colors on the dice); marker for each player

How to play Rainbow Race: Show your child the starting space on the game board. Put a marker on the board for each player. Take turns rolling the color die and identifying the color. If your child can say the color, that is good. If not, that is okay too. Advance the marker to the nearest square of matching color. Continue taking turns and moving the markers to race around the rainbow of colors.

Variation: When your child is older and can count the number of dots on the dice and can advance a marker that many spaces, you can use numbers instead of colors to play a version of this homemade board game.

Share!

When you were three years old, you enjoy this board game best: _____

_____

How we played the game was:_____

_____

Celebrate!

Celebrate your three-year-old's health and well-being.

Children this age vary widely in their interests and abilities. The motor and cognitive milestones described in this book are general and will vary from child to child. However, if your child seems to deviate widely from most or all of the milestones listed, this may be an indication of delayed development.

Check with your pediatrician if from 36-42 months you observe that your child:

- Cannot throw a ball overhand
- Cannot hold and scribble with a crayon
- Cannot stack four or more blocks
- Doesn't use sentences of more than three words
- Cannot play with other children
- Cannot pedal a tricycle

Play!

Building Towers

Why this playtime activity is good for your child: Using wooden blocks to build and stack is good fine motor practice. It also gives you an opportunity to count and sort with your child. In this informal game and follow-up discussions you can teach your child that colors, shapes, and numbers/numerals are different from each other, and that each has a different name.

What you'll need to play this activity: wooden blocks (different colors and shapes)

How to play Building Towers: Challenge your three-year-old to stack blocks to build a tower. Count as each block is added to the structure. When the tower collapses say, "You built a tower of six blocks!" Look at the blocks together. Sort the square ones from the rectangles. Name the different colors, and make a pile of each color. Count out loud the number of blocks in each pile. Show your child a block and ask her/him to find another one the same color (shape). Show your child two blocks and ask, "Are these blocks the same color?" Or, "Are these blocks the same shape?" Show your child three blocks and ask her/him to point out the two that are exactly the same. Build towers side by side and talk about the number of blocks in each tower. "Which is taller, the tower with four blocks or the tower with six blocks?"

Share!

When you were three years old and we played with wooden blocks, you would:

_____

_____

_____

Celebrate!

Celebrate your three-year-old's sensory activities.

During this developmental stage children begin demonstrating an interest in their five senses and like participating in sensory discrimination activities. Don't be surprised if your child notices if you wear a new perfume or a different color lipstick. S/He may ask about the change. S/He may enjoy experimenting with new flavors and will definitely have favorite flavors. Activities using foods will be highly motivational for your three-year-old.

From 36-42 months you will observe that your child:

- Can distinguish between different aromas and flavors
- Can distinguish between basic colors and shapes
- Can distinguish between objects with different weights or sizes
- Can distinguish between different sounds

Play!

Name That Food

Why this playtime activity is good for your child: This activity will give you an opportunity to show your child how things compare with each other in regard to weight, sound, aroma, texture, flavor, and shape.

What you'll need to play this activity: two lunch-sized bags; aromatic, textured foods such as an orange, apple, dill pickle, vanilla cookie, chocolate bar, peanut butter sandwich, raisins, crackers, bowl of popcorn, pretzel sticks, peppermint stick, tea bag

How to play *Name That Food*: Line up the foods in front of your child, and talk about each one. Ask your child to close her/his eyes. Place two of the foods in separate lunch bags. For example, put the orange in one bag and the popcorn in another. Close the top of each bag so your child cannot see inside them. Then have your child open her/his eyes. Have your child lift and shake each bag to see which one is the heaviest. Then ask, "Which bag contains the orange?" If your child doesn't know, without looking inside the bags, have your child smell the aroma of each food. Then ask again, "Which bag contains the orange?" Put a new item of food in a bag. Have your child reach inside and using the sense of touch, try to determine the name of the food. Vary the game by having your child close her/his eyes, taste one of the foods, and determine what it is. Or have your child close her/his eyes, and hold one of the pieces of food to determine by weight, texture, and shape which food it is. Using nonvisual clues such as weight, aroma, texture, shape, size, and flavor, have your child identify different kinds of food.

Share!

When you were three years old and we played "Name That Food," the nonvisual clue that helped you determine foods correctly the most often was:

Celebrate!

Celebrate your three-year-old's natural artistic abilities.

At this age the best approach for developing your child's full potential for art is to offer her/him a wide range of learning opportunities. This is the perfect age to introduce her/him to great works of art. If your child seems very artistic, take her/him to art museums and galleries, or enroll her/him in a preschool art class. Check out books in the library with photographs of works of the masters. Visit arts and crafts supply stores to look at different kinds of materials. If you know an artist, take your three-year-old to visit and see first hand the artist's studio. Always praise every effort your child makes to be creative.

From 36-42 months you will observe that your child:

- Will be free and uninhibited in her/his artistic endeavors
- Will enjoy the art process as much as the finished product
- Will enjoy having her/his art work displayed in the home

Play!

Classical Scribbling

Why this playtime activity is good for your child: These are the creative years. If creativity is not stimulated and encouraged during these early years, the desire to create gradually fades.

What you'll need to play this activity: classical music; crayons and white paper, or felt markers and construction paper, or chalk and chalkboard

How to play *Classical Scribbling*: Choose a medium like crayons, markers, or chalk. Give your child a large sheet of paper. Play classical music. Show your child how to scribble to the rhythm of the music–long swirling lines, short vertical dashes, bouncy loops, or points of color. See how many different creative ways you and your child can move the crayon (marker/chalk). Vary your medium and try other kinds of music as well. Record some of your child's musical scribbles below.

Share!

When you were three years old and we scribbled to music, here is how it looked:

Celebrate!

Celebrate your three-year-old's musical talents.

Children's musical skills increase dramatically during the early years. In addition to displaying improvements in singing and dancing abilities, they enjoy experimenting with rhythm instruments and playing them with other children in groups. They can also play a wider variety of instruments including castanets and xylophones.

From 36-42 months you will observe that your child:

- Enjoys reciting portions of a few simple nursery rhymes
- Can carry a tune and remember the words of simple songs
- Enjoys dramatizing nursery rhymes

Play!

Nursery Rhyme Finger Plays

Why this playtime activity is good for your child: Repetition of nursery rhymes impresses young minds, develops language, and encourages memorization. Repeated use of poetry and rhymes will motivate your child to play with rhymes and create original rhymes.

What you'll need to play this activity: nursery rhyme books (with big, colorful pictures)

How to play *Nursery Rhyme Finger Plays*: The "action" in many nursery rhymes can be dramatized, such as "Jack and Jill," "Heigh, Diddle, Diddle," and "Jack Be Nimble." Use the actions suggested below or create your own actions to encourage your child to interpret words with movement in her/his own way as you are reciting the rhymes. See example below.

Heigh, Diddle, Diddle

Heigh, diddle, diddle,	*(Put hands to mouth as if calling and say lines.)*
The cat and the fiddle,	*(Play make-believe fiddle.)*
The cow jumped over the moon;	*(Jump high.)*
The little dog laughed	*(Laugh and hold stomach as if laughing.)*
To see such sport,	*(Put hand over eyebrows as if looking at something.)*
And the dish ran away with the spoon.	*(Run away.)*

Share!

When you were three years old, your favorite nursery rhyme was:_____

These are the actions you performed to your favorite rhyme: _____

_____

Celebrate!

Celebrate your three-year-old's growing interest in books.

Your three-year-old should be read to each and every day. Make storytime a part of your daily routine. At this important developmental stage, books are useful for supporting social and cognitive development. As children become interested in stories, reading activities can move beyond simple labeling of objects and actions. Social interactions and feelings may be included in even very simple stories and will provide models for imitation and vehicles for representation and growing understanding.

From 36-42 months you will observe that for your child:

- Books will serve as a valuable means of broadening experiences.
- Books will facilitate understanding, promote respect for others, and nourish her/his growing self-concept.
- Books can reflect the diversity in the group and in the larger society.

Play!

Let's Go to the Library!

Why this playtime activity is good for your three-year-old: A weekly or biweekly trip to the library will give your child an opportunity to see many books, engage in a storytime, see other children, and choose her/his own books.

What you'll need to play this activity: library card

How to play *Let's Go to the Library!*: The day before the planned library visit, while gathering books to be returned, talk about the library trip. When it is time to go to the library, announce it with great ceremony. Let your child carry some of the books you checked out for her/him.

While at the library: Let your child look at books and choose some of the books you will check out. Talk to the librarian about new books and books of special interest to three-year-olds. Find out when the preschoolers' story hour takes place each week. Get on a mailing list for library happenings like puppet and magic shows. Teach your child important library rules like "reading" quietly and respecting the books. Show your child how to leave books on the table so they can be reshelved properly. Check out books for yourself, too. The more your child sees you reading, the more important the activity will become to her/him.

Share!

When you were three and we visited the library, your favorite thing to do was:

_____

_____

Celebrate!

Celebrate your three-year-old's emotional/social development.

During this time your three-year-old must face an extraordinary amount of learning. This period can be fun to watch and be a part of, if you honor your child's great spurt in development. Don't take your child's testing personally; try to see it as her/his way of learning to deal with people and find a special spot in the universe. Children this age cannot put certain concepts into words but they wonder things in general such as, "Where do I fit in? If I act out, will my parents still love and accept me? Are my parents supportive of my every need? Is the world a safe place? Is love and acceptance dependent upon my behavior?"

From 36-42 months you will observe that your child:

- Will begin to walk, talk, and have preferences very similar to one of her/his parents
- May ignore one parent while favoring the other
- May switch allegiance from the favorite parent in the blink of an eye, and switch back and forth without reasons
- May hate to lose when playing games or sports

Play!

Rock, Paper, Scissors

Why this playtime activity is good for your child: Some difficult skills, like learning to lose gracefully, require a lot of practice. This activity will give your child an opportunity to win and to lose in a safe, quiet setting. Once s/he knows the rules, your child can play this game with others.

What you'll need to play this activity: No special equipment is needed to play this game.

How to play Rock, Paper, Scissors: Teach your child how to use hands to make paper (hands out with palms up), rock (both hands in a tight fist), scissors (index and middle finger pointing out and moving fingers like the cutting blades of scissors).

Rules: Paper wraps rock; rock breaks scissors; scissors cut paper; When players show the same things—paper and paper, scissors and scissors, or rock and rock, that round is declared a tie game.

Directions: To play the game, both players put their hands behind their backs. Count to three and then both players bring their hands in front of them and indicate: paper, rock, or scissors. After each round say, "I win, you lose" or "You win, I lose." Giving your child a multitude of opportunities to be a winner and a loser will teach her/him that games are for fun and not just for winning.

Share!

When you were three years old and we played "Rock, Paper, Scissors," you would:

_____

_____

Celebrate!

Celebrate your three-year-old's developing spatial awareness.

By age three a child's spatial awareness will have developed quite a bit. You may notice that your child is more sensitive to the relationships between objects. For example, s/he may position toys with great care and carefully control the way s/he holds utensils and tools to perform specific tasks. This increased sensitivity and control will allow your child to perform new fine motor skills. At this age children are mastering the use of spatial words and concepts such as "back," "front," "under," "over," "on," "behind," etc.

From 36-42 months you will observe that your child:

- Can build a tower of eight or more cubes
- Can pour water from a pitcher into a cup without spilling it
- Can put together puzzles with five or more large pieces

Play!

Setting the Table

Why this playtime activity is good for your child: Most children this age glean a sense of accomplishment from helping with household chores. Setting the table is a good spatial awareness activity because the child must place the eating utensils, cup, and napkin in a particular place in relationship to the plate.

What you'll need to play this activity: lightweight, plastic (non breakable) place settings; eating utensils; cups; paper napkins

How to play *Setting the Table*: The precision of the placement of the cup, utensils, and napkin in relationship to the plate will depend upon the ability of your child. Begin by making a place setting the way you want it. Provide one of each item so your child can duplicate the setting. After s/he learns how to organize a place setting, encourage your child to help you set the dinner table each evening.

Variation: Use play dishes to perform this task on a child-sized table for tea parties, snacks, etc.

Share!

When you were three years old and you set the table, this is how you did it:

_____

_____

_____

_____

Celebrate!

Celebrate your three-year-old's desire to explore and experiment.

Life-long habits begin in the very early years. If you introduce the wonderful world of nature to your child and explore it together today, you will be establishing a positive lifestyle that will fill her/him with great satisfaction for the rest of her/his life.

From 36-42 months you will observe that your child:

- Will probably enjoy outdoor exploration and short hikes
- Will be interested in anything connected to nature
- Will enjoy looking at the stars at night and clouds in the daytime
- Will like watching animals

Play!

⧊ Twinkle, Twinkle, Little Star

Why this playtime activity is good for your three-year-old: Exploring the world and nature with your child will bring her/him to many interesting discoveries.

What you'll need to play this activity: No special equipment is necessary to play this activity.

How to play *Twinkle, Twinkle, Little Star*: Go outside on a starlit night, and look at the stars with your child. Sing the song "Twinkle, Twinkle, Little Star." During the day, go outside and explore the world of nature. As you and your child hike around and make new discoveries, sing new words to the tune: "Twinkle, Twinkle, Little Star."

Examples:

Lady, lady, ladybug, I am glad when I see you.
In the grass below my toes, like a speckled spot of dew,
Lady, lady, ladybug, I am glad when I see you.

Little, little, little ants, how I wonder what you do.
On the ground around my feet, like the wind's pushing you,
Little, little, little ants, how I wonder what you do.

Ocean, ocean, ocean waves, I wonder where you begin.
Washing up on the beach, all around my little feet,
Ocean, ocean, ocean waves, I wonder where you'll end.

Share!

When you were a child and we went exploring in nature, this was your favorite thing to observe:

_____

_____

Celebrate!

Celebrate your three-year-old's ability to learn rules and apply them in different situations.

As children get older, they remember responses and reactions that they have previously experienced. For example, if your child always says a good-night prayer at home, while on an overnight trip to Grandmother's house, s/he may insist on saying a good-night prayer. Being consistent with rules and routines will be comforting for your child and provide much-needed security.

From 36-42 months you will observe that your child:

- Will remember things learned on previous days
- Will learn that things work the same day after day
- Will discover that things have attributes that make them the same or different

Play!

Find Another One

Why this playtime activity is good for your child: Playing with blocks of varied attributes (shape, sizes, and colors) is fun and will give your child an opportunity to discover similarities and differences.

What you'll need to play this activity: primary colored blocks of different shapes such as squares, rectangles, and triangles. If you do not have this kind of blocks, you can use construction paper to make the four shapes (circle, square, triangle, rectangle) of various colors (red, blue, and yellow) and sizes (big and little).

How to play *Find Another One:* Place a pile of blocks (paper patterns) on the floor in front of your child. (There must be at least two of each shape and color.) Pick one block (paper pattern) from the pile. For example: a blue square. Say, "Find another one just like this one." Talk about the block. "This is a blue square (cube)." Help your child find another blue square (cube) in the pile of blocks. Repeat with red triangle, yellow rectangle, etc. If this seems too difficult for your child, begin by finding blocks that have just one shared attribute like color, shape, or size. After working with the blocks and one shared attribute, try playing "Find Another One" again.

Share!

When we played with your colored blocks, you seem to like this shape and color of block best:

_____

When we built with the colored blocks you liked to build: _____

_____

Celebrate!

Celebrate your three-year-old's development of a positive self-image.

As the parent of a three-year-old, your most important job will be to watch your child with adoration. As much as possible, while s/he is at play, stay in the background and let her/him learn at her/his own unique child's pace. Avoid pushing your child into early learning skills that may lead to a feeling of failure. The most important thing your child will be learning this year is that s/he is important. Remember to daily admire, approve of, and demonstrate unconditional love for your child.

From 36-42 months you will observe that your child:

- Will begin to value friendships with peers
- Will begin learning appropriate ways to deal with aggression
- Will begin learning how to identify with everyone around her/him
- Will tease, test, dare, hug, and learn from peers

Play!

Play Groups

Why this playtime activity is good for your child: Exploratory play and experiences with other children will give your child a surer sense of self. Make an effort to get your child together with children her/his age. A three-year-old will treat playmates as rivals, as babies to be mothered, as parents, and as every possible partner. Through this fantasy play, your child will determine how to deal with fears and aggression. Coming together in play groups–learning to take turns, cooperating, sharing–your child will begin a very important cognitive process called altruism.

What you'll need to play this activity: small group of peers; toys enough for everyone to have a variety of her/his own

How to arrange for *Play Groups*: Play groups should be small. If you arrange for the group to meet at your house, organize the play environment so there is supervision from a distance, which allows the children complete privacy during play.

Share!

When you were three years old, these were your favorite friends:_____

_____

_____

_____

Celebrate!

Celebrate your three-year-old's gross motor development.

Most children three and a half years old can move forward and backward with agility. By this age children can go up and down stairs without support. As children get closer to age four, they learn how to pump a swing, climb a rope ladder, and climb up an inclined board.

From 42-48 months you will observe that your child:

- Will be able to hop and stand on one foot for up to five seconds
- Will be able to throw a ball overhand
- Will be able to kick a ball forward
- Will be able to catch a ball bounced to her/him

Play!

Kick Ball Tag

Why this playtime activity is good for your child: Three-year-olds have many new and improved abilities. Better developed gross motors skills allow them to engage in a wider variety of "sports" activities. This activity will be fun and provide practice kicking a ball forward and running.

What you'll need to play this activity: large, soft rubber ball

How to play *Kick Ball Tag:* The object of the game is to kick a ball and then tag a designated base (tree) before the other player can retrieve the ball and tag the runner. Instead of rolling the ball to be kicked, just sit it in front of your child. It is easier to learn how to kick a stationary ball than a moving one. To begin this game teach your child how to kick the ball forward. After s/he has mastered the skill of kicking the ball, add running to a base to the game.

Variation: Give your child a turn at trying to tag you after you kick the ball.

Share!

When you were three years old and we played Kick Ball Tag, you would:

_____

_____

_____

_____

Celebrate!

Celebrate your three-year-old's maturing social/emotional skills.

Most three-year-olds play fantasy and role-playing games more than with toys. Fantasy play makes cooperation easier for playmates since they do not have to cooperate and share toys. Children this age assign roles to each other. For example, "I am the mommy. You be the daddy." Elaborate games of make-believe using social skills such as taking turns, paying attention, communicating, cooperating, and responding to one another's actions will do much to advance your child's social/emotional development.

From 42-48 months you will observe that your child:
- Will become interested in new experiences
- Will engage in increasingly inventive fantasy play
- Will begin cooperating and negotiating solutions to conflicts with peers
- Will become more and more independent

Play!

Animal Charades

Why this playtime activity is good for your child: Many children this age like to move like animals and make animal sounds. Animal charades give children the opportunity to make animal movements and sounds.

What you'll need to play this activity: No special equipment is necessary for playing this game.

How to play *Animal Charades*: Imitate an animal, and let your child guess what animal you are pretending to be. If s/he cannot verbalize her guess, give her choices from which to choose. "Do you think I am a pig, horse, or spider?" Then encourage your child to imitate an animal. The charades may include both movements and sounds that the animals make.

Variation: Use the song "Old MacDonald Had a Farm" to teach and reinforce a variety of animal sounds. Sing the song with the following animals and the sounds they make.

Pig–oink, oink	Horse–neigh, neigh	Cow–moo, moo
Cat–meow, meow	Dog–bow, wow	Chicken–cluck, cluck
Chick–peep, peep	Rooster–cock-a-doodle-do	Lamb–baa, baa
Mouse–squeak, squeak	Frog–ribb-it, ribb-it	Bear–growl, growl

Share!

When you were three years old, your favorite animals to imitate were: _____

Celebrate!

Celebrate your three-year-old's role-playing and dramatic play.

Children this age are capable of cooperative and dramatic play with peers. They increasingly engage in make-believe play, acting out a variety of play themes and portraying characters very dramatically with exaggerated feelings. Gender roles often become more important in play, and, when divided by gender, boys and girls will frequently focus on different play themes.

From 42-48 months you will observe that your child:

- Likes to role-play familiar settings such as house, store, and school
- Will also role-play about professionals such as doctors/nurses, police officers, and fire fighters
- Will play games about themes they view on television such as outer space, cowboys/Indians, or war

Play!

School

Why this playtime activity is good for your child: Children this age enjoy playing school, and this game is a good way to prepare for preschool and kindergarten.

What you'll need to play this activity: child-sized desk or small worktable; school supplies such as paper, pencils, crayons, rulers, glue stick, safety-scissors, etc.

How to play *School:* To begin this game, play with your child awhile so s/he understands the idea of using the supplies to "write," "do schoolwork," "finish homework," and create art projects. Then let her/him use the school supplies to play independently.

Variation #1: Now is an excellent time to hang a chalkboard on the wall in your child's bedroom. Having a chalkboard available will enhance your child's fun when playing school.

Variation #2: Honor the "schoolwork" your child does. Ways of honoring her/his work include: spending time looking at it and talking about it, hanging it on the refrigerator door, putting it in a scrapbook, and rolling it up, tying it with a ribbon, and putting it in a safe place. Have your child use a pencil to do some "schoolwork" below.

Share!

When you were three years old and you played school, you did "work" like this:

Celebrate!

Celebrate your three-year-old's natural curiosity in nature.

Children in this age range are interested in naming, classifying, and collecting natural forms such as seashells, stones, leaves, gemstones, etc.

From 42-48 months you will observe that your child:

- Enjoys learning more about the physical world
- Enjoys exploring nature and measuring and magnifying materials
- Enjoys collecting things from nature like stones, seashells, and gemstones
- Enjoys observing pets such as goldfish, hamsters, or small frogs

Play!

Ant Safari

Why this playtime activity is good for your child: This activity will give your child an opportunity to closely study an ant colony.

What you'll need to play this activity: ant hill; strong magnifying glass

How to play Ant Safari: Show your child how to sit back–without disturbing the ants–and quietly observe ants working in and around an ant hill. (Sit where neither of you will get ants in your pants.) Use strong magnifying glasses to study the ants more closely. Make sure the sun is not shining through the magnifying glass or the heat will endanger the ants. Be careful to leave the ants undisturbed during the observation. After the ant safari talk about what you observed. If s/he wants to draw a picture of the ants, give your child a sheet of paper and a black crayon.

Variation: Help your child begin a natural collection. Choose a theme and provide boxes, a scrapbook, etc., or whatever is needed for organizing the collection. Appropriate collection themes for children this age include: sea shells, smooth stones, pressed flowers or leaves, gemstones, etc.

Share!

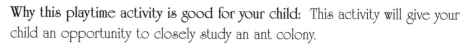

When you were three years old and we played with magnifying glasses, your favorite thing to observe was:

_____

When you used a magnifying glass to watch ants, this is what happened: _____

_____

When you began your first natural collection, you chose to collect:_____

Celebrate!

Celebrate your three-year-old's fine motor skills.

Children this age are extremely interested in finding out what they can do with tools like paper, scissors, and art mediums such as clay, paint, crayons, and markers. Most three-year-olds have the fine motor skills to manipulate these objects and will appreciate experimenting with them to make original art pieces.

From 42-48 months you will observe that your child:
- Can string large wooden beads
- Can dress and undress dolls in clothing with large zippers, snaps, and laces
- Enjoys building sand castles and mud pies

Play!

Clay Bead Necklaces

Why this playtime activity is good for your child: Using clay to make beads is fun and provides an opportunity for children to use small finger and hand muscles in an artistic and creative way.

What you'll need to play this activity: sun-dry dough (flour, salt, water); drinking straw for poking holes in beads; long shoelace for stringing beads; food coloring or powdered tempera paint; waxed paper

How to make *Clay Bead Necklaces*: Begin by having your child help you make the sun-dry dough. Mix 2 cups (474 ml) of flour with 1 cup of salt (237ml). Stir. Slowly add water until a thick dough forms. Knead the dough until it is soft and workable. (Food coloring can be added to the water or powdered tempera paint mixed with the dry ingredients.) Working on waxed paper, have your child use spoonfuls of dough to roll into large bead shapes. The beads may be square, round, oval, etc. Use the drinking straw to punch a hole through each bead. Let the beads dry in the sun until completely hard. Then help your child string the beads onto a long shoelace to create a necklace. Tie the shoelace so the necklace can be slipped over the head.

Share!

When you were three years old and you played with modeling materials, your favorite thing to make was:

_____

_____

_____

_____

Celebrate!

Celebrate your three-year-old's rapidly developing language skills.

By three and a half, your child will have an active vocabulary from three hundred to one thousand words. At this age children often chatter constantly. Be patient with your child's never-ending questions. Remember, this process is essential to her/his learning to communicate.

From 42-48 months you will observe that your child:

- Has mastered basic rules of grammar
- Enjoys telling stories
- Will speak clearly enough that even a stranger can understand her/him

Play!

Your Turn Stories

Why this playtime activity is good for your child: Using one's imagination is good practice no matter how old the child. This activity will allow your child the opportunity to contribute to your storytelling time.

What you'll need to play this activity: Nothing is needed to complete this activity except two good imaginations—yours and your child's.

How to play *Your Turn Stories*: Begin telling a story. Then when you come to an important noun or verb say, "Your Turn." Your child fills in a word. Then you use that word to continue the story. Do this often during your story. Your child doesn't have to elaborate, but if s/he is verbal and wants to add more than just a word or phrase, encourage her/him to do so.

Use basic plots of familiar fairy tales such as "The Three Bears," "The Three Billy Goats Gruff," "The Gingerbread Man," or make up whole new stories of your own.

Variation: Write down these original stories created by you and your child to reread at a later time. S/He will enjoy remembering the process of creating the original story and have fun hearing them several times.

Share!

When you were three years old and we made up new stories, one of your favorites was:

_____

_____

_____

_____

Celebrate!

Celebrate your three-year-old's cognitive milestones.

Three-year-olds cannot see an issue from two points of view. Children this age only see things from one point of view. They only know how to approach a problem from a single point of view–theirs!

From 42-48 months you will observe that your child:

- Is learning to follow three-part directions
- Enjoys recalling portions of a story
- Is beginning to understand sequencing of events in stories and daily routines
- Is learning the concept of same and different

Play!

First, Second, and Last

Why this playtime activity is good for your child: Sequencing objects first, second, and last is a good cognitive skill to teach your youngster. Ordering things from left to right in sequence will give your child an opportunity to use her/his imagination to recall the order of events.

What you'll need to play this activity: objects showing three steps (See examples listed below.)

How to play *First, Second, and Last:* Give your child three pictures or objects that show different steps. Ask, "Which came first, second, and last?" Help your child arrange the three things in the order of sequence of events. Always arrange things from the left to the right.

Examples:

1. apple with peel, peeled apple, peeled apple cut into slices
2. photo of baby, child, adult
3. supplies for making jam sandwich (jam, loaf of bread, knife), jam being spread on bread, jam sandwich with bite taken out of it
4. wrapped gift box, present being unwrapped, present out of box

Variation: Ask your child questions like, "What did you do first after your nap?" or "At lunch what food did you taste first?" "Did you eat breakfast *before* or *after* lunch?"

Share!

When you were three years old and we played sequencing games, you would:

Celebrate!

Celebrate your three-year-old's safety and well-being.

Kitchens are dangerous rooms for young children. Because you spend so much time in the kitchen, it will be impossible and undesirable to keep your youngster out of that room. To make your kitchen as safe as possible, store strong cleaners, lye, furniture polish, soap, and other dangerous products in high cabinets and out of sight. Keep knives, forks, scissors, and other sharp instruments separate from other kitchen utensils in a latched drawer. Unplug appliances when they are not in use. Turn pot handles toward the back of the stove so your child cannot reach up and grab them. Put matches out of reach of your child, and keep a fire extinguisher in your kitchen.

From 42-48 months you will observe that your child:
- Is curious and will quickly get into dangerous situations
- Will taste (drink/eat) unsafe fluids and solids if left where s/he can reach them
- Cannot distinguish between safe and unsafe tools

Play!

My Body Is Fancy

Why this playtime activity is good for your child: Children should understand that sometimes sounds are there to warn them of dangers. For example, a train whistle tells us that a train is coming. A car horn tells us that a car is very close by. When your child plays this game s/he will learn to listen, to recognize and identify familiar sounds, to distinguish between sounds, and how to duplicate the sounds her/himself.

What you'll need to play this activity: No special equipment is needed to play this game.

How to play *My Body Is Fancy*: Demonstrate sounds your body can make such as laughing, coughing, sneezing, blowing, humming, tongue clicking, singing, whistling, clapping, finger snapping, foot tapping, stomping, etc. Have your child close her/his eyes while you use your body to make a sound. Then have your child try to duplicate the sound s/he heard. Talk about warning sounds people make such as "Stop," "Stay back!," and "Help."

Share!

When you were three years old, some of your favorite sounds to make were:

_____

_____

Celebrate!

Celebrate your three-year-old's progress and development.

If you are anxious about your child's development, it can actually delay her/his progress. Your sensitivity regarding her/his progress may be making you hover or push your child. Neither approach will work; both will transmit a poor self-image to your child. If any part of your child's development–motor, cognitive, emotional, or behavioral–troubles you, see your pediatrician to find out if there is indeed a problem.

From 42-48 months it may be of concern if you observe that your child:

- Demonstrates either limp or hypertonic (overactive) muscles
- Shows a definite delay in cognitive development
- Shows a definite delay in emotional and social development
- Is emotionally withdrawn, doesn't talk or try to communicate

Play!

Nobody Is Responsible for Accidents

Why this playtime activity is good for your child: It is very important that you act warmly towards and are supportive of your child. Don't make her/him feel ashamed or tell your child s/he is a "bad girl/boy." Her/His self-confidence is in a vulnerable stage of development. Never assume when your child won't do something that s/he is being "naughty;" s/he may not know how to do what you want her/him to do or understand that you want her/him to do it.

What you'll need to play this activity: No special equipment is needed to play this activity.

How to teach your child that nobody is responsible for accidents: When your child makes a mistake, breaks something, spills something, or has an accident, reassure her/him with, "Nobody is responsible for accidents." Let your child know that s/he doesn't have to be perfect to be loved. Unconditional love is accepting, even when your child may act out or appear "unlovable." Consistently loving and accepting your child will teach her/him how to love unconditionally. Never withhold your affection because of your child's misbehavior.

Share!

When you were three years old and you made a mistake or had an accident, you would:

_____

_____

_____

Celebrate!

Celebrate your three-year-old's abilities and play interests.

Children this age are more advanced in fine and gross motor abilities. As they learn to engage in pretend play and creative activities of various kinds, an increasing number and variety of play materials will be needed to support their maturing development.

From 42-48 months you will observe that your child:

- Will enjoy materials that support her/his increasingly complex repertoire of pretend play
- Will enjoy toys that are small representations of people, animals, and vehicles
- Still needs toys that are sturdy and have no sharp edges

Play!

Racing Cars

Why this playtime activity is good for your three-year-old: Children this age have an increased interest in vehicles. Small cars are often of particular interest to small children. The activity of racing two small cars will be fun and teach your child about inclined planes.

What you'll need to play this activity: small cars; an inclined plane (can be a strip of cardboard placed on a table with three or four blocks elevating one end)

How to play *Racing Cars*: Show your child how to start the two cars racing down the inclined plane at the same time. You hold one car, and have your child hold the other. On the signal "Go," release the two cars at the same time. This starting the race procedure may take a great deal of time for you to explain and for your child to master. But once s/he understands the importance of starting a race at the exact same time, s/he will enjoy all kinds of races.

Variation #1: Explore different inclines when racing the cars. See how much the ramp can be inclined and still have the cars stay on the ramp. See how little an incline can be engaged and still move the cars forward.

Variation #2: Race plastic boats across a child-sized pool of water by splashing and making waves to propel the boats forward. (**Caution:** Always supervise all water games.)

Share!

When you were three and a half and we raced little cars, you would:

_____

_____

When we raced little boats, you would: _____

_____

Celebrate!

Celebrate your three-year-old's creative and artistic abilities.

Taking into account the wide range of abilities and interests that children have at this age, it will be important to provide your child with an increasing number of materials for artistic expression. A variety of crayons, markers, paints, chalks, and pastels plus interesting paper of varied texture, color, and sizes should be made available for your child's creative expression and enjoyment.

From 42-48 months you will observe that your child:

- Will enjoy working with graphic as well as plastic materials
- Will draw people with two to four body parts
- May begin to copy some uppercase letters and numerals

Play!

Finger Painting

Why this playtime activity is good for your child: When doing art work, it is not the finished product, but rather the process that is important to children this age.

What you'll need to play this activity: large sheets of slick surfaced paper; finger paints; newspaper or plastic wrap

How to provide pleasant finger painting experiences: Cover the work surface with newspaper or plastic wrap. Dip the paper in water, and place it on the work surface in front of your child. Place a large tablespoon of thick red finger paint in the center of the paper. Invite your child to use her/his hands and fingers to move the paint around. When your child is done with her/his painting, hang it where it can dry. Help your child wash her/his hands. Offer sincere praise, but don't overdo it. The child may not feel it is a "good" painting. A comment such as, "I like those pretty (or bright) colors you used," will please your child. Don't ask, "What is it?" Instead, ask your child to tell you about her/his picture. Then listen.

Variation: You can make your own homemade finger paints. Mix two parts of liquid laundry starch with one part powdered tempera paint or a few drops of food coloring. Or mix flour and cold water into a paste. Add food coloring or powdered tempera paint to make this homemade finger paint the color you desire.

Share!

When you were three years old and we finger painted, you would: _____

_____

_____

Celebrate!

Celebrate your three-year-old's musical talents.

Musical instruments for this age range should be carefully selected so that they support an increasingly broad spectrum of abilities and interests. As your child grows older, by a great degree, her/his musical skills and interests will be shaped by early musical experiences.

From 42-48 months you will observe that your child:

- Will enjoy using a standard rhythm instrument set
- Will enjoy playing xylophones and drums
- Will enjoy playing tambourines, castanets, and triangles
- Will enjoy hearing recorded music for singing, moving, and playing rhythm instruments

Play!

Keep the Beat

Why this playtime activity is good for your child: Using musical instruments to accompany nursery rhymes helps youngsters focus on the rhythm of the rhyme and motivates them to use rhythm when reciting rhymes.

What you'll need to play this activity: nursery rhymes with rhythm; rhythm instrument, bell, or xylophone

How to play *Keep the Beat*: Strike, ring, or blow a musical instrument on the accented (bold) words. Then recite the rhyme again this time encouraging your child to "keep the beat." If your child has trouble doing this, begin by clapping hands on the accented beat. Then hold your child's hands and help her/him play the instrument at the appropriate time. Some examples of nursery rhymes that work well with rhythm instruments follow:

Pease-Porridge Hot	Hickory, Dickory, Dock
Pease-porridge hot	Hickory, dickory, **dock**;
Pease-porridge cold,	The mouse ran up the **clock**;
Pease-porridge in the **pot**,	The clock struck **One**,
Nine days **old**.	The mouse ran **down**,
	Hickory, dickory, **dock**.

Share!

When you were three years old, your favorite nursery rhymes to accompany with music were:

_____

_____

Celebrate!

Celebrate your three-year-old's role playing and fantasy play.

Ages three and four are known as the "magic years." This is the time when your child's world is dominated by fantasy and vivid imagination. S/He'll be watching everyone in new ways. S/He will invent whole scenarios about the people s/he sees each day and assimilate these observations into her/his imaginary play. S/He'll even invent imaginary characters and interact with them in fantasy play. At first, fantasy play with imaginary characters is too vulnerable to share with parents, so remember, your three-year-old's privacy is precious and must be respected. Don't let older siblings or adults make fun of or stifle your child's fantasy play.

From 42-48 months you will observe that your child:

- May have imaginary friends who can do bad things without being punished
- May have imaginary friends who can perform miracles (fly, leap tall buildings, etc.)

Play!

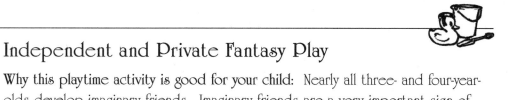

Independent and Private Fantasy Play

Why this playtime activity is good for your child: Nearly all three- and four-year-olds develop imaginary friends. Imaginary friends are a very important sign of complex thinking skills. As imagination surfaces in the third year, the child's ability to separate fact from fantasy is not yet well-developed. Fantasy play with imaginary friends is your child's way of testing the limits of her/his world.

What you'll need to play this activity: No special equipment is needed to play this game.

How to play *Independent and Private Fantasy Play:* The secret to this game is to **stay out** of it! Give your child her/his privacy when s/he is playing with imaginary friends. If your child wants to talk to you about an imaginary friend, listen. Never laugh or make light of your child's sincerity when sharing about imaginary friends. If your child shares these experiences with you, it is a sign that s/he feels safe and loved.

Share!

When you were three years old, your imaginary friends included: _____

_____

_____

_____

_____

Celebrate!

Celebrate your three-year-old's perceptual/cognitive milestones.

During this developmental stage your child's sense of time will become more clear. S/He may become aware of the time routines of others like the mail carrier (every day at noon) garbage collector (once a week in the afternoon), gardener (once a week in the morning), etc. S/He will begin to anticipate weekends when Father and perhaps siblings are home all day. Your child will become aware soon that holidays happen only once in a while–the concept of a whole year is too great for children this age to comprehend.

From 42-48 months you will observe that your child:

- Will comprehend time terminology such as "yesterday" and "tomorrow" (*Tomorrow* we will go to the library.)
- Will comprehend sequencing terminology such as "after" and "before" (*After* lunch we will go to the zoo.)
- Will begin comprehending position words such as "over," "under," "around," "behind," "out," and "in." (Put your toys *in* the toy box.)

Play!

Blowing Bubbles

Why this playtime activity is good for your child: Blowing bubbles is fun, and it will give you an opportunity to reinforce position words such as "over," "under," "around," "behind," and "in."

What you'll need to play this activity: jar of bubble liquid; bubble wand

How to play *Blowing Bubbles*: Wait for a sunny, warm day to go outside and blow bubbles. Show your child how to blow bubbles. Then when s/he blows them, narrate where they are going. For example, "Look! Your bubbles are going *over* those trees," or "Your bubbles went *under* that bush."

Variation: You can make your own bubble liquid by mixing equal parts liquid detergent and water. Place the liquid in a flat tray. Create a giant wand with a wire coat hanger. Dip the coat hanger into the tray of liquid and wave it through the breeze. Experiment with the shapes of the bubbles created by bending the coat hanger into a square, circle, and oval. Does the shape of the wand determine the shape of the giant bubbles?

Share!

When you were three years old and we played with bubbles, you would: _____

_____

_____

_____

Celebrate!

Celebrate your three-year-old's growing interest in books.

Children this age need a wide variety of books. Books can be made or borrowed from the library. Recycling centers and garage sales can provide numerous low-cost books for your child's private library. Children this age like books with familiar scenes and situations. Include in your child's library books designed to expand imaginations and vocabulary with familiar and relevant themes.

From 42-48 months you will observe that your child:

- Enjoys hearing stories told and retold, word-for-word, without changes
- Enjoys contributing ideas to stories
- Can sit for twenty minutes or longer to hear a story
- Enjoys information books about everyday life experiences

Play!

Homemade Books

Why this playtime activity is good for your child: When a child helps create a book s/he discovers that books are not magical, but rather are the thoughts and words of a person like her/himself.

What you'll need to play this activity: old magazines or books with colorful pictures that can be cut apart; paper; scissors; glue; stapler; fine-tip black marker

How to make homemade books: Have your child choose some pictures that s/he likes best in the old books and magazines. Cut out the pictures. Leaving space to write at the bottom of each page, glue each picture to a separate sheet of paper. Compile the pages into a booklet and staple it along the left-hand edge. Use construction paper or light cardboard to create a back and front cover for the book. As you turn the pages, ask your child to give you a word, phrase, or sentence about each picture. Record the words in manuscript at the bottom of each page. When the book has been "written," read it to your child.

Variation: Use photographs of your child and family members to create a personal book. Again, let your child give the "story" for each page of the book.

Share!

When you were three years old and we created a book, this is what it was about:

_____

_____

Celebrate!

Celebrate your three-year-old's maturing fine motor skills.

At age three and a half children develop both the muscular control and the concentration needed to master precision finger and hand movements.

From 42-48 months you will observe that your child:

- Can move each finger independently or together
- Will be able to trace a square, copy a circle, or scribble freely
- Will be able to coordinate hand movements with movements of other body parts

Play!

Puppet Show

Why this playtime activity is good for your child: Using puppets allows your child the opportunity to exercise small hand and finger muscles and coordinate hand movements with verbal communication skills.

What you'll need to play this activity: small hand puppets

How to play *Puppet Show*: Decide on a storyline for the puppet show. Choose puppets that you and your child will use. Your first puppet show with your child might be from an impromptu script. You can ask a question that your child is to answer. This kind of a show is a bit like an informal interview.

Example:

Parent–Brown Bear: Hello, Mr. Skunk. How are you today?

Child–Mr. Skunk: Good.

Parent–Brown Bear: How are all your baby skunks?

Child–Mr. Skunk: Good.

Parent–Brown Bear: And Mrs. Skunk? Is she well?

Child–Mr. Skunk: Yes.

Parent–Brown Bear: I am looking for some honey. Do you know where I can find some honey?

Child–Mr. Skunk: No.

At first, getting your youngster to contribute to the storyline may be tedious. But eventually, s/he will get creative, use her/his imagination, and invent stories along with you.

Share!

When you were three years old and we made up puppet shows, you would: _____

Celebrate!

Celebrate your three-year-old's social/emotional development.

During this developmental stage your child will become more aware of and sensitive to the feelings and actions of others. S/He'll gradually stop being so competitive and will learn to play more cooperatively. This is a year of practicing social skills such as taking turns, paying attention, communicating, cooperating, and responding to another's needs.

From 42-48 months you will observe that your child:

- Will understand how to take turns
- Will understand how to share
- Will understand to ask for what s/he wants instead of grabbing it
- Will be able to respond to the actions of peers during a game or fantasy play

Play!

Tea Party

Why this playtime activity is good for your child: At this age your child is interested in imitating you and doing things that please you. Tea parties give your child practice being polite and allow you the opportunity to be a good model. When your child learns good manners without pressure from you, s/he will be proud of the skills s/he has mastered.

What you'll need to play this activity: small tea set; milk or herbal tea; cookies; napkins

How to play _Tea Party_: With great ceremony, prepare the tea and cookies for the tea party. Set the table with a cloth and miniature tea settings. (If you do not have a child-sized tea set, adult tea cups and saucers may be used.) Let your child help set the table, pour the warm tea, and serve the cookies. Use lots of "pleases," "thank-yous," and "you're welcomes" during the party. Use your napkin to dab your lips after each bite of cookie and sip of tea. Ask your child, "Will you please pass the cookies?" or "May I have another cup of tea, please?" Compliment your child on the good manners s/he demonstrates during the tea party. "It makes me very proud to see that you remember to say 'please' and 'thank you.'" Use the elegant setting of a tea party to convey the pleasure of good manners to your youngster.

Share!

When you were three years old and we had a tea party, you would:_____

_____

Celebrate!

Celebrate your three-year-old's physical growth.

Most three-year-olds gain approximately 4½ to 5 pounds (2.04 to 2.27 kilograms) and grow 3 to 3½ inches (76 to 89 millimeters) between their third and fourth birthdays. However, growth varies with each child. If you have any questions about your child's physical growth, check with your pediatrician.

At the end of 48 months you will observe that your child's:

- Length of skull will increase slightly
- Lower jaw will become more pronounced
- Upper jaw will widen to make room for the permanent teeth
- Face will actually become larger and features will become more distinct
- Face will mature

Play!

Growth Milestones

Why this bi-yearly activity is good for your child: By this age most children begin to realize that they want to grow up. They want to be like everyone around them. Measuring your child's growth every six months and marking it on a growth chart, wall, tree, etc., will let your child know that you want her/him to grow up, too.

How to record growth milestones: Let your child help you record her/his growth by having her/him back up against the wall chart, bare feet flat on the floor. Her/His head should be straight so that s/he's looking straight ahead. Use a ruler, book, or other flat device to accurately line up the top of her/his head, and mark the chart. If you have not already marked the height of your child at birth and her/his birthdays and half birthdays, dig through your records to find these measurements, and add them to the wall chart. Every six months, make recording your child's height a family ritual. (Don't measure more often than every six months because your child may become discouraged with what might seem to a child to be "slow progress.")

Share!

When you were born,
you were this long: _____

When you were six months old,
you were this long: _____

When you were one year old,
you were this tall: _____

When you were one-and-a-half
years old, you were this tall: _____

When you were two years old,
you were this tall: _____

When you were two-and-a-half
years old, you were this tall: _____

When you were three years old,
you were this tall: _____

When you were three-and-a-half
years old, you were this tall: _____

When you were four years old,
you were this tall: _____

Celebrate!

Celebrate your child's fourth birthday.

This is perhaps the first birthday when your child will be old enough to appreciate a birthday party. Four-year-olds are enthusiastic party goers and tend to be cooperative if things are kept exciting enough. Kids this age are happy with simple prizes, games, and treats. The number of guests should not exceed five peers, and the party should last no more than an hour and a half.

By the end of 48 months you will observe that your child:
- Will be enthusiastic about helping you plan her/his birthday party
- Will probably prefer peer guests rather than adult family members
- Will thoroughly enjoy her/his birthday party

Play!

Ring-Around-the-Birthday Girl/Boy

Why this playtime activity is good for your child: At parties with four-year-old guests, the games should be very simple. Informal games such as "Ring-Around-the-Rosey" or "Duck, Duck, Goose" are fine for this age group. Unstructured games like blowing bubbles or tag will be better received than games with too much structure.

What you'll need to play this activity: cloth handkerchief

How to play *Ring-Around-the-Birthday Girl/Boy:* Play this game like "Ring-Around-the-Rosey" but begin by letting the birthday child be "It." The other children form a circle and hold hands with the birthday child inside the circle. They recite the verse and move clockwise around the birthday child.

> Ring-around-the-rosey,
> Pocket full of posies.
> Ashes, ashes, all fall down.

At the end of the verse, the children "fall down" in the grass. The birthday child moves to the outside of the ring of children and walks around reciting the verse again. S/He drops the handkerchief behind someone and then runs around the outside of the circle of children. The person who the handkerchief is dropped behind, retrieves the handkerchief and tries to tag the birthday child before s/he can run around the circle and sit down in the spot the runner left open. If the birthday child is tagged, s/he must be "It" again. If s/he isn't tagged, the other child is "It" and goes to the center of the circle. Repeat.

Share!

When you had your fourth birthday party, this is what happened: _____

_____

These are the names of your friends who celebrated with you: _____

_____

Celebrate!

Celebrate your four-year-old's gross motor development.

As a preschooler's gross motor skills develop, s/he is able to safely and successfully use an extended range of play materials. As motor coordination increases, children become capable of successfully using vehicle toys like tricycles and wagons, as well as simple push toys that represent adult tools.

From age 4 to 5 you will observe that your child:

- Will enjoy playing with push toys such as doll strollers, carriages, and shopping carts
- Will be able to push, balance, and steer a small wheelbarrow
- Will enjoy using real tools such as small, lightweight hammers and child-safety scissors

Play!

Construction City

Why this playtime activity is good for your child: Hammering a nail into a board takes eye-hand coordination and will give your four-year-old practice in gross motor skills.

What you'll need to play this activity: child-sized workbench or small worktable; small, lightweight hammer; small nails with large heads; a variety of blocks of wood including one very large, sturdy board for practicing hammering nails; wood glue

How to play *Construction City*: Begin by showing your four-year-old how to hold the hammer with her/his dominant hand and the nail toward the bottom with the index finger and thumb of the other hand. Tap lightly on the top of the nail to drive it slightly into the board. Her/his eyes should remain on the nail as the child is tapping the nail into the board. When the nail is securely in the board (approximately half way), remove the fingers holding the nail, and finish driving the nail into the board. Repeat this step many times until your child can successfully hammer nails into a board.

Variation: Provide models of wood construction for the child to copy. For example, a triangular piece glued to the top of the same-size cube might represent a small house. Help your child use blocks of wood to make a variety of miniature buildings. Save these wooded constructions to build a play village.

Share!

When you were a preschooler and played with hammer and nails, you would: _____

Celebrate!

Celebrate your four-year-old's abilities and play interests

Four-year-olds are especially interested in puzzles. They enjoy fit-in or framed puzzles with 20-30 pieces, large simple jigsaw puzzles with 10-25 pieces, and cardboard puzzles. Other pattern-making materials such as attribute blocks and color cubes are of high interest to this age group, too.

From age 4 to 5 you will observe that your child:

- Will enjoy pegboards with small pegs
- Will enjoy magnetic boards with forms
- Will enjoy a variety of shapes/colors/sizes of beads for stringing in patterns

Play!

Red Bead, Blue Bead

Why this playtime activity is good for your child: Children this age enjoy activities that involve many little pieces that need to be manipulated. Using fine motor skills to string large wooden beads in particular color patterns is fun and provides an opportunity for practicing eye-hand coordination.

What you'll need to play this activity: large wooden beads in a variety of colors; two long shoelaces

How to play *Red Bead, Blue Bead*: Tie a large knot at one end of each shoelace, so the beads will not slip off that end. Give one lace to your child. Begin by stringing a particular color bead on your lace. Have your child put the same color bead on her/his lace. Then make a pattern with the different colored beads and tie a knot in the other end. Encourage your child to copy the pattern you create on her/his lace. For example: red, blue, red, blue, red, blue; or yellow, yellow, green, yellow, yellow, green. The pattern should involve two colors and alternate one or two beads between colors.

Variation #1: As your child gets good at copying patterns of beads strung on a shoelace, try making a more difficult pattern such as: green, red, blue, red, green, red, blue, red; or yellow, yellow, blue, red, red, blue, yellow, yellow, blue, etc.

Variation #2: String a lace of eight to ten beads in a particular pattern and ask your child to guess what color bead comes next. For example: red, blue, green, red, blue, green. What colors come next? Have your child continue the pattern with additional beads.

Share!

When you were a preschooler and we strung colored beads, you would: _____

_____

_____

Celebrate!

Celebrate your four-year-old's language development

Four-year-olds love language and use words to help them understand and participate in the things going on around them. At this stage your youngster's vocabulary will increase by leaps and bounds, and sentence structure, grammatical usage, and correctness of tenses will improve. Children this age can name most familiar objects and enjoy hearing others elaborate on familiar terms. Preschoolers love to talk, to rhyme, to whisper, to sing, to shout, to boast, and use verbalization to get attention.

From age 4 to 5 you will observe that your child:

- May have a vocabulary of 1500 words or more
- Will talk to objects such as toys
- Will exaggerate when verbalizing ("*biggest* in the world," or "*best* I ever tasted," etc.)
- Will perfect some of the more difficult speech sounds such as l, r, s, t, sh, ch, and j
- Will enjoy doing silly things with words

Play!

Tongue Twisters

Why this playtime activity is good for your child: You can help expand your four-year-old's vocabulary by providing practice saying difficult sounds and playing with rhymes and rhythm.

What you'll need to play this activity: book of tongue twisters

How to play *Tongue Twisters*: Begin by teaching your child only a line or two of a tongue twister. Then when s/he knows it well, add the next line or two. Make up original tongue twisters that include your child's name.

Tongue Twister
Peter Piper picked a peck of pickled peppers;
A peck of pickled peppers Peter Piper picked;
If Peter Piper picked a peck of pickled peppers,
Where's the peck of pickled peppers Peter Piper picked?

Share!

When you were a preschooler your favorite tongue twister was: _____

_____

_____

_____

Celebrate!

Celebrate your four-year-old's communication skills.

This is a noisy age; four-year-olds love to communicate. Preschoolers are outgoing, and they don't especially enjoy solitary play time. Even when children this age are alone, they pretend they are playing with others and talk to their toys and imaginary playmates. If there are no children to play with, a four-year-old will engage in an elaborate, imaginative game with an adult.

From age 4 to 5 you will observe that your child:

- Will speak less of ownership and will ask permission to use things that others are playing with
- Imaginative play involves verbal fantasies
- Will verbalize strong expressions of friendship for those they like
- Enjoys whispering secrets
- Likes to hear and say nonsense words

Play!

Telephone

Why this playtime activity is good for your child: Telephone is a game of whispering, and children this age love to whisper. This activity will give your child an opportunity to improve listening and language skills.

What you'll need to play this activity: a group of three or four people

How to play *Telephone*: Begin by whispering a secret message to your child. S/He is to whisper the secret to another person. That person whispers the secret to yet another person until everyone has had the secret whispered to her/him. The last person recites what s/he believes to be the message. More than likely, the message will have changed in the process of passing it along from one person to the next. To get you started, here are some examples of lines to whisper:

> Ladybug, ladybug, fly away home.
> A dog and a cat went out to play in the rain.
> There was an old woman who lived in a shoe.
> Goosey, goosey, gander, where do you wander?
> Birds are all singing and morning's begun.

Share!

When you were a preschooler and we played Telephone, a secret you told was:

_____

_____

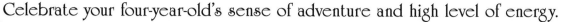

Celebrate!

Celebrate your four-year-old's sense of adventure and high level of energy.

Four-year-olds love adventure! You, too, may suddenly find life more adventurous because of your preschooler. Take time for exciting excursions and adventures with your four-year-old. Set aside an hour on a particular afternoon each week or part of a morning that is for just the two of you to go on adventures. Four is not too young to begin to appreciate Mother Nature's gifts–birds, trees, and flowers. Take daily hikes around your yard in search of interesting things to observe.

From age 4 to 5 you will observe that your child:
- Will enjoy a good place to dig with a supply of excavating tools
- Sees every day as an exciting new opportunity for fun and adventure
- Will be filled with awe for the world around her/him
- Will believe that all things–even finding buried treasure–is possible

Play!

Digging to China

Why this playtime activity is good for your child: Not all, but most children this age, enjoy playing in the dirt and digging big holes. Digging is good exercise for children, and the level of adventure is heightened by discussing what might be buried in the hole.

What you'll need to play this activity: a place to dig a deep hole; small child-sized shovels; gardening tools like spades and hoes; peers to help dig

How to play *Digging to China*: Children like to dig, but they especially enjoy digging when they have help. Begin the project by talking about what might be buried underground in your backyard. For example: "China is on the other side of the world–could we ever dig all the way through the world?" "Could anyone?" "What is in the center of the earth?" "Could we discover oil buried in the backyard?" "Could we find a buried pirate's treasure chest?" "What would a pirate put in a treasure chest?" "When we get the hole really deep, could we bury a time capsule in it?" "What is a time capsule?" (Tell your child about time capsules.) "What would you include in a time capsule?"

Share!

When you were a preschooler and you dug a deep hole, what you said about the adventure was:

_____

_____

Celebrate!

Celebrate your four-year-old's developing social skills.

At this age your child's friends will actively influence her/his thinking and behavior. Because s/he wants to be accepted by peers, s/he may violate rules and standards s/he has been taught at home. For the first time ever, your child is beginning to realize that there are other values and opinions besides yours. S/He may test this new discovery by demanding new independence.

From age 4 to 5 you will observe that your child:

- Wants other children to like her/him
- Wants to please her/his friends
- May willingly agree to rules and occasionally disobey them

Play!

Sleep-Over

Why this playtime activity is good for your child: Children this age enjoy entertaining other children at her/his home. An overnight sleep-over will provide your child an opportunity to share several meals and a whole night with a friend.

What you'll need to play this activity: sleeping bags, pup tent set up in child's bedroom (or facsimile)

How to have a sleep-over: Have your child help you plan and prepare for the sleep-over. A day before the event, talk to your child about what s/he thinks would be fun to serve for dinner and breakfast. Go shopping for the food together. The morning of the sleep-over, set up the tent or prepare a place where the children can sleep comfortably in sleeping bags on the floor. When the happy time arrives, let your child entertain her/his guest without interference.

Variations: Talk to your child ahead of time to find out how s/he plans to fill the evening hours before bedtime. If the children get bored, a rented video or a stargazing trip will be entertaining. Some board games with easy-to-follow rules, cards for "Go Fish," or puzzles might be included in the evening's recreation. A flashlight hike around the backyard is exciting for some children, but might be threatening for others.

Share!

When you had your first sleep-over, this is what you did: _____

_____

_____

Celebrate!

Celebrate your four-year-old's ability to distinguish between reality and make-believe.

Four-year-olds can move back and forth between fantasy and reality without confusing the two. A little girl this age will sometimes compete with her mother for her father's attention, while a little boy will challenge his father for his mother's attention.

From age 4 to 5 you will observe that your child:

- Will often role-play "Mom" or "Dad" in fantasy games
- Will be aware of sexuality
- Will be able to distinguish fantasy from reality
- Will bounce back and forth between being demanding and cooperative

Play!

Tall Tales

Why this playtime activity is good for your child: Imaginative thinking will help your youngster build a secure foundation as s/he prepares to go to kindergarten. This activity will combine imaginative stories with distinguishing between reality and make believe.

What you'll need to play this activity: books of tall tales or original tall tales

How to play *Tall Tales*: Read tall tales or tell original tales of exaggerated situations. Fairy tales are often good tall tales. Stories with animals that talk, sleep in beds, and wear clothes are fanciful. After you tell a tall tale, talk about the things in the story that are fact and fantasy. Ask your child questions to help her/him distinguish the things in the story that were possible and impossible.

For example:

"The Three Bears"–Do bears live in houses? Do they sleep in beds? What else in this story could never happen? Do bears sleep? Do little girls take walks in the woods? Are some little girls curious?

"The Gingerbread Man"–Can a gingerbread cookie run about? Do farmers' wives bake gingerbread men? Do people like eating gingerbread?

Share!

When you were a preschooler and I read you tall tales, you would: _____

_____

Your favorite tall tale was: _____

Celebrate!

Celebrate your four-year-old's interpersonal relationships.

Four-year-olds love other children. Preschoolers enjoy playing with peers so much that often playtime will happen without a hitch. Friendships are very strong at this age. Some four-year-olds have a best friend. While cooperating as a group to build a common structure, often one child will emerge as the leader and boss a "gang" of workers.

From age 4 to 5 you will observe that your child:

- Can cooperate quite easily
- Will share and take turns
- Can play cooperatively with peers most of the time

Play!

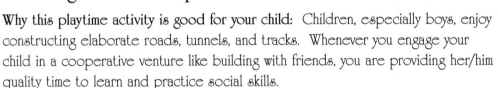

"Building" Relationships

Why this playtime activity is good for your child: Children, especially boys, enjoy constructing elaborate roads, tunnels, and tracks. Whenever you engage your child in a cooperative venture like building with friends, you are providing her/him quality time to learn and practice social skills.

What you'll need to play this activity: large construction set of big blocks; miniature trucks, cars, etc.; peers

How to play *"Building" Relationships*: Building with big blocks is a favorite physical, as well as constructive, activity. Encourage the children to use the big blocks to build structures such as houses, stories, forts, etc. Combine structures with miniature trucks and wagons, or cars and trains.

Variation #1: If you do not have a set of big blocks, cardboard boxes and blankets can be used to create special hiding places where children can have privacy to giggle, whisper, and bond with each other.

Variation #2: Putting up a tent is a good exercise for small children. They will need much help and adult supervision, but once the project is completed, they will have a great place to play. Help your child and a few of her/his peers put up a small tent in your backyard or in your child's bedroom.

Share!

When you were a preschooler and you and your friends had a gathering to build, you would:

_____

_____

Celebrate!

Celebrate your four-year-old's self-care abilities.

By age four, except for cutting up meat, most children can feed themselves completely. Preschoolers can talk and eat at the same time because they no longer have to try so hard or think about the eating process.

From age 4 to 5 you will observe that your child:
- May have only a fair appetite
- Will have an increase in appetite toward age five
- Will be able to drink milk rapidly and well
- If left to eat alone, may dawdle
- Likes social eating situations best

Play!

Ants on a Log

Why this playtime activity is good for your child: Children this age enjoy preparing their own snacks. They love the kitchen, and food is a highly motivating and great learning tool.

What you'll need to make this recipe: celery sticks, peanut butter, raisins

How to make *Ants on a Log*: Prepare ahead of time–wash and cut celery sticks. Using a spoon, have your child fill the celery sticks with peanut butter. Poke "ants" (raisins) along the top of the peanut butter covered "logs."

Variations:

Cheese and Crackers–Cheese and crackers are a healthy snack. Place cheese slices (cut in quarters) between two soda crackers sandwich-style.

Jelly Pinwheels–Use a plastic, serrated knife to trim the crust off four slices of bread. Roll the bread flat with a rolling pin. Spread each with a layer of jam. Roll up jelly-roll-style. Cut into three slices, and place on a plate with jelly pinwheels showing.

Share!

When you were a preschooler your favorite thing to make in the kitchen was:

_____

This is how you made it: _____

Celebrate!

Celebrate your four-year-old's learning about safety.

Four-year-olds' self-control, judgment, and coordination are still developing. Adult supervision remains essential for children in this age range. Preschoolers can usually play safely alone in their bedrooms, but must be supervised when playing outdoors.

From age 4 to 5 you must be cautious because your child:

- Might unknowingly chase a ball into traffic
- Might run ahead and get lost in busy public places
- Might climb to heights where s/he cannot safely get down

Play!

What Might Happen Next?

Why this playtime activity is good for your child: Children this age need to be carefully led into thinking about the sequence of events and consequences of actions.

What you'll need to play this activity: picture books

How to play _What Might Happen Next?_: Sit your youngster on your lap or on the floor in front of you. Open a picture book and begin reading the story. Before turning each page, ask your child, "What might happen next?" Praise your child's imagination and foresight.

Variation: Give your child everyday, real life situations, and ask her/him, "What might happen next?" Talk about the dangerous consequences of each of the following:

Examples:

1. A little boy is playing in his front yard with a rubber ball. When the ball rolls out into the street, without looking, the boy runs into the street to get the ball. What might happen next?

2. A little girl finds a jar of liquid in the garage. It is pink, and she thinks it might be good to drink. She opens the jar, and the smell is terrible. She is thirsty and decides to taste it. What might happen next?

Share!

When you were a preschooler and we talked about dangerous situations, you responded by:

_____

_____

Celebrate!

Celebrate your four-year-old's health and well-being.

As your child gets older, traveling by car will become more and more challenging. If your child doesn't cooperate, say for example s/he refuses to wear a seat belt, do not start the car until s/he is fastened in the car seat. There should never be an exception to that rule!

From age 4 to 5 you will observe that your child:

- Might object to seat belts and car seat
- Might unbuckle seat belts and crawl out while car is in motion

Play!

Look For Something That Sounds Like . . .

Why this playtime activity is good for your child: Four-year-olds travel better and more willingly if they are distracted. This game will keep your child occupied looking around and reinforce rhyming sounds while driving in the car.

What you'll need to play this activity: No special equipment is needed to play this game.

How to play *Look For Something That Sounds Like . . .*: As you are driving along, ask your child to find something that sounds like (rhymes with) another word. When s/he sees the rhyming object, s/he points to it and names it.

Examples:
Find something that sounds like *pie.* (sky)
Find something that sounds like *toad.* (road)
Find something that sounds like *fine.* (sign)
Find something that sounds like *bee.* (tree)
Find something that sounds like *loud.* (cloud)
Find something that sounds like *far.* (car)
Find something that sounds like *fan.* (man)
Find something that sounds like *toy.* (boy)
Find something that sounds like *curl.* (girl)
Find something that sounds like *log.* (dog)

Share!

When you were a preschooler and we played the rhyming game in the car, you would:

Celebrate!

Celebrate your four-year-old's abilities and play interests.

For the four-year-old, certain adult tools are motivational. Most children this age enjoy playing with real screwdrivers, lightweight hammers, flashlights, magnifying glasses, eggbeaters, and digging with garden tools.

From age 4 to 5 you will observe that your child's:

- Fine motor skills allow her/him to use tools correctly
- Special interests will begin to emerge
- Positive self-esteem will be enhanced when s/he learns to do new things

Play!

Strawberries and Whipped Cream

Why this playtime activity is good for your child: By age four, children have enough fine motor skills to operate an eggbeater, and they are fascinated to make the eggbeaters work.

What you'll need to play this activity: whipping cream; strawberries; sugar; vanilla

How to make *Strawberries and Whipped Cream:* Place several large strawberries in a colander. Let your child rinse them under cold water. Show your child how to pull the stems off of each berry. Using a plastic, serrated knife, have your child slice the berries in several pieces. Place the berry pieces in a small bowl and set aside. Pour the whipping cream into a bowl. Show your child how to turn the handle of the eggbeater to whip the cream. If s/he gets tired, take turns whipping the cream. When the cream is stiff, add a tablespoon (15 ml) of sugar and a teaspoon (5 ml) of vanilla. (Be careful your child doesn't keep beating the cream after it is whipped or it will turn to butter.) Place the berries in the whipped cream and stir.

Variation #1: Make instant pudding–Following the directions on the back of a small box of instant pudding, add milk to the pudding mix. Stir. Then help your child use an eggbeater to whip the pudding until thick. Chill.

Variation #2: Make honey butter–Combine equal parts butter and honey. Stir. Use an eggbeater to whip the mixture into honey butter. Use honey butter on toast, hot biscuits, or waffles.

Share!

The first time you used an eggbeater to make whipped cream, this is what happened:

Celebrate!

Celebrate your four-year-old's natural artistic abilities.

Creativity is learned in the early years. The more art supplies you can supply for your four-year-old, the more opportunities s/he will have to celebrate her/his artistic talents and plant creative seeds that will grow throughout her/his lifetime.

From age 4 to 5 you will observe that your child:

- Will enjoy making collages with paste, cardboard, old magazine pictures, and scissors
- Will enjoy molding with clay/dough and tools
- Will enjoy playing with a chalkboard and large chalk
- Will enjoy using paper and markers to create a variety of projects

Play!

Paper Bag Pig Puppets

Why this playtime activity is good for your child: Paper bag pig puppets are easy and fun to make. Then, use them to tell stories and put on puppet shows.

What you'll need to play this activity: lunch-size paper bags; pencil; white craft glue or glue stick; construction paper; child safety scissors; markers

How to make *Paper Bag Pig Puppets:* Help your child sketch where the pig's eyes, nose, and mouth will be on the bottom flap of a paper bag. Cut construction paper circles for eyes, nose, and nostrils. Help your child glue them in place. Draw on the mouth with a marker. Glue little, paper triangle cutouts for ears on the top edges of the bag's bottom flap. To give the pig clothes, decorate with buttons and bow-shaped paper cutouts down the front of the bag.

Variation: Use a large cardboard box for a puppet stage. Cut away the entire top of the box for the rear of stage. Lay the box on its side. Cut a large opening in the bottom of the box for the stage. Paint the box with poster paint. When the stage is dry, set it on a table, and present a puppet show in style.

Share!

When you were a preschooler and you played with puppets, you would: _____

_____

_____

Celebrate!

Celebrate your four-year-old's interest in books.

Children in this age range enjoy picture books, simple stories, rhymes (abundant with detailed illustrations), and complex pop-up books. Although many four-year-olds sincerely want to learn to read and will begin to recognize certain familiar words, there is no hurry to teach your child to read. At this stage of development it is better to provide a rich, varied source of books and invite your child to look at the pictures and hear you read the stories.

From age 4 to 5 you will observe that your child:

- Will enjoy wild stories
- Will like to hear silly and humorous, nonsense stories
- Will enjoy informational books

Play!

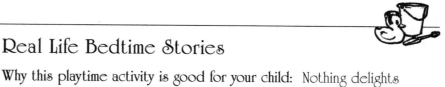

Real Life Bedtime Stories

Why this playtime activity is good for your child: Nothing delights children this age more than hearing true stories, either about her/himself, her/his parents, or people the child knows.

What you'll need to play this activity: Nothing is needed to play this game except a good memory of your own childhood or someone's that you know.

How to share *Real Life Bedtime Stories:* Prepare ahead by reminiscing about something that happened to you when you were a child. Go over the details in your mind so you will be ready to share the real life tale with your child at bedtime.

Variation #1: Four-year-olds cannot remember things they did when they were babies of two or even three. Sharing a funny event in her/his past will delight and amuse your youngster. This kind of sharing is a good way to let your child know how much s/he is developing and growing in her/his abilities. For example: "When you were nine months old, and I left you on a blanket in the yard, you ate a big bug."

Variation #2: Strengthen family bonds by sharing real life stories about other family members, too. How Mother and Father met and fell in love is a story many girls this age are interested in hearing over and over. A boy may enjoy hearing about interesting jobs that Grandfather and Father performed when they were youngsters.

Share!

When you were a preschooler, your favorite real life story was: _____

_____

Celebrate!

Celebrate your four-year-old's cognitive skills.

Everything a four-year-old does is an example of her/his mind in action. It is not necessary for a four-year-old to know the letters of the alphabet or recognize numerals before s/he goes to kindergarten. Fear of failing can make children anxious and sometimes leads to stuttering or low self-esteem. When your child makes a language mistake, repeat the sentence correctly so s/he can hear it spoken correctly, but do not emphasize the mistake or point out the correction. For example, if your child says, "I put the socks on my feets," you might say, "You put the socks on your feet."

From age 4 to 5 you will observe that your child:

- Will have an insatiable curiosity about everything around her/him
- Uses conversations to enrich her/his life and relationships
- Has enough understanding of the relationship of parts to the whole to be able to tell what is missing from an ordinary object

Play!

What's Missing?

Why this playtime activity is good for your child: Practice in remembering a series of items as a whole will help develop your preschooler's cognitive skills.

What you'll need to play this activity: tray; cloth cover for tray; six or seven items

How to play *What's Missing?*: Place six or seven items that relate to a theme (see suggestions below) on a tray. Cover them with a cloth. Then have your child sit on the floor or at a worktable in front of the tray. Remove the cover, and let your child study the items on the tray. Talk about them. How do they all relate? Then have your child close her/his eyes. Remove one object from the tray, and put it under the cloth. When your child opens her/his eyes, ask, "What's missing?"

Theme Suggestions: Sports, Kitchen, Toys, Art Supplies, Clothing, Rainy Weather Gear, Tools, Fruit

Variation: After your child gets good at playing this game, play it another way. Uncover the six or seven items. Give your child several minutes to memorize what is on the tray. Then cover the tray again. Have your child name the items that s/he remembers seeing.

Share!

When you were a preschooler and we played What's Missing? you liked to:

Celebrate!

Celebrate your four-year-old's high level of energy.

Four-year-olds have tremendous energy. They have no sense of property. To a four-year-old, all things seem to belong to her/him. Children this age are not thieves or liars; they simply believe that possession means ownership.

From age 4 to 5 you will observe that your child:
- May prefer hopping, running, or somersaulting to walking
- May be learning how to skip with alternating feet

Play!

Making a Parade

Why this playtime activity is good for your child: Four-year-olds are the happiest when engaged in active gross motor play, preferably out-of-doors.

What you'll need to play this activity: Hand-held instruments such as whistles, fifes, bells, or kazoos will add to a parade. You will need a drum for the leader of the parade to keep the beat, and a recording of some good marching music.

How to play *Making a Parade*: This activity will be fun for you and your child, but it will be even more fun if your child has several friends or siblings to make the parade a bit longer. Before putting on the music, pass out the instruments. Remember, the leader will need a drum. If you don't have a drum, use a pot and strike it with a wooden spoon or homemade mallet. The basic drum beat is to keep everyone in step. It should be loud and booming but not so loud that it drowns out the other instruments. Begin the music and step off with the left foot. Practice marching in place to the music for awhile before proceeding with the parade.

Good marching songs:

"When the Saints Go Marching In"   "Yankee Doodle"
"Grand Old Flag"   "Strike Up the Band"
"Yellow Submarine"

Share!

When you were a preschooler and you marched in parades, you especially enjoyed:

_____

Your favorite marching song was:_____

Your favorite marching instrument was:_____

Celebrate!

Celebrate your four-year-old's safety and well-being.

Children this age act impulsively without thinking. They are easily distracted and rush into unsafe situations. For preschoolers, safety rules must be taught and reinforced often until they become second nature.

From age 4 to 5 you will observe that your child:

- Might run ahead when out in public and get lost without thinking
- Might rush out into traffic to retrieve a ball
- Might cross a street without looking both ways

Play!

Red Means Stop!

Why this playtime activity is good for your child: Incorporating safety rules into everyday games will give your child practice using the rules.

What you'll need to play this activity: newspaper; five small paper plates; red, green, and yellow poster paint; paint brush; glue; long, cardboard, gift wrap tube

How to play *Red Means Stop!:* Before you play this game, have your child help you create a traffic light. Cover the work surface with newspaper. Glue the paper plates to the gift wrap tube. Let dry. Paint the top plate red. Paint the center plate yellow. Paint the bottom plate green. Let dry. Teach your child that *red* means "stop," *yellow* means "slow down and stop," and *green* means "proceed but use caution." When playing the game, place the traffic light in the dirt outside near a tricycle path. Hold the two extra plates to cover two of the colored "lights" so just one is showing at a time. Have your child follow the commands of the "light" as s/he approaches the "intersection" on a tricycle.

Variation: Talk to your child about what to do if s/he becomes lost in a busy place. Who is safe to approach? What should the child say? (Does your child know her/his full name and your name?) A few four-year-olds know their telephone numbers, but most do not.

Share!

When you were a preschooler and we played traffic light, you would: _____

_____

Celebrate!

Celebrate your four-year-old's exploration and mastery of play materials.

From age 4 to 5 you will observe that your child:

- Will especially enjoy fantasy play in sand/water
- Will enjoy playing in the water–bathtub, sprinklers, pool, etc.

Play!

Sandbox Fun

Why this playtime activity is good for your child: Sand and water play is especially appropriate for the four-year-old.

What you'll need to play this activity: large, plastic tubs for sand and water play, plus an extra tub for storing sand tools; tools such as funnels, strainers, tubes, mills, molds, and water pump

How to have *Sandbox Fun:* If you don't have a sandbox, a child-size pool of sand or large dishpan full of sand will provide hours of fun for your four-year-old. Here are some sand games to try with your preschooler:

Sand Castles–When building sand castles, the sand must be very wet. Use molds such as plastic glasses and small bowls to mold sand castles. Your child will need plenty of water to keep the sand wet. Add sticks, seashells, and other natural objects to the sand castle scene.

Sandbox Paintings–Food coloring stirred in sand will change its color. Add drops of food coloring to the sand and stir with a wooden spoon. Create large sand designs by coloring areas of sand with different colors.

Sandbox Villages–Use a sandbox. miniature plastic people, and wooden blocks to create a village. The sand will keep people and buildings erect. Roads can be added by smoothing the sand between the buildings.

Share!

When you were a preschooler, your favorite game to play in the sandbox was:

_____

This is how you played the game: _____

_____

_____

Celebrate!

Celebrate your four-year-old's good, healthy body.

By around four years, since children have the vocabulary to describe different sounds, they can take a hearing test. Children this age can also understand directions and cooperate well enough for a formal vision screening. One way to teach your child about good health habits is to let her/him know how wonderful her/his body is. Celebrate your child's beautiful, miraculous body.

From age 4 to 5 you will observe that your child:

- Should have vision of 20/40 or better, which will improve to 20/30 by age five
- Should be given a DTP; one was given around 18 months
- Should see a pediatrician once a year

Play!

I'm an Extraordinary Musical Instrument

Why this playtime activity is good for your child: This activity will teach your child that her/his body is an extraordinary musical instrument all ready to make music.

What you'll need to play this activity: No special equipment is needed to play this game.

How to play *I'm an Extraordinary Musical Instrument*: Explain to your child that from the tip of her/his head to the bottom of her/his feet, s/he is filled with musical powers waiting to be expressed. Show your child how to make a variety of sounds with her/his body. How many new ones can you think of? How many can your child invent?

> **Face**–Pop cheeks, bibble lips, drum face
>
> **Mouth, Lips, and Tongue**–Whistle, sing, hoot, click, squeak, whisper, hum, chant, yodel
>
> **Hands and Fingers**–Clap, slap, rap, click fingers, rub hands together fast like sand blocks, strum on table
>
> **Feet and Toes**–Tap, stomp, drum, shuffle
>
> **Heart**–Keeps the beat and rhythm of body

Variation: Use your musical instrument–body sounds–to keep time to original songs sung to the familiar tune "Jingle Bells."

Share!

When you were a preschooler and you used your body as a musical instrument, you would:

_____

_____

_____

Celebrate!

Celebrate your four-year-old's developing audio/visual interests.

Live piano music is appropriate for children this age. They also enjoy recorded music for their singing, movement, dancing, and imaginative play activities.

From age 4 to 5 you will observe that your child:

- Will enjoy recorded music used with rhythm instruments
- Will enjoy recorded music, songs, rhymes, and stories for listening
- Will enjoy short, high-quality films and videos, such as those that show animals in their natural environments

Play!

Sing-Along, Skip-Along

Why this playtime activity is good for your child: Youngsters this age especially enjoy games that combine singing and moving around.

What you'll need to play this activity: No special equipment is needed to play this game.

How to play *Sing-Along, Skip-Along:* Use the words to the song "The Mulberry Bush" to practice different body movements. Begin by teaching your child the words to the song and the ways it can be varied with new verbs. (See the examples below.) As you sing the song, move like the verb you are singing in the song.

The Mulberry Bush
This is the way we wash our clothes,
Wash our clothes, wash our clothes.
This is the way we wash our clothes,
Early in the morning.

Other Verses:
This is the way we skip around, . . .
This is the way we clap our hands, . . .
This is the way we stomp our feet, . . .
This is the way we sing a song, . . .
This is the way we tap our toes, . . .
This is the way we reach up high, . . .
This is the way we whisper quietly, . . .

Share!

When you were a preschooler, you enjoyed singing songs like: _____

_____

Celebrate!

Celebrate your four-year-old's developing self-esteem.

An extremely important part of any four-year-old's individuality is her/his sense of self–the way s/he feels about her/himself. The best way to help your child feel good about her/himself is to let your child know that you like her/him and that what s/he does pleases you. Arrange learning situations where your child will glean a lot of success. Encourage your child to be a good person in her/his own way without trying to make her/him into something or someone else.

From age 4 to 5 you will observe that your child:

- Will begin to recognize and verbalize her/his own feelings
- Will be proud of her/his own accomplishments
- Will be highly motivated to understand her/his own feelings

Play!

One, Two, Buckle My Shoe

Why this playtime activity is good for your child: When you celebrate your youngster's milestones it will boost her/his positive self-esteem.

What you'll need to play this activity: your child's shoes

How to play One, Two, Buckle My Shoe: Use this rhyme when you and your child are putting on her/his shoes. Don't ask her/him to memorize the words; just recite them and someday s/he will be counting along as s/he performs dressing skills.

One, Two, Buckle My Shoe
One, two, buckle my shoe;
Three, four, shut the door;
Five, six, pick up sticks;
Seven, eight, lay them straight;
Nine, ten, a good fat hen;
Eleven, twelve, who will delve;
Thirteen, fourteen, maids are courting;
Fifteen, sixteen, maids are kissing;
Seventeen, eighteen, maids are waiting;
Nineteen, twenty, my stomach's empty.

Share!

When you were this old, you began learning how to put on your own shoes: _____

When you were this old, you began learning to tie your shoes: _____

When you were this old, you began counting: _____

Celebrate!

Celebrate your four-year-old's vivid imagination.

Four-year-olds' dramatic play is of the most creative sort. No game of pretend is too "far-out" for children this age. Preschoolers enjoy playing monsters, astronauts, robbers, storekeepers, doctors, pirates, etc. Dressing up is a very popular pastime for children this age. Boys enjoy games where they can be people such as cowboys or astronauts. Girls often prefer to play wedding and be the bride, or house and be "Mother." Children this age spend a great deal of time talking about monsters, dragons, and other imaginary people.

From age 4 to 5 you will observe that your child:

- Will enjoy playing with dolls
- Will often play games based in familiar settings such as home or school
- Will enjoy playing store and "selling" things to each other

Play!

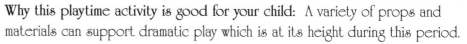

Dress Up

Why this playtime activity is good for your child: A variety of props and materials can support dramatic play which is at its height during this period.

What you'll need to play this activity: full-length mirror, wide variety of props, and dress up clothes

How to play *Dress Up:* Provide a full-length mirror and a variety of dress-up clothes with different themes. Goodwill, Grandma's attic, costume shops, and toy stores are good sources for interesting costumes. Change the clothes in the dress-up box after a few weeks. Variety is the key.

Examples of costume themes:

Sports–football helmet, ball cap, knee pads, sports equipment

Fairy Tales–crown, cape, magic wand, costumes decorated with glitter and gems

Astronaut–helmet, one piece jump suit, goggles

Dancers–tutu, soft slippers, tap shoes, top hat, music

Western–cowboy hat, boots, harmonica, banjo, rope, stick horse

Farmer–straw hat, gardening tools, wheelbarrow

Share!

When you were a preschooler and you dressed up, your favorite thing to pretend was:

Celebrate!

Celebrate your four-year-old's motor skills.

Four-year-olds are fairly proficient at a variety of catch-and-throw games. However, they do not have the coordination or the interest to play group or team ball games with competition and rules.

From age 4 to 5 you will observe that your child:

- Will be able to kick a ball from a stationary position
- Will be able to catch a large ball if it is tossed gently
- Will be able to throw a ball underhand
- Will be able to bat a ball from a stationary position

Play!

Tee-Ball

Why this playtime activity is good for your child: Batting a moving target is very difficult and almost impossible for a four-year-old. But, tapping a ball off of a tee with a large, plastic bat is something children this age can learn.

What you'll need to play this activity: lightweight (hollow plastic) softball; large, plastic bat (with constant supervision); Tee-ball stand

How to play *Tee-Ball:* Have your child bat the ball off the tee and run to a base. The base might be a tree or spot marked on the ground. Try to retrieve the ball and tag the child before s/he touches the base and scores a point. Take turns being batter and catcher.

Variation #1: Play kick ball by having your child kick a stationary ball and then run to a base. The other player retrieves the ball and tries to tag the runner before s/he can touch the base.

Variation #2: Give your child lots of practice throwing, batting, and catching a variety of sizes and shapes of balls. Foam footballs are fun to toss back and forth. Try batting tennis balls with tennis rackets.

Share!

When you were a preschooler and you played Tee-ball, you would: _____

_____

_____

Your favorite ball game was: _____

Celebrate!

Celebrate your four-year-old's maturing social skills.

Most four-year-olds have an active social life. They have many friends and may even have a best friend. A child this age may do things that are considered socially unacceptable such as sticking out her/his tongue, making faces, and saying obnoxious things. The only way your child can learn how to be social is to have friends and spend time interacting with them. Always supervise play between youngsters, but do not be quick to jump in to settle differences. As much as possible, let children verbally work out their differences.

From age 4 to 5 you will observe that your child:

- Will like entertaining friends in her/his home
- Will begin acting out like her/his friends
- Will be establishing positive or negative self-esteem

Play!

Unbirthday Party

Why this playtime activity is good for your child: When your child turns four and a half, celebrate her/his half birthday with an unbirthday party. (No present required.) It will give your child an opportunity to socialize and entertain her/his friends in a pleasurable way.

What you'll need to play this activity: unbirthday cake such as cupcakes decorated with "dirt" (chocolate cookie crumbs) and "worms" (candy worms); a candle for each cupcake; ice cream

How to have an *Unbirthday Party*: Invite two or three of your child's peers to share cake and ice cream and celebrate the unbirthday. Before the party, let your child help you decorate the cupcakes with "dirt" and "worms." Ice each cupcake with chocolate icing. Your child can use a rolling pin to make the cookie crumbs. Then sprinkle the cupcakes with chocolate cookie crumbs. Position several candy worms on each cupcake so that it looks as though the worms are crawling out of the ground. Put a candle on each cupcake. When the guests arrive, play some run-around games like tag, hide-and-seek, or "Red Rover, Red Rover." When it is time to eat, take turns singing "Happy Unbirthday" to each guest. Then light everyone's candle on her/his cupcake so that everyone has a chance to make a wish and blow out a candle. After all, it is everyone's unbirthday!

Share!

When you were four and a half years old and you had an unbirthday party, this is what it was like:

_____

_____

These are the children who came to your unbirthday party:_____

Celebrate!

Celebrate your four-year-old's skill-development.

Four-year-olds need a great deal of play materials designed for matching, sorting, and ordering (by color, shape, size, texture, aroma, taste, picture, number, letter, or other category concepts such as "fruits" or "animals.")

From age 4 to 5 you will observe that your child:

• Will enjoy playing with geometrical concept materials, including simple shapes and fraction materials
• Will enjoy measuring materials such as a balance scale and graded cups for measuring liquids
• Will enjoy simple mechanical devices such as gears, levers, and pulleys

Play!

What Cries?

Why this playtime activity is good for your child: Most children this age can respond correctly to simple categorical questions like "What cries?" Those who can't answer the questions yet will enjoy the challenge and discussion that takes place during the game.

What you'll need to play this activity: No special equipment is needed to play this game.

How to play *What Cries?*: Ask your child categorical questions, and help her/him come up with several answers that fit the category. If this activity is too difficult for your child, use picture books of animals or magazines with people as visual clues.

Examples:

What cries?–babies, sad people, an animal that is hurt
What swims?–fish, people, frogs
What sleeps?–babies, people, bears, animals
What flies?–fly, airplane, birds, bats
What has eyes?–people, animals, potatoes, needles
What needs water?–people, animals, plants

Share!

When you were a preschooler and we played categorical question games, you especially enjoyed the category:

_____

You played the game like this:_____

_____

Celebrate!

Celebrate your four-year-old's developing sense of responsibility.

Preschoolers glean a great deal of pleasure and experience about life when they care for a family pet. Four-year-olds will learn about responsibility when caring for a cat, dog, or other simple and relatively undemanding pets such as snakes, frogs, lizards, or turtles. Caring for sturdy plants can also provide a certain amount of practice in responsibility.

From age 4 to 5 you will observe that your child:

- May need to be reminded regarding the feeding and watering of a pet or plant
- May need a parent to take the major responsibility for the pet's or plant's health
- Will feel good about an animal or plant growing because of the care s/he provides

Play!

Plant a Garden

Why this playtime activity is good for your child: No matter what a person's age, it is a healing process to see seeds turn into plants, which grow and bloom.

What you'll need to play this activity: pots filled with potting soil or a flower bed; flower or vegetable seeds

How to *Plant a Garden*: Talk with your child about planting a garden. Ask your child, "Do you want to grow flowers or vegetables?" Let your child help you cultivate a small space in your yard, or if you choose to grow an indoor garden, fill some planters with potting mix. Go to a nursery or hardware store, and let your child pick the kind of vegetable or flower seeds s/he wants to grow. Once home, read the directions on the back of the seed package to your child. Use your fingers to poke holes in the ground and plant the seeds. Water the seeds. Place the pots in a warm, sunny place. Check each day to make sure the soil is moist. When the plants begin to poke through the soil, discuss their growth. Each day look at the plants and discuss their progress with your child.

Share!

When you were a preschooler and we decided to plant a garden, this is what you chose to grow:

_____

_____

This is what you did:_____

_____

_____

Celebrate!

Celebrate your four-year-old's emerging scientific curiosity.

Four-year-olds continue to enjoy playing with natural materials such as rocks, seashells, seeds, and leaves. Many begin serious play on computer software/hardware by age four.

From age 4 to 5 you will observe that your child:

- Will especially enjoy playing with a magnifying glass and prism
- Will enjoy viewing objects using special equipment like telescopes and microscopes
- Will enjoy playing with a flashlight, kaleidoscope, periscope, and stethoscope

Play!

Scientific Experiments

Why this playtime activity is good for your child: Early exposure to scientific principles such as capillary action, absorption, friction, jet propulsion, and magnetic attraction will increase your child's scientific curiosity. There are a number of simple science experiments you can demonstrate for your child which need only common household objects. Don't demonstrate more than one principle during a session. Use the proper name for each scientific principle you are demonstrating.

What you'll need to play this activity: Check each experiment to determine what you will need.

How to conduct *Scientific Experiments*: Gather the needed equipment, then demonstrate the principle. Give your child time to experience the principle for her/himself.

Simple Scientific Experiments:

Capillary Action–Fill two glasses half-full of water. Use food coloring to color one dark red and the other dark blue. (To make certain your water is dark enough, use several drops of food coloring.) Cut a celery stick up the middle, halfway up the stick. Put half of the celery into the red liquid and the other half into the blue liquid. Leave overnight. The next day discuss the color change of the celery.

Spectrum of Color–Place a full glass of water on a window ledge in bright sunshine. Allow the glass to hang over a little on the inside edge of the ledge. If the sun is shining on the glass, there will be a spectrum band or rainbow of colors projected onto the floor. Discuss the colors of the band with your child. "What color is at the top?" "Bottom?" Talk about rainbows.

Share!

When you were a preschooler, one of your favorite scientific experiments was:_____

Celebrate!

Celebrate your four-year-old developing a strong self-concept.

Four-year-olds enjoy boasting of their own abilities: "See me jump high." "I can count and write my name." "I can stand on my head; watch me!" Providing things that your child can do well will help her/him develop a positive self-image. Games and toys should allow your child plenty of opportunities for successful play.

From age 4 to 5 you will observe that your child:

- Will ask for help learning how to do something
- If not complimented by adults, will praise her/himself
- Will feel exaggerated pride with new accomplishments
- Will enjoy telling adults what s/he can do

Play!

NATHAN'S
"can do"
List

1. run
2. Jump
3. skip
4. throw ball
5. Count to 10
6. Knows his A-B-C's
7. Climb
8. Loves Books
9. Swings
10. helps cook

Can Do!

Why this playtime activity is good for your child: Acknowledging your child's developmental skills and abilities will give her/him a sense of well-being. Listing and posting a written acknowledgment of your child's newly acquired abilities will help build her/his positive self-image. Add to the list as your child learns new skills.

What you'll need to play this activity: a long sheet of paper such as shelf liner; markers

How to play Can Do!: Tell your child how impressed you are with all the new things s/he has learned to do. At the top of a long sheet of paper (2 to 4 feet or 62 to 124 centimeters long) write your child's name and the words "Can Do." Encourage your child to help you list some of her/his skills. For example: talk, walk, run, kick a ball, drink from a cup, etc.

Number each accomplishment and write them in a variety of colors so the list is pleasant to view. Hang the list where everyone can see it, perhaps on the refrigerator door. As family members read the list, ask them to think of additional skills to add to the list. When the paper is full, roll it up, tie it with a ribbon, date it, and place it in a safe place. Begin a new list for the things your child is learning each day. Celebrate all of your child's accomplishments and s/he will grow to know that s/he is capable.

Share!

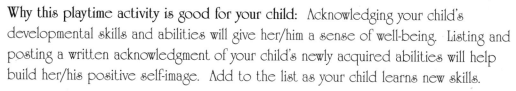

When you were a preschooler and we made a list of things you could do, it included:

_____

_____

Celebrate!

Celebrate your four-year-old's health and physical growth.

Children this age begin to understand that eating is a natural response to hunger. They usually enjoy mealtime and have healthy attitudes toward food and nutrition.

From age 4 to 5 you will observe that your child:

- Will no longer use eating or not eating to demonstrate defiance
- Will be good company at mealtimes
- Will know and practice basic table manners

Play!

I Have a Little Shadow

Why this playtime activity is good for your child: One good way to celebrate your child's physical growth is to look at her/his shadow. Children this age love to look and play with their shadows. Shadows can grow tall or become miniature in the same day.

What you'll need to play this activity: flashlight; dark room

How to play *I Have a Little Shadow*: Go into a dark room with your child. Turn on the flashlight and place it on a table or surface. Show your child how to put her/his hand in front of the flashlight. Observe the shadow of your child's hand. Have your child move her/his hand toward the flashlight. Does the shadow get larger or smaller? Move the flashlight away from your child's hand. Does the shadow get larger or smaller?

Variation #1: Use hands and a flashlight to make shadows in the shapes of animal bodies. Can your child guess the animal shape?

Variation #2: Have your child sit on a chair directly in front of a wall. Have the flashlight placed so you can get a clear shadow of her/his profile. Tape a black sheet of paper to the wall where the profile falls. Draw the shadow of your child's profile on the black paper. Cut it out and paste it on a sheet of white paper.

Variation #3: Take a walk on a sunny day. Look at shadows of people, trees, buildings, and animals. Have your child take note of her/his shadow.

Share!

When you were a preschooler and we played with shadows, your favorite thing to do was:

_____

_____

Celebrate!

Celebrate your four-year-old's creative and artistic abilities.

When shopping for art supplies for your four-year-old think COLORFUL. An assortment of colorful paints, markers, and paper will delight the child this age. Preschoolers enjoy creating directed projects as well as original works of art.

From age 4 to 5 you will observe that your child:

- Will enjoy coloring with large nontoxic crayons and markers
- Will enjoy painting with various sizes of paintbrushes and different kinds of paint
- Will enjoy using an assortment of large sheets of colored paper
- Can handle a pair of blunt-ended safety scissors
- Can use glue sticks and paste

Play!

Jeweled Crowns

Why this playtime activity is good for your child: Four-year-olds enjoy fantasy play, and crowns are great costumes for make-believe play. With a little help, your child can easily make a crown.

What you'll need to play this activity: light cardboard; aluminum foil; construction paper cutouts; plastic gemstones; glitter; glue; stapler

How to make *Jeweled Crowns*: Prepare the basic crown ahead of time. Use scissors to cut a band of light cardboard 12 inches (31 centimeters) wide. Measure the length to fit around your child's head (with a little extra for overlapping). Then cut a zigzag shape into the top of the crown. Let your child wrap the crown in aluminum foil. Decorate with plastic gems, paper cutouts, and glitter. Overlap the ends and staple together.

Variation: Make a crown of paper or plastic flowers, or braid and weave daisies or dandelions together to make a lei which can be worn like a crown in the hair.

Share!

When you were a preschooler and you made a crown, it looked like this: _____

_____

_____

_____

_____

Celebrate!

Celebrate your four-year-old's musical talents.

Children this age show a great increase of skill, and respond to music with increasing interest. Their musical skills increase dramatically during the preschool years.

From age 4 to 5 you will observe that your child:
- Will spend a great deal of time singing
- Will move to the beat of music when s/he hears it
- Will have preferences for certain kinds of music

Play!

Tap Dancing

Why this playtime activity is good for your child: Dancing feet are happy feet, and children, this age especially, like to make a sound when they dance.

What you'll need to play this activity: You can make tap shoes by gluing pennies (or quarters, or slugs) on the toes and heels of old sneakers. You will need to use very strong glue such as an epoxy or a hot glue gun so the coins won't fall off. Glue three coins on each toe and one on each heal.

How to play *Tap Dancing:* There are basic movements of tap dancing. Try teaching your child some of these:

Step–Step down on one foot like taking an ordinary step.

Stamp–Pick up a foot and stamp it hard in front.

Shuffle–Lift a foot off the floor a little and kick it forward. Slap the sole of the foot on the floor, then pull the foot back and slap the sole on the way back. (This step is a 1-2 count.)

Slap–Make a tiny kick and slap the sole down on the floor in front. This is a moving forward step.

Ball–Put the ball of the foot on the floor.

Heel–Lift the heel without lifting the rest of the foot, and click it down on the floor.

Share!

When you were a preschooler and you tried tap dancing, you would: _____

_____

Celebrate!

Celebrate your four-year-old's role-playing and fantasy play.

Children in this age range enjoy rich fantasy play and have a voracious appetite for the dramatic. Relevant role-playing materials to support this fantasy play include: dress-up materials (hats, capes, grown-up clothes), role-relevant props (cash register, doctor's equipment, office materials, school supplies), miniature housekeeping equipment (stove, refrigerator, ironing board and iron, telephone, pots and pans, flatware, serving dishes, cleaning equipment) and doll equipment (bed, baby carriage, stroller, high chair).

From age 4 to 5 you will observe that your child:

- Can play simple singing games
- Demonstrates increased voice control
- Can recognize and sing whole songs
- Can sing on pitch and keep time

Play!

Fairy Tale Operas

Why this playtime activity is good for your child: Although four-year-olds are beginning to separate fact from fantasy, they still enjoy fairy tales. Dramatizing fairy tales will give preschoolers an opportunity to role-play different characters.

What you'll need to play this activity: To dramatize a fairy tale into an opera will require that your child be knowledgeable about a particular story and enjoy singing.

How to perform fairy tales as operas: Decide on which fairy tale you will do, for example, "Little Red Riding Hood." You do not have to perform the whole story; just rehearse a small scene in the story. You and your child might perform the kitchen scene when Little Red Riding Hood is getting permission to take her grandmother a basket of food. The thing that makes fairy tale operas different from other plays is that there is no talking; all of the lines are sung. In these fairy tale operas, the actors are to make up the lines as they go along.

Example of Red Riding Hood kitchen scene:
Mother: Little Red Riding Hood, why are you putting that food in a basket?
Little Red Riding Hood: I am going to Grandmother's house.
Mother: Little Red Riding Hood, you know I do not like you walking through the woods.
Little Red Riding Hood: Mother, I want to go.
Mother: Little Red Riding Hood, I worry about you.
Little Red Riding Hood: Please Mother, let me go to see Grandmother; she is sick.

Share!

When you were a preschooler, and we did opera fairy tales, you would: _____

Celebrate!

Celebrate your four-year-old's gross motor milestones.

Four-year-olds no longer need to concentrate on the mechanics of walking. Most children this age are agile and use a regular heel-toe motion when walking. Preschoolers walk erect and move easily up and down stairs. Both boys and girls, but especially boys, appreciate any vigorous physical activity. By four-and-a-half, most children can play outside in their own yards unsupervised, with only occasional checking by a parent. Children this age have an abundance of energy, a vivid imagination, and the ability to turn almost anything into a good play opportunity. The outdoors provides them the space needed for active play.

From age 4 to 5 you will observe that your child:

- Will enjoy a jungle gym for hanging upside down or holding on with one hand
- Will need a flat surface for ride-on toys like tricycles
- May still need to make a conscious effort to stand on tiptoes or on one foot
- Will enjoy active games like tag, racing, and playing ball

Play!

Ball

Why this playtime activity is good for your child: Most children this age can catch a large ball and throw a small ball overhand with ease. They enjoy playing with balls and practicing these skills.

What you'll need to play this activity: an assortment of balls such as a beach ball, a foam football, small rubber ball, tennis ball, soccer ball, etc.

How to play *Ball*: When playing ball, let your child choose the ball and the skill to be practiced. A variety of throwing, tossing, catching, and kicking will keep the ball game interesting.

Variation #1: In the warm summertime, passing a water balloon back and forth is exciting and fun. It is a great way to cool off, and most children enjoy the extra excitement added by the possibility of getting wet.

Variation #2: Many children this age enjoy watching others play ball. Take your child to a Little League, professional, or local school ball game. When watching ball games, talk about the equipment and the way the game is scored.

Share!

When you were a preschooler, your favorite ball game was: _____

_____

Celebrate!

Celebrate your four-year-old's love of books.

Books should make up a big part of your four-year-old's play. Many children this age have special favorites and can listen to a single book for an extended time. Preschool children begin to have individual and well-defined tastes in book preferences.

From age 4 to 5 you will observe your child might especially enjoy hearing these stories:

- *Danny and the Dinosaur* by Syd Hoff (New York: Harper & Row)
- *Bedtime for Frances* by Russell Hoban (New York: Harper & Row)
- *Ten, Nine, Eight* by Molly Bang (New York: Greenwillow)
- *Corduroy* by Don Freeman (New York: Viking)
- *The Gingerbread Boy* by Paul Galdone (New York: Houghton Mifflin)
- *Pancakes for Breakfast* by Tomie DePaola (New York: Harcourt Brace Jovanovich, Inc.)

Play!

Bookstore Shopping

Why this outing is good for your child: Most bookstores have a children's book section, and although the public library will have a multitude of titles, the bookstore is where you will find the newest titles. Purchase copies of your child's very favorite books for her/his own private collection.

What you'll need to play this activity: No special equipment is needed for this playtime activity.

How to conduct *Bookstore Shopping:* Go to a bookstore and show your child the children's books. Explain that s/he must look at the books very carefully because they are new and eventually someone will buy each one. Give your child plenty of time to look through the latest arrivals. If possible, let your child choose a book to buy. Make note of titles that your child would like to have so when her/his birthday arrives, you will be able to surprise your child with a favorite new book.

Share!

When you were a preschooler, your favorite books were: _____

_____

_____

_____

Celebrate!

Celebrate your four-year-old's fine motor development.

Four-year-olds need quiet time activities that can help improve their hands' abilities. Activities such as building with blocks; playing with simple jigsaw puzzles and pegboards; stringing large wooden beads; coloring with crayons and chalk; painting; modeling with clay; and dressing and undressing dolls with large zippers, snaps, and laces are all good play activities to reinforce eye-hand coordination.

From age 4 to 5 you will observe that your child:

- Will begin projects with a purpose in mind
- Will be able to play quietly for extended periods of time

Play!

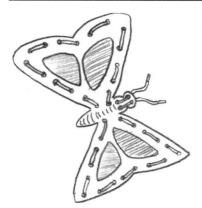

Sewing Cards

Why this playtime activity is good for your child: Sewing is excellent practice for eye-hand coordination and exercises small finger and hand muscles.

What you'll need to play this activity: fine-tip black marker; scissors; long shoelaces; light cardboard; hole punch; patterns of basic shapes

How to make and play *Sewing Cards*: Trace large basic shapes such as a star, heart, or leaf on a sheet of light cardboard. Outline the shape with the marker. Cut out the shape. Using the hole punch, put holes around the edge of shape as far into the center as possible. Tie a knot in one end of a shoelace. Use it to weave in and out of the holes to outline the picture.

Variation: Cut out pictures from magazines and glue them to light cardboard. Punch holes around the edges and "sew" these pictures, too.

Share!

When you were a preschooler and we made sewing cards, you played with them like this:

_____

_____

_____

_____

Celebrate!

Celebrate your four-year-old's self-care skills.

Children this age often dress and undress themselves without much help. Bath time is an easy routine by age four. Children in this age range can wash and dry themselves fairly well. They can do a reasonably good job of brushing teeth, combing hair, and washing and drying their hands and faces.

From age 4 to 5 you will observe that your child:

- May need help distinguishing the front from the back of clothing
- Will probably enjoy choosing clothing and dressing her/himself
- May be able to tie a knot in a shoestring, but may not be able to manage a bow

Play!

Beat the Clock

Why this playtime activity is good for your child: Children this age are highly motivated when they are racing against time.

What you'll need to play this activity: time piece to measure three minutes such as an egg timer, a stopwatch, or a three-minute hour glass

How to play *Beat the Clock*: Make certain your child wants to race against time when doing a self-care activity. Don't challenge your child if s/he doesn't want to play the game. For the child who is willing, clearly state what s/he must do in three minutes. Set the egg timer for three minutes (or tip over the three-minute hour glass or use a stopwatch), and give a signal to begin the race such as "Go!" Make certain the task can be accomplished in the set time limit. It would be too frustrating if the time allowed was not appropriate for the task at hand.

Example of things to try to do in three minutes:

Undress for a bath   Pick up a small amount of toys
Dry off with a towel   Put away a tricycle
Put on socks or shoes   Put crayons back in a box
Brush teeth   Finish drinking a small glass
Comb hair   of juice or milk

Share!

When you were a preschooler and we played Beat the Clock, you would: _____

_____

Celebrate!

Celebrate your four-year-old's physical growth.

The average four-year-old gains 4½ pounds (2.04 kilograms) and grows 2½ inches (64 millimeters) between her/his fourth and fifth birthdays. Mark your child's growth on a growth wall chart every six months. It will be great fun for you and your child to look back and see how much s/he's grown.

From age 4 to 5 you will observe that your child:

- Will continue to lose baby fat and gain muscle
- May begin to look skinny and fragile, but will gradually fill out

Play!

Looking Back

Why this playtime activity is good for your child: Children are proud of the way they grow and develop. Taking time to review photographs of your child's growth and development will be fun and exciting for both you and your child.

What you'll need to play this activity: photographs of your child from birth

How to play *Looking Back***:** Pick three photographs of your child at different developmental stages. Together, look at each photograph. Talk about how old your child was in each photograph. If it is a recent photograph, see if your child remembers where the photograph was taken. Name other people in the photographs. Have your child help you arrange the three photographs in chronological order.

Variation #1: Choose three other photographs to share with your child. Have your child look at the photographs to see if s/he can put them in chronological order.

Variation #2: Share a photograph of you when you were pregnant with your child. Tell your youngster stories about the day you learned you were going to have a baby. Share humorous things that happened to you while you were pregnant.

Variation #3: Look at photographs of you and your spouse when you were children. Show the photographs to your child. Tell your child stories about you when you were her/his age.

Share!

When you were a preschooler and we looked at photographs, you were fascinated that:

_____

_____

Celebrate!

Celebrate your five-year-old's birthday.

Although preschoolers vary widely in individual differences, it would probably be safe to say that this past year has been wild and wonderful! Your "baby" is becoming a person with a very unique personality and distinctive nature. Does s/he have high energy or low drive and limited energy? Is s/he highly focused or does she find it hard to concentrate and settle down to a task for more than a few seconds? Does s/he persevere or flitter from task to task? Is s/he organized from within, or is s/he chiefly influenced by others? Is s/he controlled by her intellect or emotions? Is s/he messy or immaculate? Is your four-year-old a perfectionist or is s/he careless and easily satisfied? No matter where your child falls between these wide ranges, it is perfectly okay! Remember, every child has the right to be exactly who s/he is. S/He is PERFECT–perfectly her/himself.

By age 5 you will observe that your child:

- Will be developing her/his unique personality
- Will have an emerging basic nature
- Will begin dealing with the world in a consistent way
- Will love parties, socializing, and entertaining in her/his own home
- Will demonstrate a strong identification with a play group

Play!

Happy Birthday Five-Year-Old!

Why a birthday party is a good idea for your child: Birthday celebrations are milestones of development punctuated with cake, ice cream, family, and friends. Don't let your child's fifth birthday slip by without a gathering of celebration!

What you'll need for a five-year-old's birthday party: small prizes such as candies, plastic toys, or miniature toy cars; party hats; refreshments; decorations

Planning the party: Children this age enjoy planning parties; however, their ideas may not be feasible. Preschoolers have great imaginations. To a five-year-old, inviting Superman to come to the party and give each guest a flying ride would not seem too unreasonable. Talk over the possibility of entertainment, refreshments, and games with the birthday child. Most children this age have a favorite color, and you may want to use that color when decorating with balloons and streamers.

How to give a five-year-old's birthday party: For a successful party you will need a great deal of planning in advance. Have all materials and props ready before the party begins. Have games and activities planned for every minute. The party should not last more than two hours and accommodate more than six guests. For a good party, the key is to keep everyone busy. Children this age like costume parties and parties with themes. Ask your child to help you make these important decisions about the party. Appropriate party games are found on the next page.

Play!

Relay Races–Races of teams with two or three members is fun for this age group. A box of clothes (identical for each team) at one end of the room that can be put on and then taken off quickly is a good relay game. The box of clothes might include things such as boots, gloves, a coat, and hat.

Follow the Leader–This is a great game for children this age. Add to the fun by giving each member of the parade a musical instrument to play. Then form a line so each child can follow the actions and rhythm of the leader. Let the birthday child be the first leader. Then on a signal, have the leader go to the end of the line, and the next person in line becomes the leader. Give every child a chance to be the leader.

Elephant Walk–Tape pieces of paper in a circle on the floor with a number written on each one. Have the children mimic elephants and march around the circle to the music. When the music stops, everyone stands on a number. Draw a number from a hat, and the child who is standing on the space with the matching number receives a small prize. Prizes might include: individually wrapped chocolates or candies; or prizes such as a comb and brush for a doll, lip balm, crayons, coloring books, miniature toy cars; or party favors.

Treasure Hunt–Children this age love treasure hunts. Hide some treasures such as foil-covered coin-shaped chocolates or plastic jewelry in your backyard. Draw a treasure map and indicate where the treasures are hidden. Copy the maps, and give each team of two children a map. See which team can find the most candies.

Refreshments–Make sure the table is set ahead of time. Small sandwiches, cut with cookie cutter shapes such as stars or hearts; fresh fruit or vegetable sticks; and juice or milk are good refreshments for a birthday party. End by blowing out the candles and serving birthday cake and ice cream. Don't forget to sing the birthday song!

Share!

When you turned five years old and we planned your birthday party, your ideas were:

_____

Your fifth birthday party was: _____

The names of your friends who came to the party were: _____

_____

_____

The games we played at the party were: _____

_____

Your birthday cake was: _____

Celebrate!

Celebrate your five-year-old's gross motor development.

At age five children's gross motor activities are well developed. Children this age are poised and controlled physically. Their eyes and head move simultaneously as they direct their attention to something.

By age 5 to 6 you will observe that your child:

- Can handle a full-size wagon, can balance and steer a scooter
- Will be able to descend stairs and skip with alternating feet
- Will begin learning how to turn and skip a rope

Play!

Jump Rope

Why this playtime activity is good for your child: Jumping rope is good exercise and improves coordination skills.

What you'll need to play this activity: jump rope

How to play *Jump Rope:* Begin by teaching your child to jump an imaginary rope. Hold the imaginary rope out to the sides of the body at shoulder height. Turn the imaginary rope and jump up with both feet off the floor at once when the pretend rope is on the floor. When a real rope is introduced, have your child turn the rope slowly and step over it, and keep repeating this process until it is comfortable to move hands and jump at the same time. Practice this basic activity before actually trying to jump over a fast moving rope. When your child can jump rope, recite some jump rope rhymes while s/he jumps. Jumping on the accented beat (bold syllable or word), try some of the rhymes below. Talk to grandparents, aunts, and uncles to find out which jump rope rhymes they used when they were children. Teach your child these rhymes, too.

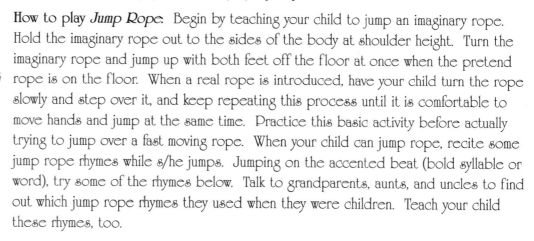

To **mar**ket, to **mar**ket,
To buy a plum **cake**,
Home again, **home** again,
Market is **late**.
To **mar**ket, to **mar**ket,
To buy a plum **bun**,
Home again, **home** again,
Market is **done**.

I **love** my love with an **A**,
Because he is a**gree**able.
I **love** my love with a **B**,
Because he is **beau**tiful!

Share!

When you first learned to jump rope, you enjoyed:

Celebrate!

Celebrate your five-year-old's fine motor skills.

Playing with most types of interlocking building systems such as fitting notched logs, interlocking cogs, snapping or pressing together plastic bricks, inserting flat pieces into slots, using nuts and bolts (2 to 3 inches or 51 to 76 millimeters long), connecting straws, and popping tubes together will all improve your child's emerging eye-hand skills. As s/he "works" to create interesting constructions, your child's self-esteem will grow.

By age 5 to 6 you will observe that your child:

- When drawing, will hold the paper with one hand and the pencil or crayon in the other
- Will enjoy building complex structures with many small blocks
- Will still enjoy playing with small wooden blocks

Play!

Kitchen Cupboard Construction

Why this playtime activity is good for your child: Providing a broad range of opportunities will give your five-year-old an opportunity to explore all of her/his abilities and celebrate her/his creativity.

What you'll need to play this activity: an assortment of foods that can be used for building (See individual projects to note materials needed.)

How to play *Kitchen Cupboard Construction*: Use foods and food-related objects for construction. There are hundreds of ways to combine foods for building materials; below are two projects you will want to try with your child.

Marshmallow Construction Toys–Use miniature marshmallows and grapes to connect spaghetti pasta the way you connect other building toys. Break the pasta into different lengths. For variety, use colored marshmallows and regular-sized marshmallows. For a sturdier construction, dip each pasta end in white glue before sticking it into a marshmallow or grape.

Graham Cracker Barns–Use icing to connect graham cracker squares to create a building. Mix confectioner's sugar with a few drops of water (enough to make a paste). The icing can be used as mortar to hold the walls of the building together. Use with miniature farm animal figures or animal crackers.

Share!

When you were five years old and we built things with food, you liked to:

_____

_____

Celebrate!

Celebrate your five-year-old's language development.

Most preschoolers have a vocabulary of around 1,500 words which will grow by another 1,000 words over the course of the kindergarten year. Language–for its own sake–is now meaningful to the child. Five-year-olds like new words–big words! They will often ask what a word means or how to spell a word.

By age 5 to 6 you will observe that your child:

- Will be able to tell elaborate stories using relatively complex sentences of up to eight words
- Will be able to describe the things s/he wants and relate her/his dreams and fantasies
- May begin to pick up and use swear words

Play!

Word Games

Why this playtime activity is good for your child: Your child is learning language from listening to you and others. Playing word games will increase her/his vocabulary and provide many hours of fun for your child. Playing word games will give you an opportunity to introduce and reinforce new vocabulary.

What you'll need to play this activity: No special equipment is needed for these word games.

How to play Word Games: See the rules for each individual game described below. Make sure your child understands the object of each game. Give your child a chance to ask you questions, too. Play the games on different days; playing them on the same day can be confusing or frustrating for children this age.

Same or Different?– Give your child two words, and have her/him tell you if the words mean the same or are different. Examples: happy–sad; sick–ill; fast–slow; up–down; television–TV; salt–pepper; child–adult

Opposites–Give a word, and have your child name an opposite word. Remember, there will be a variety of acceptable responses. Examples: night–day; dark–light; sad–happy; little–big; cold–hot; boy–girl

Rhymes With–Give your child a word and a clue about another word that rhymes with the word. The child is to name a word that fits both clues. Example: Color that rhymes with bed. (red)

Share!

When you were five years old and we played word games, you especially enjoyed:

Celebrate!

Celebrate your five-year-old's developing social skills.

It is important to remember that your child's friends are not just playmates. Your child's peers will influence her/his thinking and behavior. Most kindergartners want to be well-behaved and usually succeed in doing so. For children this age, each day is a challenge to do everything exactly right.

By age 5 to 6 you will observe that your child:

- Wants to please her/his peers
- Wants to please parents and family
- Will imitate things her/his friends do
- Is more likely to agree to rules than s/he was at age four

Play!

Self-Portrait–Autograph Book

Why this playtime activity is good for your child: Five-year-olds treasure things they have that represent their family and friends. Creating an autograph book with contributions by friends and family will be fun and provide your child with a childhood keepsake.

What you'll need to play this activity: autograph book or 20 sheets of 6-inch (15 centimeter) square paper stapled together along the left-hand edge; colored pencils

How to create a *Self-Portrait–Autograph Book*: Give your child the book, and explain how autograph books are used. Explain that since many of her/his friends cannot write yet, they can draw a self-portrait on the pages. Those who can write their names can do that also. Have your child take the book and colored pencils to school and collect self-portraits on each page. Your child will probably ask you to draw and write in the book, too. Other family members can add self-portraits to help get the autograph book started.

Follow-Up: When your child brings the book home, sit down, and look through it with her/him. Talk about each friend who contributed to the book. If your child wants you to, write each child's name under her/his self-portrait. Have your child draw a self-portrait in the space below.

Share!

This is a self-portrait you drew when you were five years old:

Celebrate!

Celebrate your five-year-old's developing communication skills.

Five-year-olds generally have very positive attitudes. You may often hear your kindergartner saying, "Yes," "Great," and "Let's do it!" Kids this age often adore certain adults, especially their parents, and they are quick to accept the uniqueness in others. Their acceptance of the world is expressed in their positive communications with those they come in contact with each day–neighbors, family, teachers, and even strangers.

By age 5 to 6 you will observe that your child:
- Will tell spontaneous stories
- May talk constantly
- Will enjoy reciting rhymes, limericks, poems, and singing songs

Play!

Creating Original Nursery Rhymes

Why this playtime activity is good for your child: Children this age are very creative and can improvise to create new and original rhymes, sayings, and songs.

What you'll need to play this activity: nursery rhymes

How to create *Original Nursery Rhymes*: Recite one rhyme at a time. When your child is familiar with a rhyme, recite it again leaving blanks to be filled in by your child. Instead of giving a noun or verb in the rhyme, point to your child and let her/him fill in a word. Then recite the new rhyme together.

Example of Rhyme:	Way to Improvise:
One, two, three,	One, two, three,
Mamma loves coffee,	Mamma loves _____,
And I love tea.	And I love _____.
How good we be!	How good we be!
One, two, three,	One, two, three,
Mamma loves coffee,	Mamma loves _____,
And I love tea.	And I love _____.

Share!

When you were five years old, this is a silly original rhyme you created:

_____

_____

Celebrate!

Celebrate your five-year-old's musical talents.

Children this age respond to music with increasing skill. Their movements become more graceful and varied until by about age six they are doing real dancing.

By age 5 to 6 you will observe that your child:

- Will enjoy reciting or singing rhymes and jingles as well as songs
- Will enjoy the mastery of melodies and tunes and may sing well
- Will enjoy acting out a story in dance form

Play!

Cut a Record!

Why this playtime activity is good for your child: Children in this age range like to record their own voices and listen to themselves.

What you'll need to play this activity: tape recorder; blank tape; CD of a favorite song

How to *Cut a Record*: Tell your child you plan to record her/him singing a favorite song. Play the background music. Have your child practice singing the words to the music. Help her/him memorize the words. Then record the music and your child's voice singing the song.

Variation #1: Tape record your child telling a story or chatting with a person who lives a long way away. Birthday messages are especially nice to tape and tuck into a greeting card. Your child will probably enjoy "cutting a record" so much s/he'll want to make lots of tapes to send to friends and family.

Variation #2: Have your child make a tape of her/his favorite songs, stories, and rhymes. Put it away as a keepsake. Someday the tape will be cherished by you and your child.

Share!

When you were five years old, you loved to tape your own voice. When you "cut a record," you:

_____

_____

_____

Celebrate!

Celebrate your five-year-old's high level of energy.

Children this age especially enjoy outdoor gym equipment. They like to run around and exert great amounts of energy at recess. Favorite games include tag; running races; hide-and-seek; Red Rover, Red Rover; and jumping rope. Five-year-olds need ample opportunity to release energy, and running games provide a safe expression of angry and aggressive feelings.

By age 5 to 6 you will observe that your child:

- Enjoys life
- Will see every day as a new adventure
- Will be fairly willing to stay within prescribed boundaries

Play!

Timed Relay Races

Why this playtime activity is good for your child: Children like racing, especially racing against time. They enjoy being timed so they can break their own records.

What you'll need to play this activity: stopwatch; scorecard; pencil

How to play *Timed Relay Races*: Think up several running courses like those described below. Time your child running each course and record her/his score. Praise your child each time s/he finishes a race. Encourage your child to practice running the course several times each day. Then once or twice a week, have your child run the course again. Time her/him, record each new time, and note any improvements. Relay races will vary depending on your child and your play area.

Examples of relay races:

Run around the house three times.

Run from one end of a fence to another.

Run around two distant trees five times.

Skip around the house once.

Share!

When you were five years old, your favorite racing game was: _____

_____

_____

Celebrate!

Celebrate your five-year-old's fantasy play.

By age five most children can create houses, offices, and schools from large blocks or cardboard boxes and can use crayons, markers, paints, and paper cut-outs to create added effects. They can use preconstructed play puppet stages effectively in play but are increasingly capable of making their own stages.

By age 5 to 6 you will observe that your child:
- Will spend a great amount of time preparing a place for play
- Will like to play within a construction such as a playhouse, tree house, tent, etc.

Play!

Build a Secret Hide-Out

Why this playtime activity is good for your child: As they become capable, it is desirable for children to construct their own play settings. This activity requires planning (often in interaction with others), mental representation, and creative efforts.

What you'll need to play this activity: building materials such as appliance boxes, large sheets of cardboard, lightweight boards, blankets, etc.

How to organize *Build a Secret Hide-Out*: A good family video called *The War* is about some children who build a tree house. You might want to share this video with your child. Encourage your youngster to create a hide-out. Unless your child asks you for help, providing the materials is all the assistance you should give to this project. Let your child and her/his friends create the secret hide-out.

Variation #1: Hide-outs can be places created under a large bush, in the low branches of a tree, in a garage attic, under a porch, bed, or large trampoline–anywhere a child enjoys hiding. Encouraging your child to have special places that are hers/his alone will enrich your youngster's role-playing and fantasy world.

Variation #2: A small pup tent or a family-size camping tent set up in the backyard makes a great place to play. If your child would enjoy a few days in a tent, assist your child putting it up.

Share!

When you were five years old, your favorite hiding place was: _____

Celebrate!

Celebrate your five-year-old's learning about safety.

The best way to avoid accidents is to design an environment in which the hazards have been removed. But even the most conscientious parents cannot be there every second to monitor their child's movements. Child proofing your home will reduce the opportunities for injury, and taking time to teach your child how to use tools properly will prevent many accidents; however, children this age still need some supervision.

By age 5 to 6 you will observe that your child:
- Will be curious and want to explore–especially forbidden areas
- Will enjoy spending time in the most dangerous room in the house–the kitchen
- Will want to use adult tools such as kitchen utensils

Play!

Cooking Up a Storm

Why this playtime activity is good for your child: Teaching your child how to use kitchen tools and utensils correctly is the best way to safeguard against accidents.

What you'll need to play this activity: Check the materials needed for each recipe.

How to play *Cooking Up a Storm:* Let your child choose one of the recipes s/he wants to try. Then have your child wash her/his hands. After cooking with your child, require that s/he help you clean up the work area and put everything away. Try these three recipes:

Grilled Cheese Sandwiches–Use a cheese grater to grate about ½ cup (118 milliliters) of cheese. If supervised, a five-year-old can do this. If you do not want your child using a grater yet, use sliced cheese. Help your child use a toaster to toast two slices of bread. Show your child how to carefully remove the hot toast from the toaster. Teach your child that a toaster is a hot appliance. Place the toast on a plate and have your child spread it with butter or margarine, and then sprinkle grated cheese or layer sliced cheese between the pieces of buttered toast. Put the sandwich in a microwave oven for 20 seconds or until the cheese melts. Let it cool slightly before serving.

Circus Sandwich–Make this dessert sandwich. Place a graham cracker on a glass plate. Cover it with miniature marshmallows and chocolate chips. Then put another graham cracker on top. Put it in the microwave oven until it melts, about 20 seconds.

Apple Sauce–Peel and chop ten apples. Place them in a slow cooker with a spoonful of cinnamon and sugar. Cook the apples with the lid off until done.

Share!

When you were five years old, your favorite thing to cook was: _____

Celebrate!

Celebrate your five-year-old's learning about feelings.

Five-year-olds generally know how to cooperate, take turns, and share–but no one is perfect! At times your child's anger, impatience, or frustration may become physical. If your child strikes out aggressively at another child, quickly restrain her/him. Take your child aside and talk about her/his feelings. Explore what feeling your child is experiencing. Through conversation, try to discover what caused your child to lose her/his temper. Acknowledge that everybody at times feels angry, impatient, and frustrated. Talk about socially acceptable ways of dealing with these feelings like talking it out, exercising, punching a pillow, etc. Expressing turmoil openly is healthy.

By age 5 to 6 you will observe that your child:

- Will sometimes act out in aggressive ways if angry, frustrated, hungry, sleepy, sick, etc.
- Will need guidance about ways to deal with negative feelings
- Will have the language to express basic feelings

Play!

Getting Out My Tension–Yah, Yah, Yah!

Why this playtime activity is good for your child: Children need safety valves in a stressful world, and dancing is a good way to release tension and stress. Although children don't need a special occasion to rock 'n' roll, if your child is experiencing a lot of pent-up hostility, bring out the rock 'n' roll records and rock around the clock.

What you'll need to play this activity: You will need rock and roll music. Try to get the song that first launched rock and roll music–"Rock Around the Clock." Also look for Elvis Presley's "Jailhouse Rock," Chuck Berry's "Johnny Be Good," or "Great Balls of Fire" by Jerry Lee Lewis.

How to play *Getting Out My Tension–Yah, Yah, Yah!*: Let your child lip sync and play air guitar (pretend to hold a guitar and play it) to rock 'n' roll music played as loudly as "Mother can stand it." Encourage your child to move around, dance, shake, rattle, and roll! Some children like to perform in front of a full-length mirror. Have your child practice a few times. Then sit down and watch the show s/he has created. The more you can encourage your child to move around when s/he is having a "bad feelings" day, the more likely s/he is to relax and let go of the stress.

Share!

When you were five years old and you played rock 'n' roll music, you enjoyed:

Celebrate!

Celebrate your five-year-old's learning to count and understanding numbers.

Five-year-olds take a giant leap in the kindergarten years. Many can count by ones, at least a little ways. During the kindergarten year many children learn to count to twenty. Children this age also learn to add and subtract small numbers. Some enjoy writing numerals, but often some numerals and letters are reversed.

By age 5 to 6 you will observe that your child:

- Will recognize numerals from 1 to 10.
- Will count from 1 to 20 or even higher
- May use fingers to count, add, and subtract

Play!

Mother, May I, Please?

Why this playtime activity is good for your child: This game will teach your child to count and reinforce asking permission and using "Please" and "Thank you."

What you'll need to play this activity: No special equipment is needed to play this game.

How to play *Mother, May I, Please?*: Have your child stand back about twenty-five to thirty feet (eight to ten meters) away from you. Give your child a command as listed below. Your child is to ask, "Mother, may I, please?" before advancing the number of steps given. When you tell your child, "Yes, you may," s/he is to say, "Thank you," before advancing. If your child forgets to ask permission, or say "Please" or "Thank you," s/he goes back to the starting point. When your child tags you, let her/him have a turn at giving the commands.

Examples:

Take five giant steps forward.   Advance four skips.
Take six scissor steps forward.   Run to that tree.
Take two rabbit hops forward.   Take two kangaroo leaps forward.
Take three little, baby steps sideways. Take seven bird hops forward.
Take a frog leap forward.   Take three giant leaps forward.

Share!

When you were five years old and we played Mother, May I, Please? you would:

Celebrate!

Celebrate your five-year-old's natural artistic abilities.

As children's representational ability expands, their fantasy and art activities become more imaginative and creative. Interest in creating patterns with materials and drawing or constructing representations of the world also grows.

By age 5 to 6 you will observe that your child:

- Can use smaller crayons and markers
- Can use watercolor paints
- Can manipulate simple sewing forms with large, blunt needles

Play!

Citrus Critters

Why this playtime activity is good for your child: Using natural objects like fruits to make art projects is an enjoyable and aromatic way to express creativity.

What you'll need to play this activity: orange, tangerine, lemon, or grapefruit; whole cloves; craft sticks; construction paper or felt; pasta pieces; glue; child's safety scissors; ribbon

How to make *Citrus Critters*: First discuss what kind of a critter your child wants to make. A porcupine, sea urchin, snail, or other animal with a round body will work well. Show your child how to push whole cloves into the fruit peel. Decorate the fruit to look like the body of an animal. Use broken craft sticks to make legs. Add paper (felt) cutouts for head, neck, antlers, antennae, or other details. When the critter is finished, tie a ribbon around it so it can be hung in your child's closet like a potpourri ball.

Share!

When you were five years old and we made citrus critters, yours looked:

Celebrate!

Celebrate your five-year-old's musical talents.

Five-year-olds have increased skills in the area of music and dance. They enjoy making a variety of sounds and keeping time to a strong beat. Silly songs hold a special fascination for the kindergarten-age children. Encouraging your child to create and play a musical instrument will enhance her/his musical enjoyment.

By age 5 to 6 you will observe that your child:
- Will recite rhymes and sing rhymes and jingles
- Enjoys playing a variety of musical instruments
- Can learn the words to simple, progressive songs

Play!

Mountain Music

Why this playtime activity is good for your child: Jug band instruments can be made from many things found in the kitchen, and creating one's own musical instrument is interesting and fun.

What you'll need to play this activity: You and your child can make homemade musical instruments such as a jug to blow across the top, jars filled with beans or rice to shake, a tissue box with rubber bands wrapped around it to be played like a guitar, spoons to clack together, glasses filled with varying amounts of water to tap with a spoon, etc. Look around; you'll see many things in your kitchen that can be used to make beautiful, mountain music.

How to play *Mountain Music*: Experiment to make sounds with things you find in the kitchen. Let your child think of things to use, too. Try them all out. Find out which ones please your child the most. Then teach her/him the words to a mountain song that has been sung for over one hundred years. Sing and accompany the song with homemade instruments.

"She'll Be Coming 'Round the Mountain."
She'll be coming 'round the mountain when she comes. *(Echo: when she comes!)*
She'll be coming 'round the mountain when she comes. *(Echo: when she comes!)*
She'll be coming 'round the mountain,
She'll be coming 'round the mountain,
She'll be coming 'round the mountain when she comes!

Share!

When you were five years old and we made homemade musical instruments, you liked playing:

Celebrate!

Celebrate your five-year-old's expanding attention span.

This developmental stage is a peak interest period for creating play scenes and developing extended pretend sequences with them. Children enjoy prepackaged scenes (house, school, garage, airport, farm, zoo, etc.), but they can also construct these scenes using unit blocks or play bricks with people and animal figures, vehicles, and a variety of additional props (fences, trees, road signs, barn/room enclosures, etc.).

By age 5 to 6 you will observe that your child:

- Will construct increasingly elaborate and detailed scenes
- Will engage in longer and more complex play sequences
- May participate with several friends in construction and fantasy play

Play!

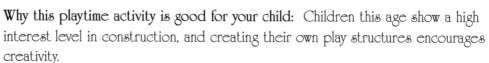

Cardboard Village

Why this playtime activity is good for your child: Children this age show a high interest level in construction, and creating their own play structures encourages creativity.

What you'll need to play this activity: an assortment of tiny boxes such as match boxes, and food containers like tea and cookie boxes; white bond and construction paper; glue stick and clear adhesive tape; child's safety scissors; markers or crayons

How to play *Cardboard Village:* Ahead of time, prepare the boxes by covering them with white paper. The easiest way to do this is to wrap them as if they are tiny gifts, with the tape on the bottom and top. Use folded construction paper rectangles to make roofs for the buildings. Decorate the sides of the boxes with paper cut-outs of doors and windows. Look at pictures of buildings in magazines to see how barns, houses, buildings, etc., are designed. Let your child decorate the buildings. Create buildings of many different sizes and shapes. Use these to set up small villages. Use with miniature people and animal figures.

Share!

When you were five years old and we used tiny boxes to build a village, you would:

_____

_____

_____

Celebrate!

Celebrate your five-year-old's well-developed gross motor skills.

Children this age show great interest in playing with vehicles. Their increased manual skills allow them to operate more complicated mechanisms, such as large cranks. Kindergarten-age children typically incorporate transportation toys into fantasy and dramatic play.

By age 5 to 6 you will observe that your child:

- Will enjoy outdoor gym equipment like hanging bars, rings, and climbing equipment
- Will enjoy playing with outdoor building materials

Play!

Obstacle Course Follow the Leader

Why this playtime activity is good for your child: Children this age love to be challenged to do physically difficult stunts. As the adult, you will have to set the limits and decide what equipment your child is ready to use.

What you'll need to play this activity: park or playground with an assortment of gym equipment

How to play *Obstacle Course Follow the Leader:* Move around the park on different equipment, and have your child follow and perform the stunts you perform.

Examples:
Climb the steps of the slide and slide down.
Go to the swings and pump until swinging quite high, then gradually slow down the momentum, and stop.
Propel yourself under the crossbar by hand-over-hand movements.
Run around two trees that are fairly far apart.
Climb to the top of the jungle gym and take a rest.

Variation: Give your child a turn at being the leader. Try to follow her/his activities.

Share!

When you were five years old and we went to the park, your favorite things to do were:

_____

_____

_____

_____

Celebrate!

Celebrate your five-year-old's desire to explore and experiment.

Children learn best who learn for themselves, not for others. Play is a child's way of learning. Learning by playing requires that the child try different techniques to discover what works best for her/him. If a five-year-old can't do something, s/he will get frustrated. Frustration drives humans to find out how to do something. When a child finally learns how to do something for her/himself, s/he will feel elated, and her/his self-esteem will soar.

By age 5 to 6 you will observe that your child:

- Will enjoy puzzles with up to 50 pieces
- Will enjoy number and letter puzzles
- Will enjoy clock puzzles
- Will learn patience from working difficult puzzles

Play!

Puzzle Corner

Why this playtime activity is good for your child: During the preschool and kindergarten years, children develop skill in doing puzzles and move from successfully completing 12-piece puzzles to putting together 50-piece puzzles. Puzzles provide a quiet setting where the child can learn on her/his own, as well as patience and tenacity.

What you'll need to play this activity: puzzle worktable where a puzzle can be left until completed; boxes of puzzles with 40-50 pieces

How to play *Puzzle Corner:* Set up a puzzle corner in your child's bedroom. You will need a table large enough for one puzzle to rest, plus extra space for holding the unused pieces around the edges. The puzzle corner should have a light directly overhead or be placed in a spot where sunlight comes into the room, providing plenty of light for matching colors and shapes. When your child completes a large puzzle by her/himself, celebrate the occasion with great fanfare. Provide a variety of puzzles from which your child can choose.

Share!

When you were five years old, you thought playing with puzzles was: _____

_____

_____

_____

_____

Celebrate!

Celebrate your five-year-old's curiosity about science.

Kindergarten-age children enjoy playing with measuring tools. They can successfully use balance scales, trundle wheels, and unbreakable thermometers. Children this age can make use of a plan in their play and hold the plan in mind over time. They engage in intellectual exploration of objects, experiment, and remember basic principles learned through play activities.

By age 5 to 6 you will observe that your child:

- Will enjoy specimen collections (rocks, shells, leaves)
- Will learn from the care of a pet (ant farm, aquarium) and plants
- Will learn best by experimenting and testing methods on her/his own
- Will remember lessons learned through experience and experimenting
- Will be able to transfer a lesson learned in one situation to another completely different situation

Play!

Kitchen Laboratory

Why this playtime activity is good for your child: You can introduce your child to basic scientific principles with things found in your kitchen.

What you'll need to play this activity: Look at each experiment to see what materials you will need.

How to play *Kitchen Laboratory*: Gather the materials you will need for one experiment. It is best to do one demonstration per session. Explain to your child what you are going to do, and always use the appropriate scientific terms for the principles you are demonstrating. After your demonstration, allow time for your child to use the materials to experience the scientific principle for her/himself. Try these simple scientific experiments:

Static Electricity–You will need a dry, cold day to do this experiment. Rub a comb with a piece of wool. Fill a balloon with air and tie it so the air cannot escape. See if the balloon will cling to the comb. Use a stopwatch to see how long the comb will attract the balloon. Test some other objects such as a table tennis ball, bits of paper, or hair on your head to see if they are affected by the static electricity in the comb. Recharge the comb by rubbing it with the wool between each test item.

Dissolving–Experiment with sugar, salt, and sand to find out which one dissolves in water the quickest. Will they dissolve without stirring them? Which one does not dissolve in water? Try dissolving each in cold, lukewarm, and hot water. What water temperature works the best?

Share!

When you were five years old and we did science experiments in the kitchen, you would:

Celebrate!

Celebrate your five-year-old's developing a positive self-image.

It is important to occasionally give your child a small task that you know s/he can successfully perform. Kindergartners can set the table, clean their own rooms, pick up and put away toys, wash or dry dishes, rake leaves, etc. When you give your child a task to help with the household chores, you are sending her/him a clear message that s/he is a valuable asset to the family. Always praise your child for a job well done. Don't expect your child to do very much work around the house; one small task every other day or twice a week is enough. Remember, a child's work is to play!

By age 5 to 6 you will observe that your child:

- Will enjoy certain household chores
- Will still think tasks like washing dishes are a game and not work
- Will be highly motivated when preparing food for the family

Play!

Fancy Cookies

Why this playtime activity is good for your child: Although cutting out cookies from cookie dough is difficult, most five-year-olds can do it if the dough is rolled out for them.

What you'll need to play this activity: tube of refrigerated sugar cookie dough; floured board; cookie cutters; can of vanilla icing; sprinkles; food coloring; waxed paper; baking sheet

How to make *Fancy Cookies*: On a floured board, roll out the chilled cookie dough. Let your child use large cookie cutters to cut out fancy-shaped cookies such as stars, hearts, or gingerbread men. Use a spatula to place the cookies on a baking sheet. Bake as directed on the cookie package. When done, remove from the oven, and place the warm cookies on waxed paper to cool. Divide the icing into three or four bowls, and add food coloring to each bowl of icing. Let your child stir the food coloring into the icing in the bowls. Have your child use the colorful icing and sprinkles to decorate each cookie. Leave flat on the waxed paper until the icing sets.

Variation: If you do not have time to bake cookies, you can let your child decorate store-bought sugar cookies, animal crackers, or graham crackers with icing and sprinkles.

Share!

When you were five years old and you decorated cookies, you enjoyed:

_____

_____

Celebrate!

Celebrate your five-year-old's abilities and play interests.

Action figures (super heroes) and fashion dolls are not appropriate toys for children this age because they are typically violent and stereotyped. These toys are fragile and have many small parts to be lost. They represent teen-age or adult role-play activities rather than activities that are appropriate for young children. To promote creative imaginative play, which is at a height during this age, dolls should be generic rather than detailed and specific.

By age 5 to 6 you will observe that your child:

- May be interested in dolls that look like a child her/his own age (especially for dressing and undressing)
- Will still be interested in dolls that look like babies

Play!

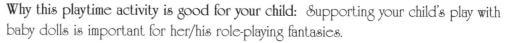

Baby Dolls

Why this playtime activity is good for your child: Supporting your child's play with baby dolls is important for her/his role-playing fantasies.

What you'll need to play this activity: washable rubber/vinyl dolls with accessories for caretaking tasks such as feeding, diapering, and sleeping. Housekeeping toys like a playhouse with miniature furniture, especially a table and chairs, doll bed, etc. will make playing with baby dolls even more enjoyable.

How to play *Baby Dolls*: There is no right or wrong way to play with baby dolls. Each child will bring to the game her/his own level of interest. Some children this age, especially girls, have a doll that they pretend is their very own live baby. They carry the baby doll around, dress and undress it, and even pretend to feed it. Other children have dolls that they periodically take out, play with, and then put back on the shelf again. Your participation in your child's playing with baby dolls will be up to you and her/him. If your child has a playmate around, s/he probably won't be anxious to have you join in; however, if she is alone, s/he may very much enjoy your presence in such an activity. Follow her/his lead. If s/he wants to be the Mother/Father, you take the opposite role. This is a good time to talk to your child about safety rules and keeping babies safe.

Share!

When you were five years old and we played Baby Dolls, you enjoyed:

_____

_____

Celebrate!

Celebrate your five-year-old's emotional development.

Crying is an active, healthy response to sadness. It is okay for a sad child to cry. Sometimes it is the best way of dealing with sad feelings. If there is good reason for the sadness, the child has every right to feel sad and to express her/his misery.

By age 5 to 6 you will observe that your child, when sad:

- May on occasion demonstrate withdrawal or lack of energy
- May occasionally experience feelings of hopelessness, guilt, or fear
- May express sadness with tears and anger with aggression

Play!

I'm Here, and I Love You

Why this activity is good for your child: Sadness should be taken seriously. Don't joke or make light of a situation that makes your child sad. Listening and discussing feelings is the best way you can help elevate your child's feelings.

What you'll need to play this activity: rocking chair

How to practice *I'm Here, and I Love You*: When your child shows signs of sadness, loneliness, inadequacy, inexpressible anger, or depression, know that these are normal feelings that occur in most children. Holding your child in your arms while rocking her/him and giving soothing and encouraging messages may help her/him deal with the negative feelings. It is comforting to a child to know that her/his parents understand the sadness and can protect her/him from the fears and guilt that are compounded by a sense of helplessness. Begin by telling your child, "I'm here, and I love you." Ask your child to tell you about why s/he is so sad. If she can verbalize her feelings, listen closely. Encourage her/him to get it all out. Listen, listen, listen. Tell your child that all human beings experience sad feelings sometimes. Explain that feeling sadness is okay. Explain that there are some things we can do to make ourselves feel better after we are through crying and letting out the sadness. To end this together session, nurture your child in one of the following ways:

- Back and shoulder massage
- Close the blinds/curtains, light some candles, and listen to some soft music
- Brush your child's hair lightly with a soft brush

Share!

When you were five years old and you were sad, one thing we did to elevate your feelings was:

Celebrate!

Celebrate your five-year-old's developing fine motor skills.

Kindergarten children begin exhibiting order and balance in their art, building projects, and constructed play worlds. They begin to plan and create intended effects and have increasing interest and pride in the products they produce.

By age 5 to 6 you will observe that your child:

- Will enjoy using beginning weaving materials such as looms and yarn
- Will enjoy weaving simple paper designs
- Can handle and use tools that require fine muscle skills

Play!

Weave Paper Mats

Why this playtime activity is good for your child: Weaving paper takes eye-hand coordination and thinking skills. Designing weaving patterns is creative and fun.

What you'll need to play this activity: construction paper of varying colors; child's safety scissors

How to *Weave Paper Mats*: Prepare ahead of time by cutting one sheet of paper into strips. Fold the other sheet of paper in half. Starting at the fold, cut slits across the paper, stopping about one inch from the edge. After you cut six to ten slits, open the page and lay the paper down flat. Show your child how to weave strips of paper in and out of the slits, first over one slit, then under the next slit, through to the other side. Repeat with the next strip, starting under the slit, then going over, alternating each strip until mat is completely woven.

Variation #1: For a unique pattern, cut wavy or zigzag slits in the construction paper instead of straight lines.

Variation #2: Have your child weave a place mat for each member of the family. Cover both sides with clear adhesive paper slightly larger than the mat. Trim around the edges so that the mat is sealed between the two sheets of adhesive paper. Use the place mats at dinner, on special holidays, or for party table decorations.

Share!

When you were five years old and you weaved place mats, this is what you did:

_____

_____

Celebrate!

Celebrate your five-year-old's maturing social skills.

Five-year-olds are beginning to try to figure things out on their own. At this age children begin making generalizations. For example, if the family's pet cat is black and female, and a neighbor has a black cat that is also female, your child may generalize that all black cats are females. Most children this age still believe in Santa Claus, and many believe that wishes come true.

By age 5 to 6 you will observe that your child:

- Will show high interest in dramatic play—recreating adult occupations, using costumes and props
- Will show increasing interest in group pretend play
- Will engage in social play that is typically cooperative, practical, and conforming

Play!

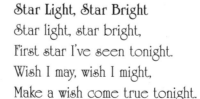 ### Star Light, Star Bright

Why this playtime activity is good for your child: It is important to teach your child that things do not happen because someone wishes they would.

What you'll need to play this activity: No special equipment is needed to play this game.

How to play *Star Light, Star Bright*: You don't need a dark night to spot the planet Venus in the sky. Unlike any other planet, Venus can be seen by the naked eye in full daylight during many months of the year. To find Venus, look at the sky in the early evening. It is the first "star" visible and is about ten times the typical brightness of Sirius, the brightest star in the sky. Teach your child how to spot Venus. Say the rhyme and make a wish.

> **Star Light, Star Bright**
> Star light, star bright,
> First star I've seen tonight.
> Wish I may, wish I might,
> Make a wish come true tonight.

Share!

When you were five years old, the thing you seemed to wish for the most was:

_____

_____

Celebrate!

Celebrate your five-year-old's gross motor skills.

Children this age like all kinds of balls and ball games. Ten- to twelve-inch (twenty-five to thirty-one centimeters) rubber balls for kicking, throwing, and catching are especially popular with kindergarten-age children. Most kids this age, especially boys, enjoy using a lightweight (hollow plastic) softball with a large, lightweight bat.

By age 5 to 6 you will observe that your child:

- Will enjoy catch-and-throw games
- Will be able to kick a ball hard
- Will be able to catch a large ball
- Will be able to throw underhand

Play!

Ball Bouncing

Why this playtime activity is good for your child: Street rhymes are good for counting out beats and ball bouncing. When children use rhymes to play bouncing ball games, they practice both eye-hand coordination and rhythm.

What you'll need to play this activity: large, rubber ball

How to play *Ball Bouncing:* Use street rhymes or nursery rhymes to keep time when bouncing balls. Try some of the ball bouncing games described below.

Bounce and Catch–Bounce the ball and catch it one time on each line of the rhyme.

> Great A, little a,
> Bouncing B!
> The cat's in the cupboard,
> And can't see me.

Toss Up and Catch–Use the rhyme to toss and catch the ball two times. See how high your child can toss the ball and still catch it while you recite the rhyme.

> Toss up my darling, toss the ball high.
> Don't let the ball though, hit the blue sky.

Bounce, Bounce, Catch–Bounce the ball two times and then catch it on each line of the rhyme.

1, 2, 3, 4, 5!	1, 2, (*bounce*) 3, 4, (*bounce*) 5! (*catch*)
I caught a hare alive.	I caught (*bounce*) a hare (*bounce*) alive. (*catch*)
6, 7, 8, 9, 10!	6, 7, (*bounce*) 8, 9, (*bounce*) 10! (*catch*)
I let him go again.	I let (*bounce*) him go (*bounce*) again. (*catch*)

Share!

When you were five years old and played ball bouncing games, your favorite went like this:

Celebrate!

Celebrate your five-year-old's curiosity in nature.

Five-year-olds are fascinated with animals. Many children this age own and care for a pet. Children can learn a lot about growth and responsibility by caring for a family pet. Observing other animals at zoos, farms, aquariums, wildlife parks, and exotic pet stores will be extremely educational too.

By age 5 to 6 you will observe that your child:

- Will want to observe favorite animals
- Will know habits of many different animals
- Will still enjoy stories about fantasy animals that act like people
- May have fear of some animals especially spiders, snakes, or rats

Play!

Information Scavenger Hunt

Why this playtime activity is good for your child: Observing insects and animals in nature is interesting and offers examples of laws of nature such as camouflage, hibernation, migration, hatching, etc.

What you'll need to play this activity: pencil; paper; magnifying glass; binoculars

How to play *Information Scavenger Hunt:* Write a question on paper, and then set out to see if you and your child can discover the answer.

Examples of Information Scavenger Hunts:

How many different kinds of insects live in our backyard? (Make a numbered list of the insects that you spot.)

If we throw bread into the yard, how long will it take the birds to find it? (Use binoculars to observe the birds while they eat the bread.)

If we put a bowl of sugar water on the sidewalk, how long will it take the ants to find it? (Use a magnifying glass to study the ants while they eat the sugar water.)

Variation: Look up answers to questions in animal books and encyclopedias. Example: What does a gorilla eat? (leaves; shoots; the pith of certain plants, such as bamboo; fruit)

Share!

When you were five years old, you were fascinated to learn about these animals:

_____

_____

Celebrate!

Celebrate your five-year-old's abilities and play interests.

A large variety of specific skill development materials are appropriate for kindergarten-age children. Toys, art supplies, and educational materials should be selected that support the development of a broad range of skills, but to be effective they must be integrated into play with guidance from an adult. Incorporate educational toys and games into your playtime activities, and use everyday events like driving in the car for teaching new skills.

By 5 to 6 you will observe that your child:

- Can play dominoes based on letter or number matching
- Can play bingo/lotto based on letter or number matching

Play!

X	V	J	C	P
M	F	D	S	B
Q	K	A	H	O
Y	G	T	R	L
U	W	N	E	I

ABC Bingo

Why this playtime activity is good for your child: Bingo can be a game played to introduce and reinforce the letters of the alphabet. (Play only if your child shows an active interest in learning the letters.)

What you'll need to play this activity: a bingo card (25 space grid); pencil; marker

How to play *ABC Bingo*: Randomly write the uppercase letters of the alphabet on a bingo grid. (You will have to leave one letter out or label one space with two letters—"Y and Z.") Give your child the bingo grid and a marker. As you randomly call out letters of the alphabet, s/he marks out the matching space on the card. When s/he has five letters in a row, column, or diagonally, s/he calls out "bingo" and wins the game! Later, when your child can write the letters of the alphabet, s/he can put the letters on the grid in any order s/he chooses. This game can be played as a competition between several children at once.

Variation #1: Lowercase Alphabet Bingo—Instead of writing uppercase letters on the playing card, use the lowercase letters, and play with the same rules as above.

Variation #2: Number Bingo—Instead of writing letters on the bingo card, use a four by four grid and write the numerals 0-15 on the card.

Share!

When you were five years old, your favorite way to play bingo was: _____

_____

_____

Celebrate!

Celebrate your five-year-old's developing language skills.

Kindergarten-age children have increased language skills and longer attention spans. The availability of previously learned information-processing strategies allows children to begin to solve problems mentally and plan ahead. The typical five-year-old loves to talk and will often use words to solve problems.

By age 5 to 6 you will observe that your child:

- May talk constantly
- Uses language in many meaningful ways
- Will ask questions and wants to know about everything s/he sees

Play!

The little girl who wouldn't eat her dinner.

Creative Story Writing

Why this playtime activity is good for your child: It is good for children to see their thoughts put into words.

What you'll need to play this activity: paper; pencil; markers

How to play *Creative Story Writing:* Have your child draw a picture of a fantasy, dream, or make-believe story. Encourage her/him to be as imaginative as possible. When the picture is complete, have your child tell you about it. As your child dictates the story, write it on a sheet of lined paper. When the story has been told and recorded, cut it out and attach it to the picture. While looking at your child's picture, read the story to your child.

Variation: Repeat this exercise on different occasions, and collect ten or twelve pictures with stories. Staple all of the stories together like a book. Add construction paper or light cardboard front and back covers. Have your child decorate the cover of her/his book and give it a title. Reread the stories to your child.

Share!

When you were five years old, you liked to make up stories about: _____

One story that you made up was: _____

_____

_____

_____

_____

Celebrate!

Celebrate your five-year-old's exploration and mastery of play.

Children in this age range can handle most sand and water play materials. Both large and small sand tools are appropriate, and if available, children will actively experiment with a large variety of sand and water materials such as cups, sieves, funnels, tubes, and waterwheels. They also enjoy using fantasy materials (plastic animals, boats, vehicles, etc.) in sand and water.

By age 5 to 6 you will observe that your child:

- Enjoys the texture of sand
- Enjoys manipulating sand, dirt, mud, and water
- Enjoys exploring how water and objects relate (float, sink, absorb)

Play!

Sandbox Play

Why this playtime activity is good for your child: Playing in sand is soothing and pleasurable. All children should have ample opportunity to play with sand.

What you'll need to play this activity: sandbox or large tub of sand; sand tools such as cups, sieves, funnels, tubes, sifters, scoops, etc.

How to set up *Sandbox Play*: Provide sand tools and a sandbox. Your child can have an indoor sandbox providing you don't mind sweeping up excess sand that may be scattered around the box. An indoor sandbox allows a child the chance to play in the sand no matter what the weather. Indoor sandboxes, protected from neighborhood cats, are more sanitary than the outdoor ones. Place a large tub of sand on a worktable in your child's bedroom, in a basement, or in a play area. When not in use, store the sand toys in a plastic dish tub near the sandbox.

Variation #1: If appropriate for your sandbox, water can be added to the sandbox for modeling of sand castles.

Variation #2: If for one reason or another, your child cannot have a sandbox, provide a large plastic tub of rice, beans, rock salt, or round pieces of pasta for measuring activities. The same tools can be used with these materials as with the sand.

Share!

When you were five years old, your favorite sandbox activity was: _____

_____

Celebrate!

Celebrate your five-year-old's developing social skills.

After starting school, children generally have many friends, but often they choose a very best friend with whom they spend much of their time. The best friend might be a next door neighbor, slightly older or younger sibling, or someone who lives close by. Because the five-year-old cannot go too far from home, close proximity is a contributing factor for early friendships.

By age 5 to 6 you will observe that your child:

- Will hate to lose and is not ready for organized competitive play
- Will increasingly differentiate by gender in play roles and interests
- Will enjoy the company of one or two special friends

Play!

Best Friend Scrapbook

Why this playtime activity is good for your child: Children this age enjoy dressing up and having their photograph taken.

What you'll need to play this activity: camera; dress-up clothes; child's best friend

How to make a *Best Friend Scrapbook*: Explain to your child and her/his best friend that you are going to take photographs of them in dress-up clothes for a photograph scrapbook. Let the children dress up in costumes and pose any way they choose. Leave them to their play as they get ready for each photo session. Take twelve to twenty photographs. Once the film is developed, attach each photograph to a separate page in a scrapbook. Ask your child for comments about each photograph, and record the statements with black marker on each page. When the scrapbook is finished, look at the photographs and read each page of the scrapbook to your child.

Variation: Make two scrapbooks at once. Have two copies of each photograph made. Record the comments made by the children on each page of both scrapbooks. Give the second scrapbook to your child's best friend.

Share!

When you were five years old, your best friend was: _____

The two of you spent much time:_____

_____

Celebrate!

Celebrate your five-year-old's cognitive milestones.

Kindergarten-age children are interested in classifying the world around them according to color, size, shape, etc. By the age of five, children may be able to sort using more than one criterion at the same time.

By age 5 to 6 you will observe that your child will learn:

- To count ten or more objects
- To correctly name primary and secondary colors
- To name basic shapes (square, circle, triangle)

Play!

Attribute Logic Blocks

Why this playtime activity is good for your child: Playing with blocks of varied attributes (shape, sizes, and colors) is fun and will give your child an opportunity to sort using more than one criterion.

What you'll need to play this activity: two construction paper cutouts of each of the following:

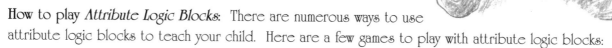

Big red circle, blue circle, and yellow circle
Big red square, blue square, and yellow square
Big red triangle, blue triangle, and yellow triangle
Little red circle, blue circle, and yellow circle
Little red square, blue square, and yellow square
Little red triangle, blue triangle, and yellow triangle

How to play *Attribute Logic Blocks*: There are numerous ways to use attribute logic blocks to teach your child. Here are a few games to play with attribute logic blocks:

Exactly the Same–Show an attribute logic block. Ask her/him to find the one exactly like it.

One-Way Train–Play this game like connecting dominoes. Make a "train" of attribute pieces that are alike in one way and unlike in two ways. For example, a large, red circle can be connected with a large, blue triangle because the common attribute is size (both are large). Work on creating a long train of attribute blocks that are similar in one attribute–color, size, or shape.

Two-Way Chain–Play this game like connecting dominoes. Make a chain of attribute pieces that are alike in two ways and unlike in one way. For example, a large, red circle can be connected with a large, red triangle because the two common attributes are color and size. The unlike attribute is shape. The next block in the chain must be like the large, red triangle in two attributes.

Share!

When you were five years old and we played with attribute blocks, you enjoyed:

Celebrate!

Celebrate your five-year-old's progress and development.

Children this age can use more fragile equipment, such as doll high chairs and bassinets, and more elaborate cooking, serving, and washing equipment. They benefit from a large variety of dress-up clothes and props for the enactment of specific roles (doctor/nurse, office equipment, play cameras, cash registers, play money, play food, etc.). A number of these props can be created (in fantasy or reality) by children this age.

By age 5 to 6 you will observe that your child:

- Will learn through her/his play
- Will learn from all of her/his experiences
- Will enjoy learning new skills
- Will often play games of familiar settings such as home or school
- Will enjoy playing store and "selling" things

Play!

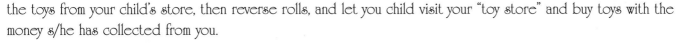

Toy Store

Why this playtime activity is good for your child: Using real money to exchange for goods while playing store, will give your child the opportunity to learn the names of basic coins.

What you'll need to play this activity: toys; real money–pennies, nickels, dimes, quarters, one dollar bills; plastic bags

How to play *Toy Store*: Have your child set up some toys on a table as if for sale. When playing "Toy Store," let your child be the merchant and you be the customer. Ask prices of toys and select some. Pay with real money. When paying ask, "This is a penny. Is that enough to buy this toy?" "This is a dime. Is this enough to purchase this doll?" etc. After making a purchase, have your child put the toys in a bag. Leave the "toy store" and go to another area of the house and place the toys on a table or shelf. When you have bought all of the toys from your child's store, then reverse rolls, and let you child visit your "toy store" and buy toys with the money s/he has collected from you.

Variation: Any merchandise that is bought and sold can become the focus of a game for your child's playtime–grocery store, clothing store, shoe store, pet shop, art gallery (sell her/his works), bookstore, etc.

Share!

When you were five years old, your favorite merchandising game was:_____

_____

Celebrate!

Celebrate your five-year-old's abilities and play interests.

Until the age of five or six children typically do not have the dexterity to operate puppets that have limbs. But by kindergarten, children can use hand, finger, and arm-and-arm puppets. They prefer soft materials and typically care little for elaborate detail on puppets as long as the facial features are clearly marked.

By age 5 to 6 you will observe that your child:
- Will enjoy using hand puppets
- Will prefer making up and acting out her/his own puppet stories
- Will use simple puppet theaters but do not make use of elaborate stages or scenery

Play!

Sock Puppets

Why this playtime activity is good for your child: Sock puppets are easy to make and manipulate. Creating sock puppets will give your child an opportunity to express her/his creativity.

What you'll need to play this activity: white or black sock; yarn; child's safety scissors; red felt scraps; scissors; white glue

How to make Sock Puppets: Ahead of time, cut out an oval shape from red felt for the puppet's mouth. Put the sock on your child's hand with four fingers on top and a thumb on the bottom. Press in between the fingers and thumb to form a mouth. Glue the red felt into the mouth. Cut out felt eyes, ears, nose, etc., for the puppet's details. Let your child glue these in place. If your child wants the puppet to have hair or a mane, sew on yarn with a needle and thread. Add any details your child suggests. When the glue dries, use the puppet to tell stories.

Examples of sock animal puppets:

Dragon–Add a scalloped piece of felt down the back of the sock.

Porcupine–Add a lot of yarn pieces sticking out of the back of the puppet in all directions.

Mouse–Add big felt mouse ears to the top of the puppet's head.

Moose–Add big brown felt antlers on top of the puppet.

Snake–Glue a variety of colored felt dots all over the sock.

Shark–Glue big, white felt teeth hanging down inside the puppet's mouth.

Pelican–Add a big, orange felt bill hanging down from under the puppet's mouth.

Turkey or Peacock–Add big, colorful felt tail feathers standing up above the wrist area.

Share!

When you were five years old and played with puppets, you enjoyed: _____

Celebrate!

Celebrate your five-year-old's creative and artistic abilities.

By kindergarten, children can do more elaborate representational drawings. A five-year-old's drawing of a house may include doors, windows, a chimney (sometimes with smoking coming out of it), and a roof. They often say what they will draw before beginning and will become more critical of their own work.

By age 5 to 6 you will observe that your child:
- Can hold a pencil, brush, or crayon in an adult-style grasp
- Will be able to draw more realistic pictures
- Can copy a wide variety of figures
- Can use scissors skillfully

Play!

Go Fly a Kite

Why this playtime activity is good for your child: All humans, no matter what age, seem to be fascinated with kites. Constructing a kite from a kit takes adult supervision and assistance, but the activity is a very bonding experience for parent and child.

What you'll need to play this activity: kite kit; kite string; glue; rags for tail

How to play *Go Fly a Kite*: Before you fly a kite, build it with your child. The basic, simple diamond-shaped kite is the easiest to build. Lay out all of the materials. Read the directions aloud for your child. Have her/him hand you things as you assemble the kite. When it is dry, go outside and fly it.

Variation: You and your child can create a paper bag kite. Use scissors to cut a small round hole (approximately 2 inches [51 millimeters] in diameter) in the bottom of a large, lightweight paper bag. Decorate the bag with brightly colored markers, stickers, glitter, etc. Use florist's wire to create a circle larger than the hole in the bag (approximately 3 inches [76 millimeters] in diameter). Tape the ends of the wire together to make a ring. Attach three bridle strings to the wire ring. Then tie the three strings into a knot about 6 to 10 inches (15 to 25 centimeters) from the wire circle. Tape the wire loop inside the sack. Pull the bridle string out through the hole in the bag. Attach kite string to the bridle string knot.

Share!

When you were five years old and we flew kites, you would: _____

_____

_____

Celebrate!

Celebrate your five-year-old's need for positive reinforcement.

Many child psychologists believe that children want attention so much that if they cannot get it by doing positive things, they will do negative things for attention. So, it is very important that you often lavish your child with praise. When needed, discipline should be time out or a lecture–not physical punishment which only creates hostility, resentment, and a desire for retaliation. It is impossible to teach children desirable behavior by arousing negative feelings.

By age 5 to 6 you will observe that your child:
- Needs lots of verbal praise
- Should receive time out as punishment
- Will need to be listened to and heard

Play!

Tracking Down the Wild Beast Within

Why this playtime activity is good for your child: Children need to be able to express negative feelings in socially acceptable ways without fear of retaliation.

What you'll need to play this activity: safari-type hats for you and your child

How to play *Tracking Down the Wild Beast Within*: When your child is feeling extremely hostile or angry, put on the safari hats and "go hunting." Sit your child on your lap or near you so you can look into her/his eyes. Ask your child to look inside her/himself and try to figure out what is causing the angry feeling. Ask questions to guide your child. Sometimes anger comes from a fear of rejection or anxiety about abandonment. Listen to your child. When you discover the cause, "tame it" like you might a wild animal. Let your child know that s/he has a right to all of her/his feelings. Validate your child's feeling by telling her/him that you understand and that you sometimes share these same feelings. Show your child how to deal with anger in socially acceptable ways. Choose one of the following and try it:

Make Loud Noises–Shout and scream where no one can hear you or will be bothered by the noise.

Dance it Away–Play loud music and move around with stomping and ponderous steps.

Punch a Pillow–Use a pillow like a punching bag. Hold it so your child can punch at it and work out her/his tension.

Exercise Hard–Do jumping jacks or other exercises for several minutes.

Be Creative–Have your child think of a way that s/he can get rid of the anger.

Share!

When you were five years old, you would deal with angry feelings by: _____

Celebrate!

Celebrate your five-year-old's cognitive milestones.

Kindergarten-age children are interested in time. They are familiar with the calendar and the clock. They can usually answer questions about time such as, "What time do you go to bed?" or "How old are you?" or "When is your birthday?" They rarely get confused with past and future.

By age 5 to 6 you will observe that your child:

- Understands the concept of time
- Knows about time devices used every day in the home—clocks and calendars
- Can name the days of the week
- Knows that there are four seasons

Play!

Look at Mr. Clock's Face

Hickory, dickory, dock;
The mouse ran up the clock;
The clock struck One,
The mouse ran down,
Hickory, dickory, dock.

Why this playtime activity is good for your child: Children like to be able to tell time. Most children this age can read on-the-hour and half-hour times.

What you'll need to play this activity: a paper plate clock

How to play *Look at Mr. Clock's Face:* Begin by making a paper plate clock. Write large numerals 1-12 around the edge of a paper plate. Use brass fasteners to attach paper strips for the "big hand" and "little hand" to the clock. Show your child that when the "big hand" is on the twelve (straight up) and the "little hand" is pointing to a number, the "little hand" indicates what time it is. Put the "big hand" on the twelve, and then move the "little hand" around to different numbers. Tell your child what time each one represents.

Variation: During the day when your child wants to know what time something will happen, you can say something like this: "When the 'big hand' points to twelve and the 'little hand' points to three, the school bus will bring your bother home from school."

Share!

When you were five years old and we played with a paper clock, you would: _____

_____

_____

Celebrate!

Celebrate your five-year-old's health and nutrition.

The basic eating habits your child is developing now will most likely become her/his lifelong habits. If your child overeats or consumes a lot of sweets and junk foods now, s/he may be an overweight child, teenager, or adult.

By age 5 to 6 you will observe that your child:

- Will have established basic eating habits
- Will have favorite foods
- Will enjoy cooking and creating recipes

Play!

Cool Treats

Why this playtime activity is good for your child: Creating imaginative desserts is fun and offers you the opportunity to introduce your child to terms such as pouring, sprinkling, layering, measuring, chopping, stirring, mixing, freezing, baking, etc.

What you'll need to play this activity: See the recipes below to determine the supplies you will need for the recipe you and your child choose to prepare.

How to make *Cool Treats*: Cool off in the hot summertime by making some frosty snacks. All of the following can be made by a five-year-old:

Favored Ice–Mixtures with real fruit juice can be frozen in ice cube trays, paper cups, or muffin tins. Use a plastic spoon or a craft stick in each flavored ice. Put flavored ice mixtures in the freezer until they're frozen. Here are some combinations to try: Crushed berries mixed with water and sugar, lemonade mixed with milk, orange juice and vanilla ice cream, grape juice and lemonade, soda and whipped topping, pineapple juice and crushed pineapple, root beer and vanilla ice cream, or cranberry juice and cream.

Pudding Pops–Freeze instant pudding, yogurt and honey, or ice cream and crushed berries.

Parfaits–In a tall, transparent plastic glass, layer ice cream and any of the following: crushed cookie crumbs, sliced bananas, hot fudge, cake slices, chopped nuts, dried fruit chunks, pudding, whipped cream, applesauce, sherbet, marshmallow creme, flavored gelatin, raisins, chocolate or butterscotch chips, jelly, peanut butter, coconut flakes, berries, grapes, granola cereal, wheat germ, vanilla wafers, candy bears, choclate candies, etc.

Share!

When you were five years old, one of your favorite frozen treats to create was: _____

_____

This is how you made it: _____

_____

Celebrate!

Celebrate your five-year-old's maturing fine motor skills.

Fine motor capacities such as cutting, drawing, and writing demand considerable neurological and emotional maturity. Although most five-year-olds are quite skilled at using basic writing and art supplies, the degree to which they practice these skills will make a difference in their self-confidence when they are placed in a group setting. Providing such learning tools at home gives your child a chance to practice in the safety and privacy of her/his own space.

By age 5 to 6 you will observe that your child:

- Will hold pencils and crayons in a correct position
- Will be able to cut large, simple shapes outlined for her/him on paper
- Will enjoy painting and modeling with clay

Play!

Build a Gingerbread House

Why this playtime activity is good for your child: The idea of a house made of candy and cookies is fascinating to five-year-olds. Creating one will be a treasured memory for your child.

What you'll need to complete this activity: graham crackers; icing; vanilla wafers; candy canes; cardboard; canned icing; confectioner's sugar; variety of candies such as peppermints, chocolate chips, licorice sticks, colorful fruit candies, chocolates, gumdrops, bubble gum, etc.

How to *Build a Gingerbread House*: Ahead of time, create the base for the gingerbread house. Cover a large sheet of cardboard with icing. Sprinkle the icing with powdered sugar for snow. Then construct the basic house. Mix confectioner's sugar with a little water to create a thick paste and use this as mortar to connect graham crackers into a house with walls and a roof. Let dry overnight. The next day, cover the roof with vanilla icing and overlap vanilla wafers like tile on the roof, or decorate with candies. Let your child's imagination do this work. The gingerbread house may not turn out to be as organized and neat as you had hoped, but your child will think it is the most beautiful thing s/he has ever seen!

Variation: Make a Zoo—Begin by creating the icing covered cardboard base for the zoo. Use graham crackers and icing mortar to make cages. Use animal crackers in each cage for the zoo animals. This will require your child to sort the animals and create cages for each kind of animal. (Animal crackers can be colored with fine-tip markers.)

Share!

When you were five years old and you made a gingerbread house, you enjoyed: _____

Celebrate!

Celebrate your five-year-old's desire to learn to read.

Is your five-year-old interested in learning the names of letters? Does s/he look through books, magazines, and at road signs and pick out certain familiar letters? Does s/he scribble "stories" and "letters?" If your child shows a strong interest in learning the letters of the alphabet, there are many games you can play to reinforce this skill. However, if your child shows no interest in reading, it may take another year or two to develop sufficient prereading skills. Don't push your child into learning the alphabet until s/he is motivated to do so.

By age 5 to 6 you will observe that your child:
- May know the names of some of the letters of the alphabet
- May know how to write her/his name
- May enjoy hearing and singing the alphabet song

Play!

ABC Hopscotch

Why this playtime activity is good for your child: Seeing the letters of the alphabet and singing them will make learning the names of the letters fun and easy.

What you'll need to play this activity: chalk; sidewalk; stone markers

How to play *ABC Hopscotch*: Begin by drawing a regulation hopscotch path on a sidewalk with chalk. Instead of putting numbers in the spaces, write twelve different letters of the alphabet. As you and your child play on the hopscotch path, use the appropriate letters of the alphabet in your conversation. "Your marker landed in the space with the letter "L." "You hopped all the way to the letter "G." "Can you get to the letter "H" on this turn?" "I hope I can jump over that letter "C."

Variation: Use combinations of two or three letters in each space on the path so that all of the letters of the alphabet are included, or extend the hopscotch pattern to make it longer, so there is room for all twenty-six letters.

Share!

When you were five years old, and we played hopscotch, you would: _____

_____

_____

_____

Celebrate!

Celebrate your six-year-old's birthday.

Although kindergartners vary widely in individual skills, personalities, and feelings, nearly every six-year-old loves a party! They like to gather to dance, sing, and make merry. For a six-year-old, any occasion is a reason for a party. Don't miss a perfect chance to let your child entertain some treasured friends on her/his birthday. Children this age enjoy theme parties and entertainment such as a clown or magician. They also enjoy surprises, so if you are thinking about giving your child a surprise birthday party, this is the perfect age to do it.

By age 6 you will observe that your child:

- Will have a best friend
- May have an adult best friend who is considered part of "the gang"
- Will have a variety of friends from school
- Especially enjoys surprises

Play!

Happy Birthday Six-Year-Old!

Why a surprise birthday party is a good idea for your child: Birthday celebrations are milestones of development punctuated with cake, ice cream, family, and friends. Don't let your child's sixth birthday slip by without a surprise gathering to celebrate it!

What you'll need for a six-year-old's birthday party: Children this age enjoy entertainment at parties such as a clown or magician, plenty of games with opportunities to win prizes, and refreshments that they help create themselves.

Planning the party: If you are planning a surprise party, don't plan too far in advance. Call parents of the children who are invited, and instruct them not to mention the party to their children until the night before the gathering. Arrange for someone to take your child out for an hour or so during the time the guests are to arrive. Have everyone hide and jump out with a big "Surprise!" when your child arrives.

Entertainment: If you have entertainment planned, such as a clown or magician, present this part of the party before games and refreshments.

Prizes: When buying prizes remember, six-year-olds are not concerned with the value of a party prize. They enjoy the winning of the prize. So include many different games with lots of inexpensive prizes so that everyone will have an opportunity to win at least one prize. Prizes might include: individually wrapped candies, cookies, or nuts; art supplies such as pencils, crayons, tablets; plastic jewelry; large, sturdy balloons; etc. Provide each guest with a small bag for collecting prizes and party flavors.

Play!

Games: Appropriate party play for six-year-olds includes the traditional birthday party games. Children this age can cooperate, take turns, line up, etc., so they enjoy any of the following:

Drop the Clothespin in the Bottle–Line up and take turns dropping clothespins from under the chin into a bottle sitting on the floor between the player's feet. Give a prize to those who get even one clothespin in the bottle.

Pin the Tail on the Donkey–Blindfold the children one at a time, and have them try to pin a tail on a donkey, nose on a clown, mustache on a man, etc. Give the ones who come closest prizes plus the one who misses by the most.

Balloon Bust–Use string to tie an inflated balloon to each child's ankle. The idea is to break everyone else's balloon without getting your own balloon popped. Give a prize to each of the last two or three children who have unpopped balloons.

Musical Chairs–Play this game the traditional way. Give the last pair of children prizes.

Name That Tune–Play (sing) familiar songs, and have the children try to name the songs.

Charades–Divide into teams, and have the children imitate different animals. Every member of the winning team can get a prize.

Refreshments–Children this age enjoy making their own desserts. Ice cream sundaes, banana splits, or parfaits are excellent party treats. Simply put the ice cream and all the toppings on a table. Let each child build her/his own sundae, banana split, or parfait. After lighting the candles on the cake and singing "Happy Birthday," serve each child a small piece of cake to eat with the ice cream treat. Have plenty of napkins available.

Share!

When you turned six years old, your birthday party was: _____

_____

At your party we played these games:_____

_____

The names of your friends who came to the party were: _____

_____

The refreshments were: _____

Your birthday cake was: _____

You received these gifts:_____

_____